Art That Dares

Gay Jesus, Woman Christ, and More

by

KITTREDGE CHERRY

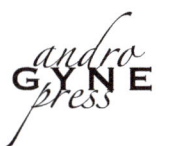

*andro***GYNE***press* | BERKELEY, CA

For more information, contact: www.JesusInLove.org

AndroGyne Press
1700 Shattuck Ave #81
Berkeley, CA 94709
www.androgynepress.com

For Audrey:
yesterday, today and forever

OTHER BOOKS BY KITTREDGE CHERRY

Jesus in Love
A Novel

Hide and Speak
A Coming Out Guide

Womansword
What Japanese Words Say About Women

Equal Rites
Lesbian and Gay Worship, Ceremonies, and Celebrations
(with Zalmon O. Sherwood)

COMING SOON

Jesus in Love: At the Cross

Contents

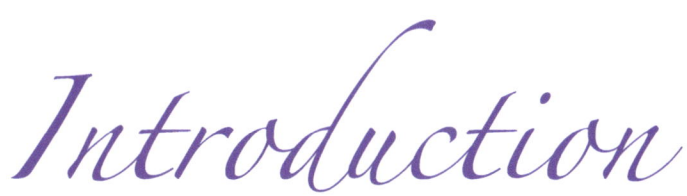

Introduction

Two dramatic new visions are coming into consciousness: the gay Jesus and the woman Christ. They break gender rules and gender roles. Their very presence stirs controversy. These radically new Christ figures embody and empower people who are left out when Jesus is shown as a straight man. They can free the minds of everyone who sees them.

Artists who dare to show Christ as gay or female have had their work destroyed—if they can find a way to exhibit it at all. Now for the first time these beautiful, powerful, sometimes shocking images are gathered together for all to see.

Art That Dares features the work of eleven brave, visionary artists who portray the gay Jesus, the woman Christ, and more. Here they tell the stories behind the images, including the controversies that erupted when the art was exhibited. In some cases the artists faced censorship, hate mail, violence, death threats, and/or vandalism that destroyed their work. Many were accused of blasphemy. Religious freedom clashed with freedom of expression, raising important legal issues. The most virulent opposition came from the religious right, but some were also criticized by feminists and queers for being too Christian.

The paintings, photographs, and sculpture selected for *Art That Dares* were done over the last thirty years by a diverse group of artists. Most work was done independently, in isolation

> Where there is no vision, the people perish.
>
> —Proverbs 29:18

from the others. Each arrived at the revolutionary images in a unique way. They run the gamut from well established to emerging artists. They are women and men of various races and ethnicities who come from both the United States and Europe. They are among the best of a growing number of artists all over the world who do queer or female Christ figures. (Comparable images from Africa and Australia could not be included due to limited resources.)

The artists in this book stand both inside and outside the institutional church. Their religious backgrounds include Buddhism and Judaism as well as Christianity. Some still claim those traditions, while others decline to label their current spirituality. A few hold official church positions. All tried to portray Jesus in a way that honors his life and teachings. The profiles in *Art That Dares* are based on the author's interviews with the artists, their written statements, and/or news reports.

Two thousand years ago a man named Jesus befriended prostitutes, lepers, and other outcasts in Palestine. He taught love and justice and was killed for it, leading to the formation of Christianity as a religion. Images of Christ as queer or female are now popping up around the globe with increasing frequency in political debate, historical research, artistic expression, and spiritual contemplation.

> The images are arising now because the conventional Jesus is no longer adequate.

The images are arising now because the conventional Jesus is no longer adequate. They're here for a reason: to heal and empower people, just as Jesus did when he walked the earth. The new images come at a time when hyper-sexual commercialism is ripping apart sexuality and spirituality. They arrive in a politically conservative period when Christian rhetoric is used to justify hate and discrimination against women and lesbian, gay, bisexual, and transgender (LGBT) people. The gay Jesus and the female Christ are not a reaction—they're a revelation.

The new images grow out of humanity's age-old desire to see ourselves mirrored in the divine. Countless versions of Jesus Christ have been created, each adapted for a particular audience and era. For example, European artists generally picture a white

Jesus, and Asians tend to make Jesus look Asian. Artists are the dreamers who can articulate an idea before any community is ready to accept or expound it. They are free to mix religious iconography with their own experiences and imagination. They can rectify the past and transform people by creating new images out of contemporary life.

Appreciation for the gay Jesus and woman Christ images is not limited to LGBT people, women, or even Christians. Many others are also turned off by dogmatic, male-dominated religions and the wars they fuel. Such people may welcome the sacred feminine and the gay-sensitive reassessments of Christ. On a deeper level, the new images aim to heal the painful split between body and soul introduced by patriarchy. Without that basic wholeness, humanity is likely to continue down the destructive path of war, economic exploitation, and ecological destruction.

legal and financial issues: blasphemy

Jesus himself was charged with blasphemy. It was one of the charges that led to his crucifixion. The stories in *Art That Dares* are just some of the latest examples in the long history of religious censorship. Men with authority have tried to regulate religious imagery at least since Moses announced the Biblical commandment against "graven images." By controlling religious images, they control people. No wonder conservatives are upset by the gay Jesus and the woman Christ. In both form and content, they prove that unauthorized images can be made by unauthorized people.

Legally, blasphemy refers to speech that is designed to transgress or express contempt for central religious beliefs. Blasphemy laws usually protect only one religion and therefore they were a key to building the pre-modern state. In Western culture the understanding of blasphemy has evolved from a crime against God to an offense against public order, and now to "hate speech" against individual believers.

The United States inherited blasphemy laws from the British during the colonial period. The laws used to be enforced, notably at the Salem witch trials of 1692. Current Supreme Court rulings affirm that the First Amendment protects freedom of expression, including artwork.

Most blasphemy laws fell out of use in the West as society became more secular starting in the nineteenth century. However, laws making it a criminal offense to commit "blasphemous libel" or "religious defamation" against Christianity remain on the books to this day in Canada, Australia, South Africa, and parts of Europe. Islamic blasphemy laws on visual images collided with Western sensibilities in 2006 when caricatures of the prophet Mohammad in a Danish newspaper sparked violent worldwide protests.

Funding is another method for suppressing unorthodox religious art. U.S. federal spending on the arts has been cut drastically since the 1990s, partly on the basis that tax money shouldn't pay for art that offends some taxpayers. Economic boycotts have also been staged against private organizations that show controversial images.

The institutional church used its role as the West's biggest art patron to exert control for most of the last two thousand years. Secularization gave artists the freedom to reject religion and even realism. Today there is a revival of realistic art and artists are beginning to resume their spiritual role, but the relationship between artists and the institutional church remains tense.

To some people, the gay Jesus and the woman Christ images look like a stunt to attract attention, but nobody's getting rich off them. In fact, for most it's a financial sacrifice to create this kind of art. Some artists declined to be in *Art That Dares* for fear of losing their livelihood or status in the church if their queer content was publicized. At the other extreme, some secular artists use Christian iconography, but refuse to let their images be displayed in a spiritual context. They want to critique religion, not create objects of worship.

a place in history

Art and spirituality were one unified whole in prehistoric times. A popular theory says that most early human communities were egalitarian, worshipping goddesses who represented the earth, natural cycles, erotic wholeness, and peaceful cooperation. A single shaman could fulfill all the roles that are now split between specialists called "artists," "priests," "doctors," "politicians"—and even "queers." Human communities have always included some people with same-sex attractions. Many believe that a double blessing of spiritual power goes with a homosexual orientation. The "two-spirited" people who have both masculine and feminine traits were honored as tribal leaders in some Native American traditions, and anthropologists have found the same pattern in various cultures throughout history.

Whether or not the golden age of egalitarianism ever really happened, hierarchies did arise with heterosexual men on top. They dominated society by censoring spiritual expression and by denigrating women, queers, and nature, including the human body with its unruly sexual needs. Virtually all mystical traditions speak of sexual ecstasy as a metaphor for union with the divine, but in Christianity the concept has been buried. Over the centuries the church taught women and queers that they were inferior to straight men. Witch burnings and gay bashings were approved in the name of Christ. In order to stay in the church, women learned to submit to male authority and LGBT people learned to hate themselves. And yet their subversive wisdom lived on. It can be glimpsed in the writings of medieval mystics such as Julian of Norwich, who adored "Mother Jesus," and St. John of the Cross, who wrote erotic poetry about ecstatic moments with Christ.

In modern times the movements for women's rights and then gay rights got rolling. Women began gaining legal equality, but religious institutions were especially slow to allow women's ordination. Churches also denied ordination, marriage, and

In order to stay in the church, women learned to submit to male authority and LGBT people learned to hate themselves. And yet their subversive wisdom lived on.

sometimes even membership to LGBT people. Some women left to form a loose-knit network of women's spirituality circles, while some LGBT people and their allies established groups with names like "open and affirming" or "welcoming." There are more than three thousand such churches and ministries in the United States alone, with countless more worldwide. Most of these gay-friendly ministries aren't ready to embrace a gay Jesus yet, but queer Christian images are beginning to find their way into the LGBT Christian movement. For instance, an interfaith spirituality group named The Living Circle carries icons of gay and lesbian saints every year in Chicago's Pride Parade.

Another catalyst for the new images was AIDS, which spread quickly in the gay community in the 1980s. Thousands died, many of them gay men, before more effective drugs were developed in the mid-1990s. The survivors felt a grief so extreme that, for some, only Christ's Passion could compare. When Christian extremists said AIDS was God's judgment, artists fought back by appropriating Christian imagery.

gay jesus

Nobody knows for sure whether the historical Jesus was attracted to other men. Being human, he must have had sexual feelings. Some groundbreaking scholars think that the historical Jesus really was gay, a term used loosely here to mean any same-sex attraction. They base their theory on Jesus' actions in the Gospels, especially his relationship with the man known only as the Beloved Disciple. They point out that Jesus gladly healed the centurion's "boy," the same word used for a homosexual lover. They pore over the little-known Secret Gospel of Mark, a text discovered in 1958 with details about Jesus and a half-naked man.

Whatever Jesus did or didn't do during his earthly life, artists over the centuries have certainly created many homoerotic images of him. Christ has been the object of homosexual fantasies, whether or not he would return the feelings. He is commonly shown almost nude or enjoying the company of other

> The homoerotic Christ has been obscured by layers of sex-negative interpretation and the artists' own efforts to disguise their queer interests, but he's hiding in plain sight for those who care to look.

men. Often he looks androgynous, even effeminate. The homo-erotic Christ has been obscured by layers of sex-negative interpretation and the artists' own efforts to disguise their queer interests, but he's hiding in plain sight for those who care to look. And now some artists are looking, drawing inspiration from the rich history of Christian art.

Contemporary artists are finding many ways to interpret the gay Jesus. He lives in the fertile, uncharted zone between two almost irreconcilable opposites: too gay for most churches, but too Christian for most of the LGBT community. He may be Jesus who is gay-positive, or Jesus who is called a "faggot," or Jesus who has a boyfriend. Some revel in the Biblical metaphor of Christ as bridegroom of all people. Certain scenes from the life of Jesus have fired queer imaginations: the male-on-male waterplay of Jesus' baptism, the Beloved Disciple resting on Jesus' chest at the Last Supper, Judas' famous kiss of betrayal, and— most common of all—the crucifixion.

Queer people can relate to the hurt and humiliation that Jesus experienced at his trial and on the cross. Traditional iconography such as the Stations of the Cross, the Man of Sorrows, and the Passion narrative have all been adapted to address gay suffering, sometimes with references to AIDS or sadomasochism. *Art That Dares* includes a sampling of images that put the crucifixion narrative in a gay context, but the theme has been used by a wide variety of artists, notably by neoclassical painter Delmas Howe of New Mexico.

woman christ

The woman Christ is a radical reimagining of the central figure of Christianity. It's possible that the historical Jesus was gay, but he definitely was not female. All artists who portray the female Christ are breaking with historical fact in order to express a deeper truth. Most say they are drawn to the Christ archetype for reasons that they cannot explain. Some note the influence of feminism or faith—the Christian belief that the risen Christ transcends gender. Some point out that the world needs to honor the sacred feminine and is cycling back to it.

A woman on the cross is still rare enough to shock, but for those who go looking, it is the most common motif for female Christ figures in art. As with the gay Jesus, crucifixions far outnumber resurrections. Female crucifixions generally express the sacrifice and suffering of women—and yet the power to overcome death is implicit in every crucifixion.

In addition to the female crucifixions in this book, artwork on the theme has been done by French photographer Bettina Rheims, Australian landscape painter Arthur Boyd, and German-born magical realist Martina Hoffman. Another outstanding image that could not be included here is *Yo Mama's Last Supper* by African American photographer Renee Cox, who appears nude in the role of Christ.

The current exploration of the female Christ is new, but not unprecedented. Some artists draw inspiration from Sophia, the female incarnation of Wisdom in the Bible. Sophia is considered a Christ figure in Byzantine tradition, and she has appeared in Byzantine churches and icons at least since the Middle Ages.

Artists who re-envision Christ often want to recast the Madonna, too. One recurring theme is the lesbian Madonna with her female lover, sometimes with references to the virgin birth and its similarity to artificial insemination. A few alternative images of the Madonna are included here to suggest the range of contemporary artistic inquiry.

my story

I grew up with art, never knowing where it would lead. I was born in Iowa City, Iowa, in 1957. My mother was an artist and art teacher who filled our home with art. She taught me to love art and to create it myself from the time I was old enough to hold a crayon. Until adolescence I wasn't exposed much to religion or to LGBT people. When I did go to church, I felt like an outsider because I was female, regardless of my sexual orientation. Men ran the church and all the Bible stories seemed to be about men. I didn't feel I had a place there.

During my first week at college I met Audrey Lockwood, the woman who became my life partner. We fell in love while taking many art history courses together at the University of Iowa. I double-majored in journalism and art history, dreaming of becoming an art critic. But the job market and a spiritual conversion experience led me down different paths.

By my mid-twenties, I was working as a journalist in Japan. My father's sudden death provoked a spiritual crisis that made me resort to church. There I met God—and feminists. Japanese feminists, raised in Buddhism, told me how conversion to Christianity set them free from sexism. Christian lesbian feminists taught me to read the Bible in a new way, focused on female images of God and Jesus' treatment of women as equals. In that highly charged atmosphere I was baptized in 1984 at Kobe Union Church, an interdenominational church with members from all over the world.

I came to believe in a God who loved me and loved truth. My Christian faith gave me the courage to come out as a lesbian, attend seminary, and minister in the LGBT community. I served as clergy at Metropolitan Community Church of San Francisco during the height of the AIDS epidemic, then I became ecumenical director for the whole denomination. I was on the cutting edge of the international debate on sexuality and spirituality. One of my primary duties was promoting dialogue on homosexuality at the National Council of Churches (USA) and the World Council of Churches. I almost forgot about art.

Suddenly Chronic Fatigue Syndrome forced me to leave my job, and I was thrust into a much more contemplative life. As my access to the physical world diminished, new spiritual dimensions opened to me. I got startling results when I tried to visualize Christ by using a method that I had learned in seminary more than a decade earlier. Back then a traditionally masculine Jesus had walked with me in remote silence through "safe

I came to believe in a God who loved me and loved truth. My Christian faith gave me the courage to come out as a lesbian, attend seminary, and minister in the LGBT community.

places" remembered from my childhood. Now in my imagination a bisexual-transgender Christ seemed to give me a guided tour of the Gospels. Like his original disciples, I felt that Jesus wanted me to tell others what I witnessed. With great physical difficulty and heroic help from others, I spent years writing *Jesus in Love,* a novel about the queer Christ.

I didn't realize my visions were part of a larger trend until I started hunting for a publisher. Back when I was an active church leader, nobody was seriously questioning Jesus' sexual orientation. I was amazed to discover a growing number of scholarly books that claimed the historical Jesus was gay (see bibliography). I began building a website, JesusInLove.org, based on the queer Christ.

Then, by some grace, art caught up with me. Audrey and spiritual director Jim Curtan introduced me to a picture of Jesus kissing Lord Rama (see Alex Donis, p. 36). It was a stunning affirmation. I could hardly take my eyes off it, and I certainly couldn't get the life-giving image out of my mind. Through the magic of online search engines, I found more images of the gay Jesus and the woman Christ. They were beautiful, strong, and true to my own experience of Jesus. They expressed meanings that I could not put into words.

The new Christ images evoked a healing response in me. I was weaving together the separate threads of my life: spirituality, lesbian identity, writing, and art. My physical strength gradually began to return as I finished my novel and began contacting the artists who seemed to have seen what I saw. Some let me display their work at JesusInLove.org, sparking an explosion of interest. Hundreds of gay news sites covered it and blogs buzzed on both sides of the issue. The response convinced me of the urgent need for *Art That Dares.*

blasphemy or blessing?

The gay Jesus and the woman Christ may come as a shock, especially to those who believe in the divinity of Jesus Christ. Some denounce them as blasphemy because they differ from

> The new images do even more than empower women and LGBT people. They liberate the Christ who dwells within every individual.

traditional images. Others, myself included, experience them as a blessing that enhances Christian faith by embodying God's wildly inclusive love for all.

Art That Dares is useful for church libraries and individual devotions because it enlarges the way readers see God. Looking at the new images makes it easier to recognize the image of God in oneself and in others, particularly women and gays. Art can open the heart in a way that traditional texts may not.

It is appropriate, even essential for Christians to explore Jesus' same-sex attractions and female side because in him God became flesh—a total, shocking identification with all people, including the sexually marginalized. Christ embodies male and female as well as humanity and divinity. The images start to compensate for the institutional church's past biases and omissions. The Bible gets translated from its original Greek, and sometimes Christ needs to be "translated" by making him female or queer.

The gay Jesus and woman Christ have a special urgency for people who have been indoctrinated with self-hatred in the name of Christ. Many LGBT people feel that God hates them, and many women feel that God requires them to suppress their gifts. Some would say *that* is blasphemy!

The new images do even more than empower women and LGBT people. They liberate the Christ who dwells within every individual. Each human being encompasses both masculine and feminine energies, and those who keep one side in shadow do so at their own peril. Queer people benefit from seeing Jesus as queer—and so do straight people. Women benefit from seeing Christ as female—and so do men. I believe that the Christ who inspired the new images will speak directly through them to bless everyone who looks at *Art That Dares*.

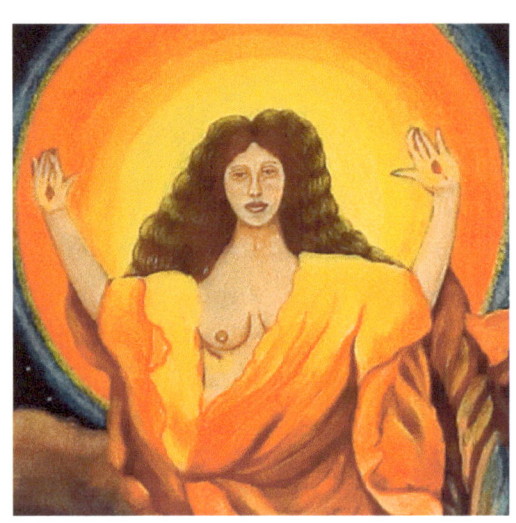

"A Tribute to Matthias," detail

Jill Ansell

b. 1944, San Francisco, CA

emale Christ figures live out the cycles of death and rebirth in the magical dreamscapes of Jill Ansell. Sometimes a complete image comes to the New Mexico artist like a flash in a waking dream. She strives to paint each vision while it lives and evolves in her mind. This creative process enabled Ansell to survive personal tragedy so devastating that she felt only Christ's crucifixion could compare. Recently she looked back on her woman Christ paintings and declared, "They saved my life. If I hadn't had that vehicle, I don't think I would have made it."

Ansell is a painter and a college art teacher whose work has been widely exhibited and collected. She has done murals for prisons, hospitals, and schools across the Southwest. She earned a master of fine arts degree from Vermont College in Montpelier, but she considers herself largely self-taught because she discovered and studied the early twentieth-century women surrealist painters on her own. Surrealists such as Frida Kahlo inspired Ansell to develop her mature style of detailed, allegorical landscapes embedded with themes of feminism and social justice.

An example of how Ansell honors the sacred feminine is *Missa Solemnis* (Latin for "Solemn Mass"). When Mass is cele-

Surrealists inspired Ansell to develop her mature style of detailed, allegorical landscapes embedded with themes of feminism and social justice.

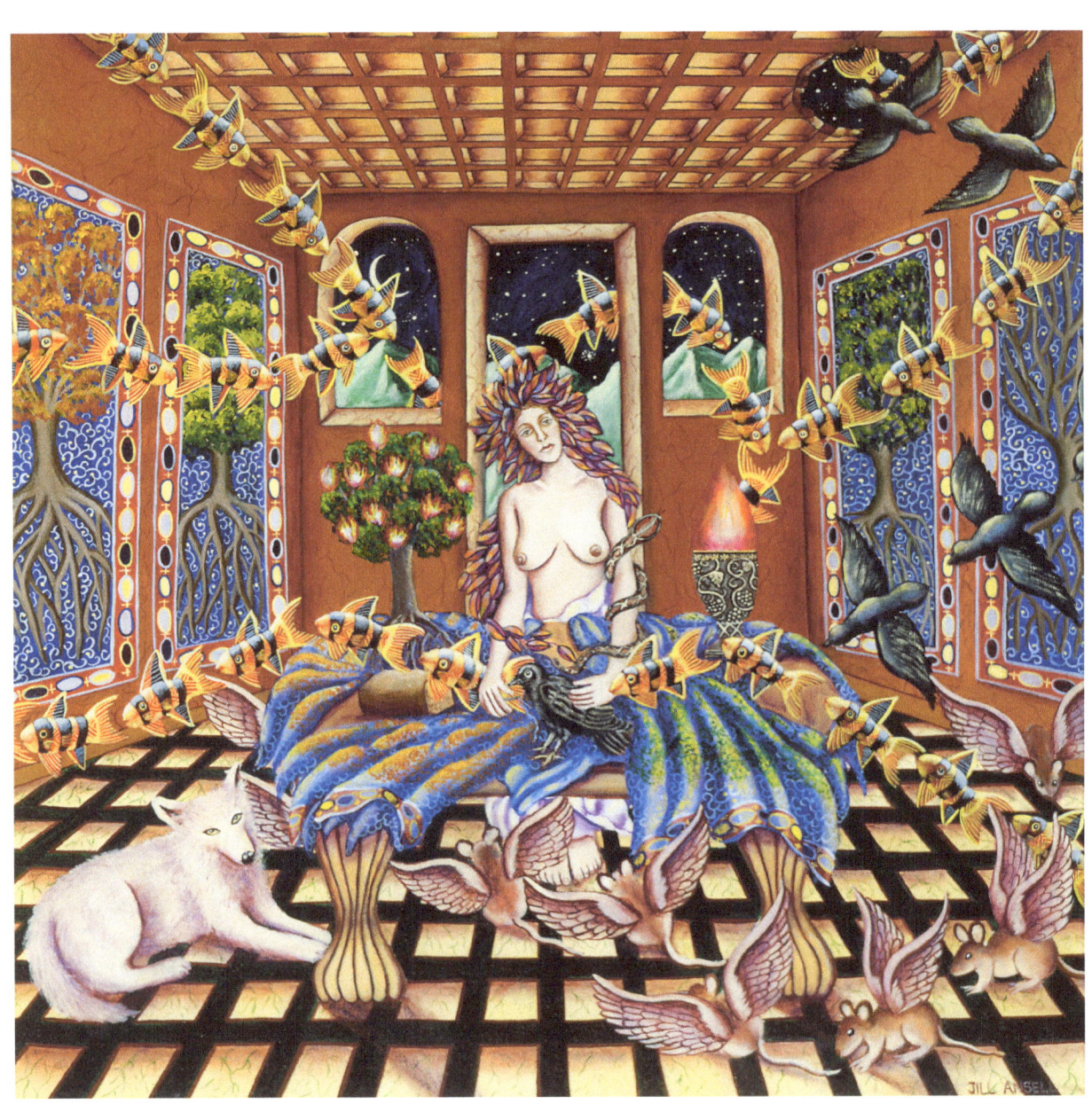

"Missa Solemnis," Jill Ansell, c. 1992.
Acrylic on canvas, 24" x 24".

brated, a priest enacts the role of Christ at the Last Supper. In Ansell's version, a female Christ figure presides over the bread and chalice, inviting all to join Her in the marvelous meal. Viewers can feast their eyes on the rich symbolism drawn from nature and the four seasons. "She represents the feminine, not in terms of men and women, but as an archetype that's connected to natural cycles, fecundity, earthiness, relatedness, warmth, birth and death, and eros as opposed to logos," the artist explained.

Ansell's art career was already well underway in the mid-1980s when her husband, journalist Michael Rosenberg, was diagnosed as HIV-positive. He was a hemophiliac who got infected by blood products. Rosenberg reported on how the pharmaceutical industry had approved the tainted products despite evidence of the danger. Virtually the entire hemophiliac population ended up dying of AIDS, including Rosenberg and his brother.

"It was like I was being crucified," Ansell recalled. AIDS dragged her into two legal battles, one for product liability damages and another for child custody after AIDS strained her marriage to the breaking point. Ansell's nightmare in the court system led her to paint the female crucifixion called *Fire and Ice*.

"That painting came out of the whole tragedy and the ineptitude of the court procedure to deal with the whole experience," Ansell said. "The court system is so icy and objective and corrupt in a certain way. How do you determine the value of someone's life, or the value of someone's relationship?! It's impossible to weigh such loss."

Fire and Ice shows a woman crucified in a burning, snake-infested bush behind a judge in a polar nightscape. Forces of life and death approach: on the right a skeleton carries a flaming heart, while on the left a pregnant woman holds an egg surrounded by sperm. A checkerboard floor emphasizes that this is a meeting of opposites. The scales of justice stand empty, for matters of the heart cannot be measured. An absurd sacrifice lies

A female Christ figure presides over the bread and chalice, inviting all to join Her in the marvelous meal.

in front of the scales: a sock monkey, based on a toy that Ansell stitched back together for her son many times. The imaginary courtroom is festooned with streams of flying fish to symbolize the subconscious.

"Out of this deep suffering, there was a resurrection, a renewal in some way," Ansell continued. She went on to paint a resurrection based on the early sixteenth-century Isenheim Altarpiece by Matthias Grünewald. The original was created for a hospital specializing in skin diseases and syphilis. Patients began their healing treatment by meditating on the altar, which features what is probably the most gruesome crucifixion ever painted. A greenish, bloated Jesus is covered with the kind of oozing sores caused by syphilis. The ghastly image is paired with an equally extreme resurrection in which a radiant Christ shoots out of the grave, fully healed. In Ansell's *Tribute to Matthias,* a woman Christ is reborn.

"I'm using that archetype of resurrection because that experience has touched me deeply as a woman. It's not limited only to Jesus. It is indeed a human process we all experience throughout life," Ansell explained.

She further emphasized the feminine by painting her Christ on a circular canvas in the company of snakes, an ancient goddess symbol. Snakes also represent renewal because they shed their old skins to be reborn over and over. These elements reflect Ansell's belief that a healing transition toward the sacred feminine is now underway worldwide.

More than a decade after she painted the resurrection, Ansell celebrates life in her most recent body of work. Colorful animals, dancers, and nomads clear open space in elaborate Tibetan landscapes, a metaphor for reclaiming the sacred places within. Instead of using Christian iconography, Ansell draws images from her Buddhist practice.

Her interfaith imagery made her laugh out loud in a recent discussion: "Would you believe I was raised a Reform Jew?!"

"How do you determine the value of someone's life, or the value of someone's relationship?!"

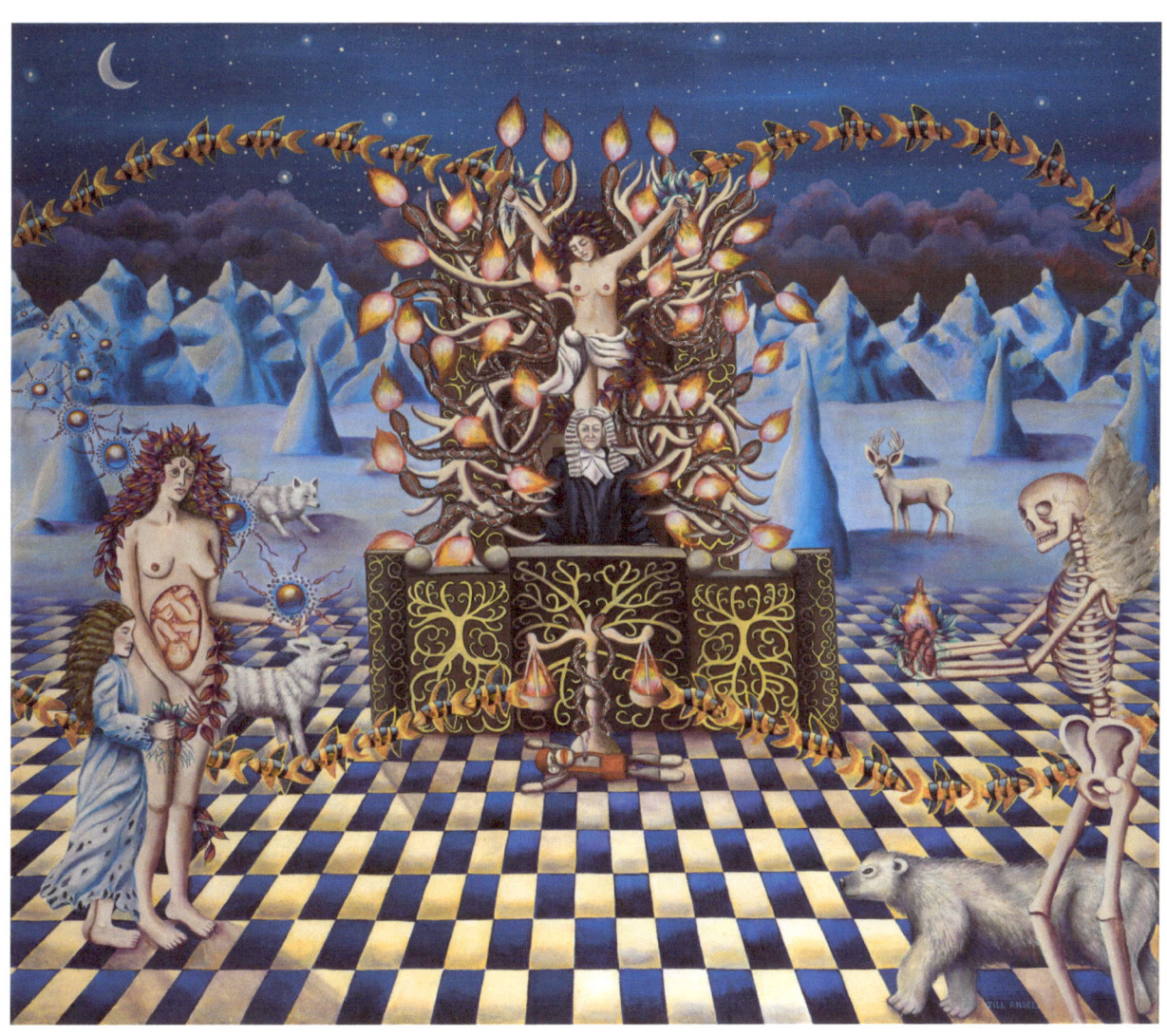

"Fire and Ice," Jill Ansell, c. 1990.
Acrylic and mixed media on canvas,
54" x 60".

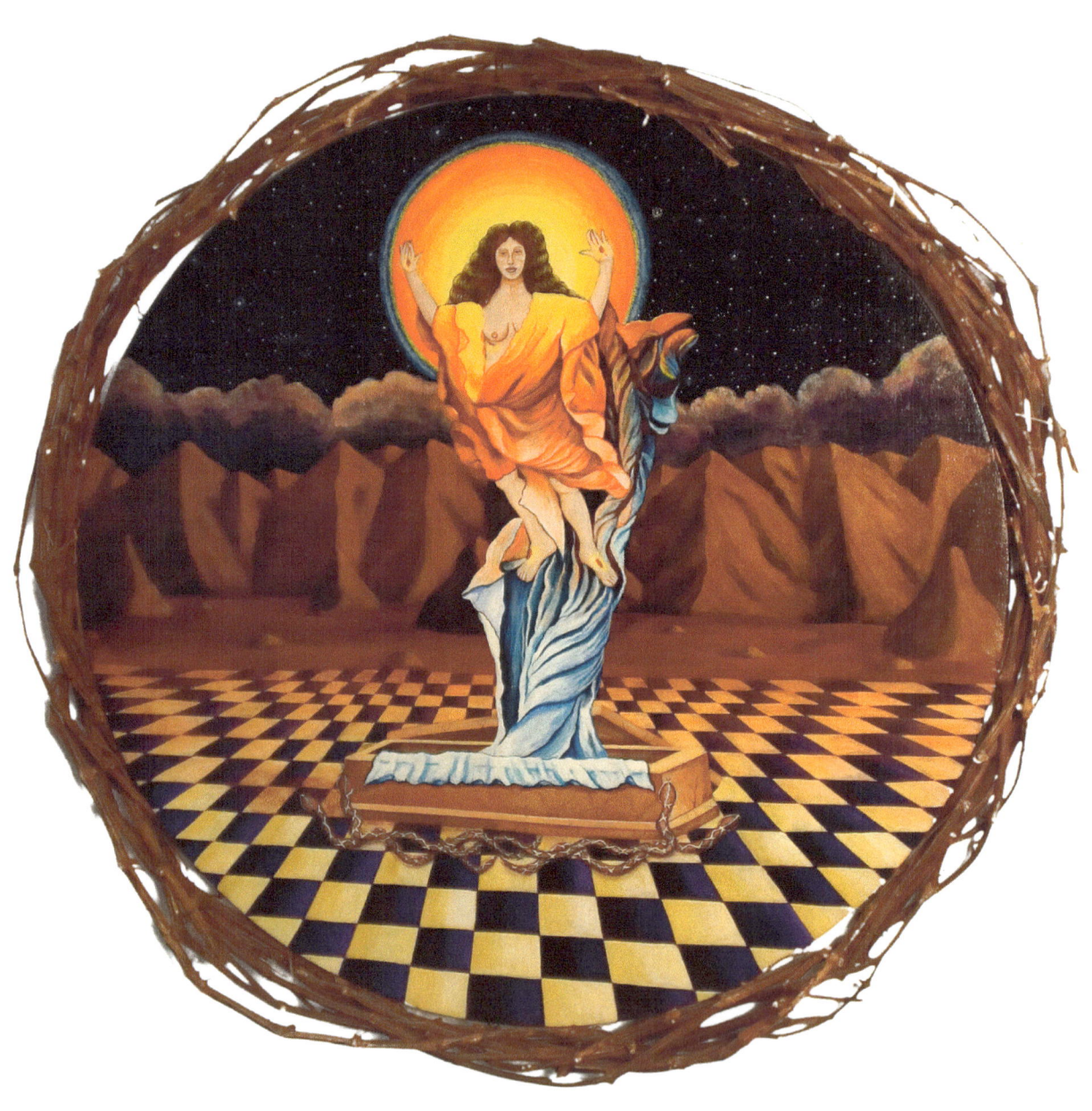

"A Tribute to Matthias," Jill Ansell, c. 1991.
Acrylic on canvas framed by branch,
36" diameter. Collection of Jack Meier
and David Haight, Nevada City, CA.

Ansell transcends the limits of religion by borrowing religious images to express universal themes such as suffering. "In our personal lives we all have deep crosses to bear. The truth is that we do deeply suffer and the only way out of suffering is to transform our states of mind. That's what these images speak to," she said.

People often tell Ansell that she looks like her own Christ figures, but she did not intend them as self-portraits. "It's absolutely a female Christ figure," she said. "Not the savior Christ, but the inner Christ, the inner Buddha that we all have."

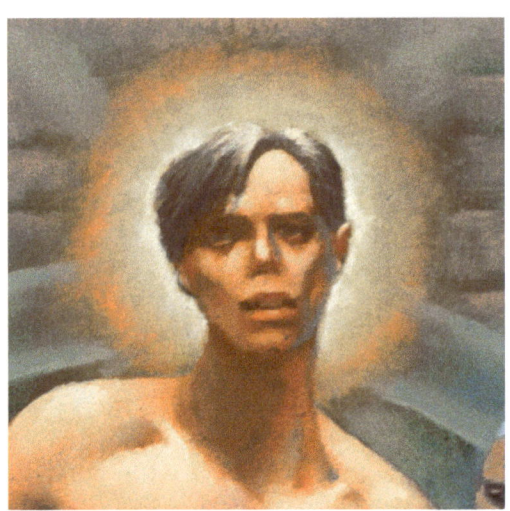

"Jesus Rises," detail

F. Douglas Blanchard

b. 1957, Dallas, TX

F. Douglas Blanchard decided to make Christ's Passion more real by painting it in his own context as a contemporary gay man. The New York artist spent four years wrestling with the story of Jesus' arrest, trial, death, and resurrection. The result is a compelling series of twenty-four paintings called *The Passion of Christ: A Gay Vision.*

"I hope to present in this series a more humane and radical vision of Christianity. What keeps me in this otherwise confounded religion is its profoundly revolutionary character. The very idea of God becoming a human being and going through everything we must go through is most revolutionary," explained Blanchard, an active Episcopalian who teaches college art history.

Raised in Dallas, Blanchard studied art in St. Louis and Kansas City before earning a master of fine arts degree from the New York Academy of Art. Much of his art explores the gay experience, such as the Stonewall uprising. He was inspired by Renaissance and Baroque artists to develop a hearty, engaging realism that is reminiscent of Thomas Hart Benton and other Depression-era muralists.

"What keeps me in this otherwise confounded religion is its profoundly revolutionary character."

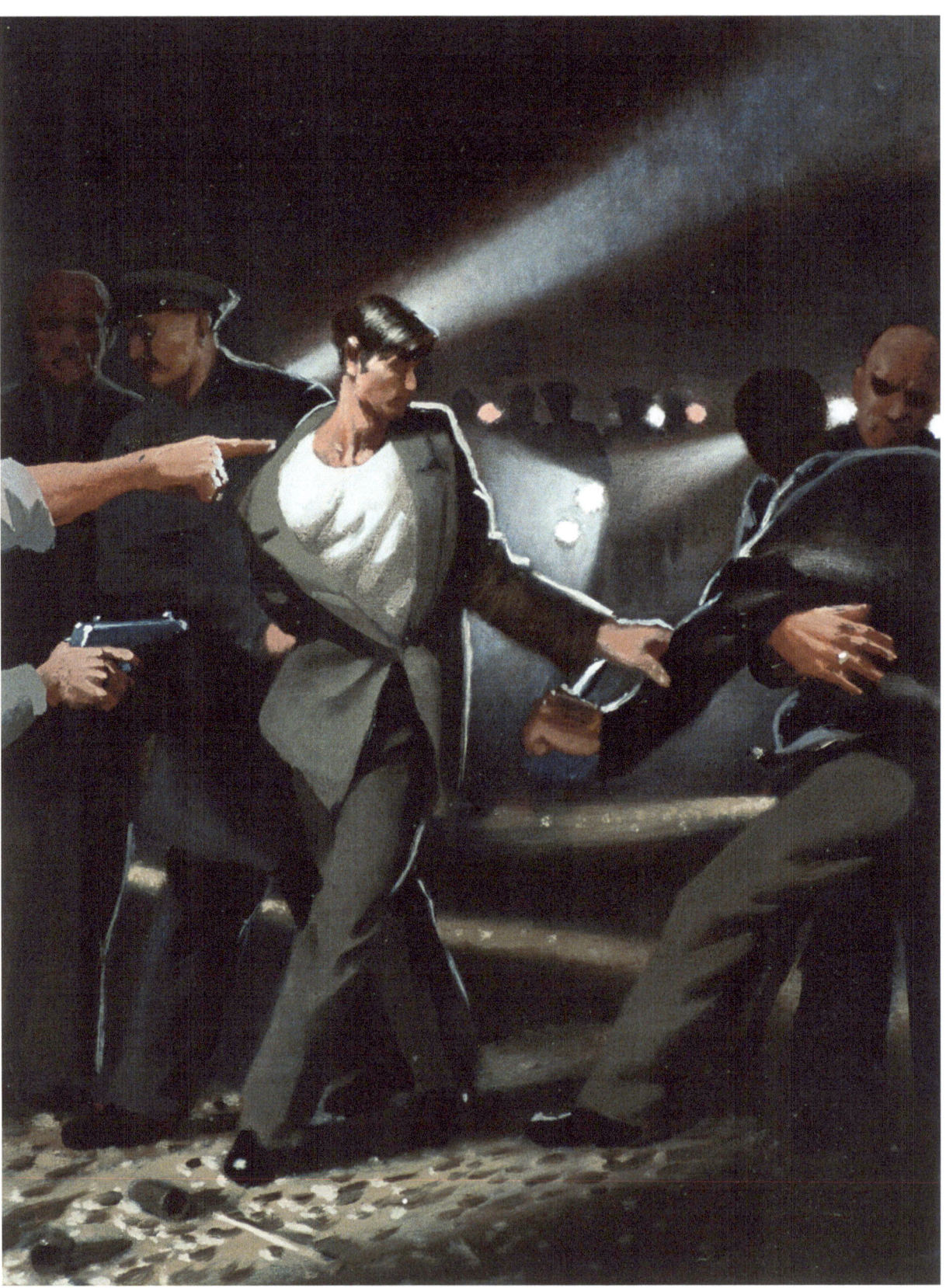

In his *Passion* series, Blanchard decided to remake Jesus into a handsome, accessible young man of today. "I didn't want him to seem in any way remote and unapproachably sacred," he said. The scope of Blanchard's *Passion* is unusually broad, starting with Palm Sunday and extending well beyond Christ's death.

His Jesus faces forms of rejection that feel familiar to contemporary lesbian, gay, bisexual, and transgender people. He stands up to priests, businessmen, lawyers, and soldiers—all of whom look eerily identical to the people holding those jobs in America today. Blanchard avoids the trap of presenting Jesus as a popular hero and instead reveals the stark truth: Jesus was harassed by crowds like those who picket at pride marches and AIDS funerals. Holy gay kisses are rarer than gay bashings in art, so the most daring part of Blanchard's vision occurs after Jesus dies. His risen Christ holds hands with another man, and goes on to a blissful homoerotic kiss with God.

The Passion series, begun in summer 2001, took on new meaning for Blanchard on September 11 when hijacked planes crashed into the World Trade Center near his studio on New York's Lower East Side. "I understand that a lot of people rediscovered religious faith after September 11th. I had the opposite reaction," he said. "I was horrified by the religious motivation of those attacks." He used the paintings to resolve his inner conflict, concluding that Christ's resurrection reverses the "grim arithmetic of power."

His Jesus faces forms of rejection that feel familiar to contemporary lesbian, gay, bisexual, and transgender people.

Left: "Jesus is Arrested" (from The Passion of Christ: A Gay Vision), F. Douglas Blanchard, 2002. Oil on panel, 18" x 14".

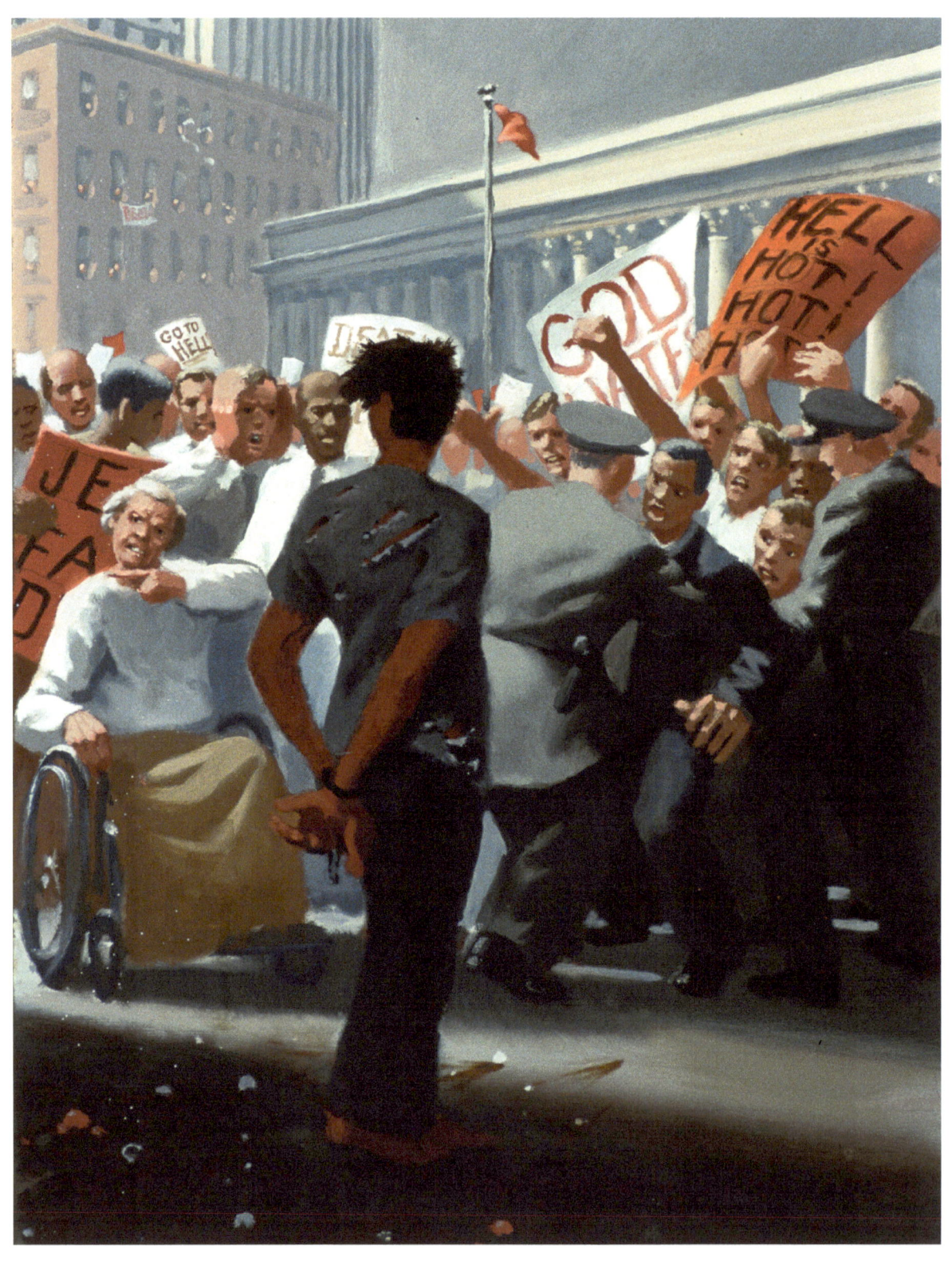

"Jesus Before the People" (from The Passion of
Christ: A Gay Vision), F. Douglas Blanchard,
2002. Oil on panel, 18" x 14".

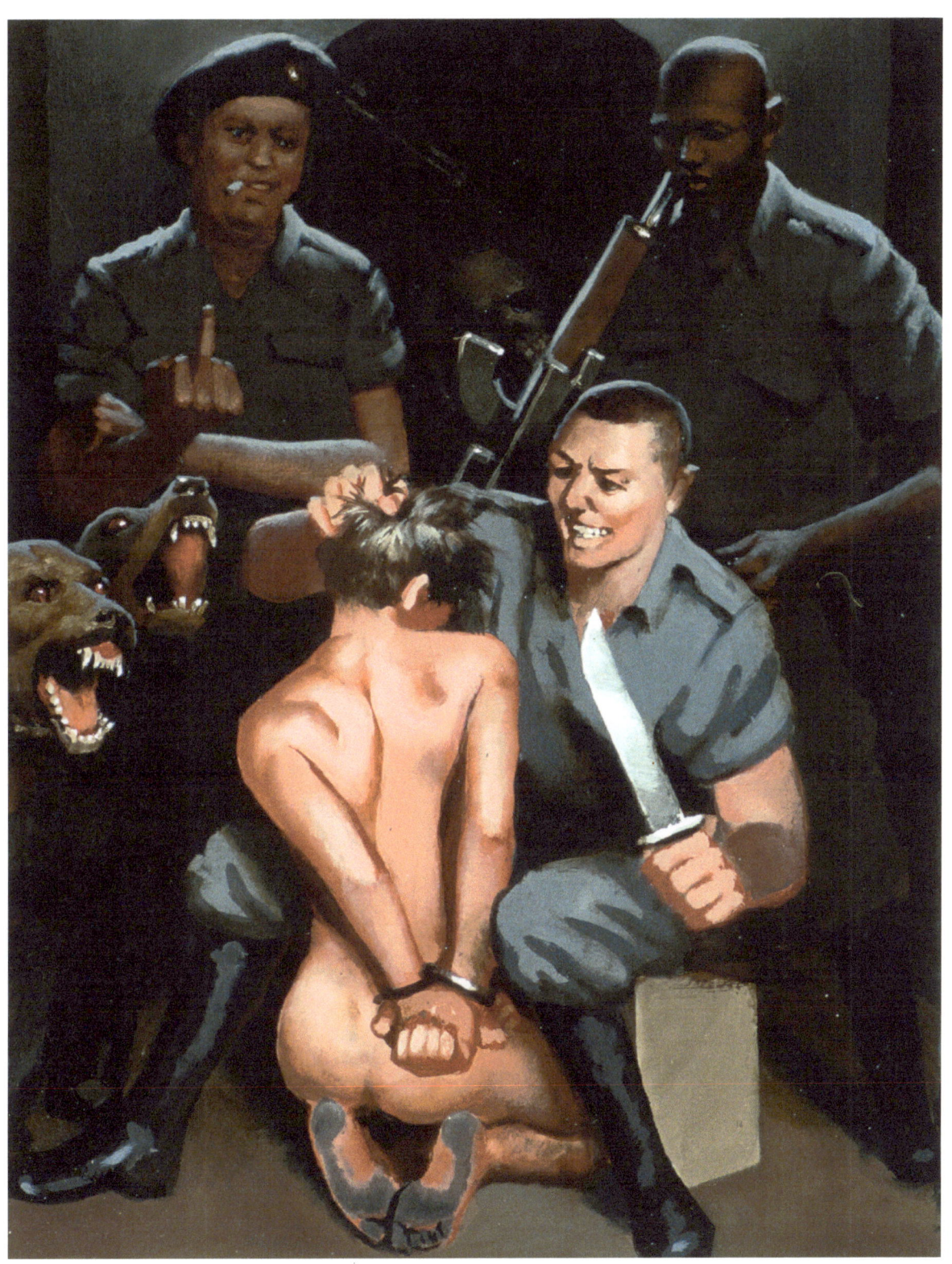

"Jesus Before the Soldiers" (from The Passion
of Christ: A Gay Vision), F. Douglas Blanchard,
2003. Oil on panel, 18" x 14".

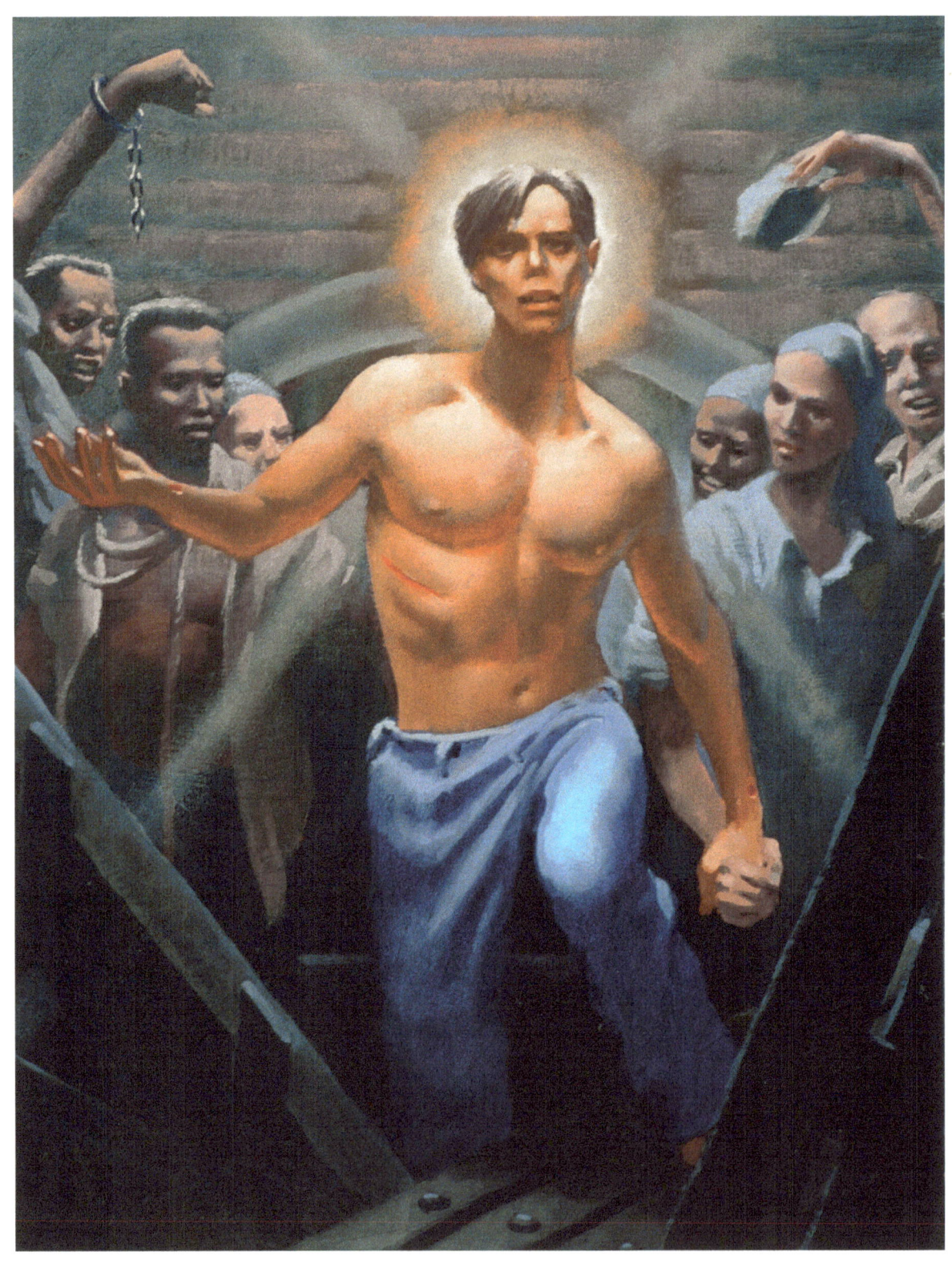

"Jesus Rises" (from The Passion of Christ:
A Gay Vision), F. Douglas Blanchard, 2005.
Oil on panel, 18" x 14".

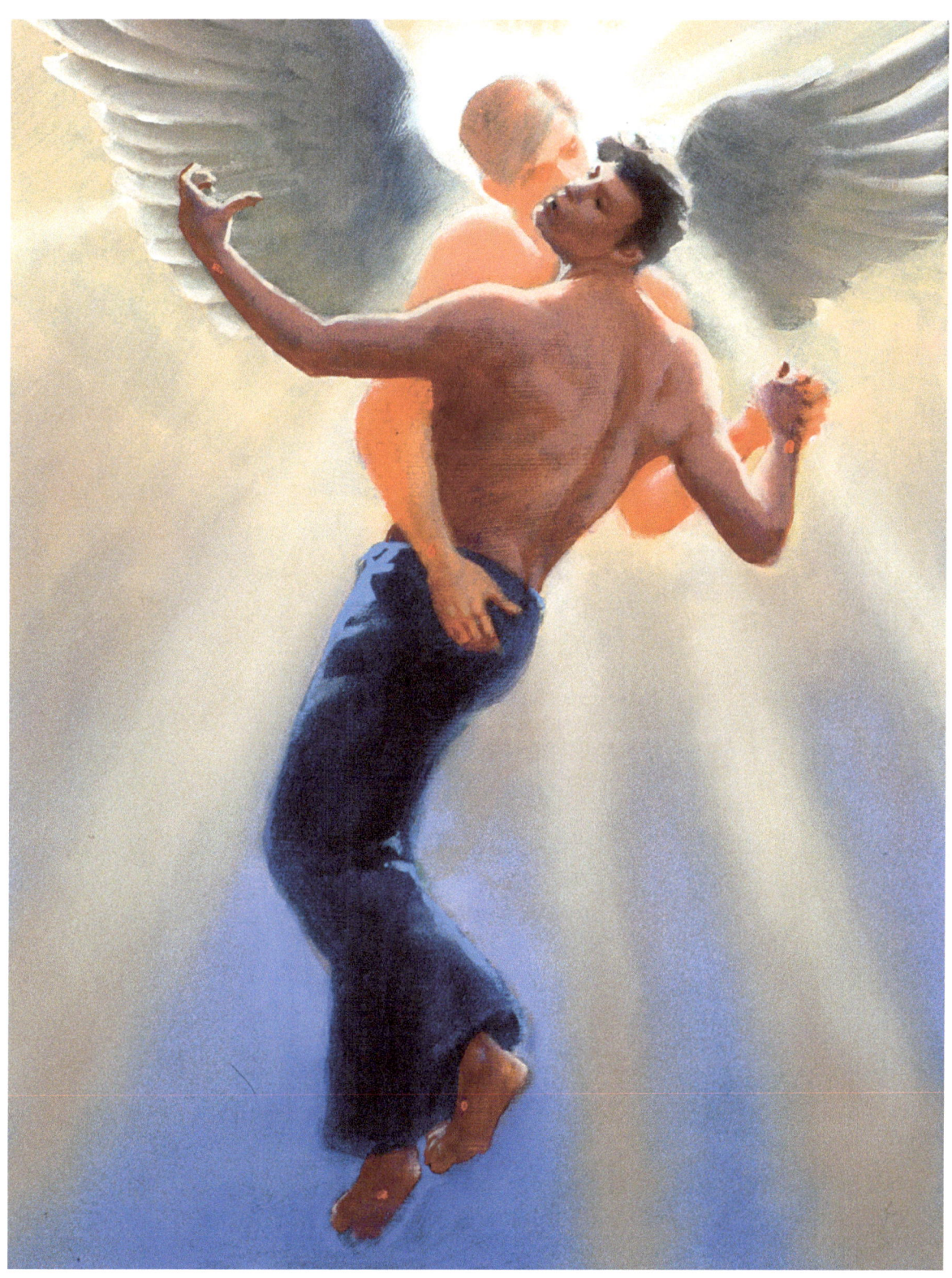

"Jesus Returns to God" (from The Passion
of Christ: A Gay Vision), F. Douglas Blanchard,
2005. Oil on panel, 18" x 14".

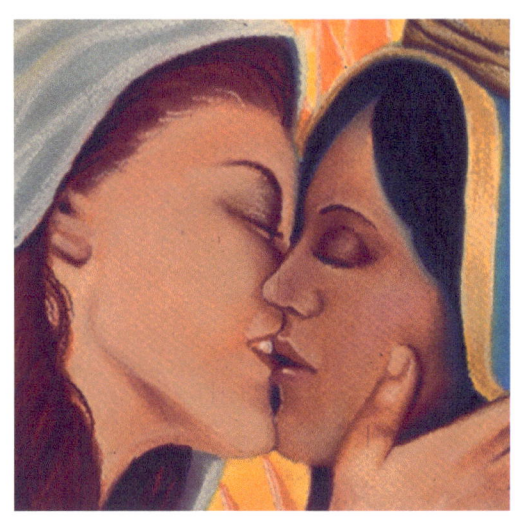

"Mary Magdelene and Virgen
de Guadelupe," detail

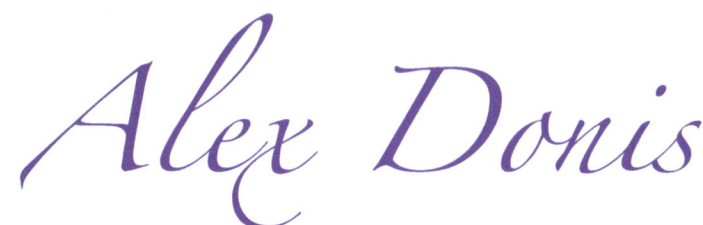

Alex Donis

b. 1964, Chicago, IL

Alex Donis wanted to show what forgiveness looks like. The Los Angeles artist imagined enemies kissing in same-sex pairs. He began sketching his favorite political, religious, and pop icons, then matching each one with a partner of the same sex, but opposite viewpoint: Jesus and a Hindu god, Martin Luther King, Jr. and a Klansman, Mother Theresa and pop star Madonna.

Donis was familiar with contradictions from his own "tri-cultural" identity: pop, queer, and Latino. Born to Guatemalan parents, he grew up in East Los Angeles where he attended Catholic school and Mass, but also joined his parents at Pentecostal services. His eclectic education included a Guatemalan military academy and an Eastern prep school, eventually leading to a master of fine arts degree from Otis College of Art and Design. Though he has been accused of being deliberately provocative, Donis comes across in person as gentle and good-humored.

He had already established a reputation as an artist by the mid-1990s when he received a commission to do an installation at Galería de la Raza, a bastion of innovative, socially engaged Latino art. His visit to the gallery in San Francisco's Mission district reminded him of the East L.A streets where he grew up: full of Spanish conversation, storefront churches, and outdoor

Donis began sketching his favorite political, religious, and pop icons, then matching each one with a partner of the same sex, but opposite viewpoint.

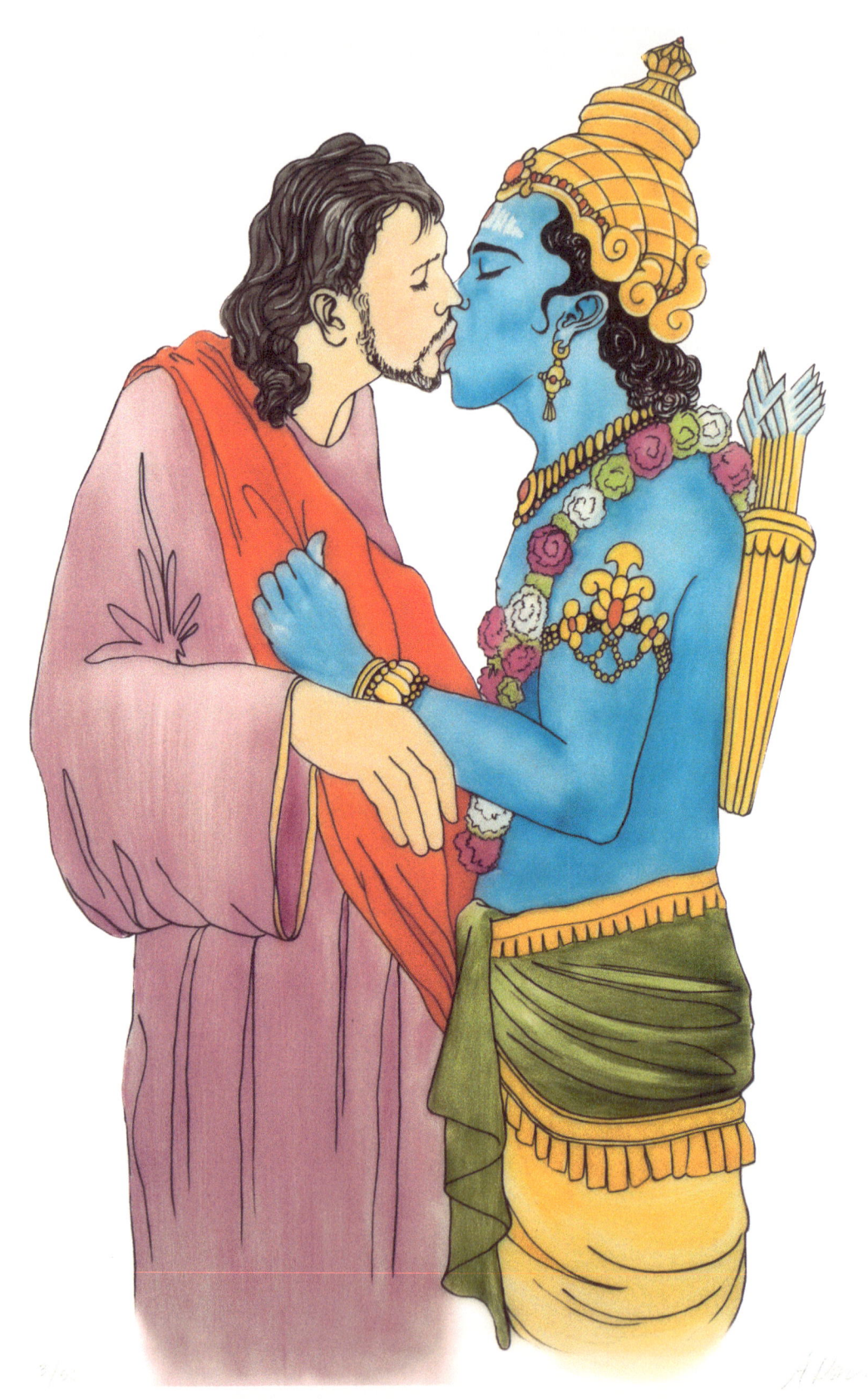

murals. He saw murals of guerilla leader Che Guevara, labor organizer Cesar Chavez, and Mexico's beloved Virgin of Guadalupe. Donis felt right at home as a Latino, but he wasn't sure if he was welcome as a gay man.

He decided to use art, video, and sound to transform the storefront Galería into a storefront church offering his own vision of what is good and holy. Donis painted his improbable same-sex couples on light-up boxes like stained glass windows. Some faced the street in window displays, while others were arranged inside like a chapel. He called it *My Cathedral*.

Opening in August 1997, the exhibit electrified viewers as soon as they saw who he had matched up: Kennedy with Castro, the Pope and Gandhi, Hitler and a Holocaust survivor, Mary Magdalene and the Virgin of Guadalupe, and so on. Heated arguments erupted in the gallery, followed by threatening phone calls and letters, and then physical violence. Vandals threw rocks and traffic barriers through the gallery windows—not once, but twice in three weeks. They smashed two of the artworks: first Jesus and Rama, and then Che and Chavez.

When gallery staff discovered the damage, they also found a spontaneous altar of candles inside a blue plastic milk crate, set up by persons unknown. Amid the broken glass, the storefront church/gallery had spilled out onto street. Donis flew to San Francisco after each attack to mark the boarded-up windows with flowers and a statement affirming the right to freedom of expression. "If these works had to be sacrificed for the cause of getting people to talk, then that's a worthy way to go for a work of art," Donis told the *San Francisco Examiner* at the time.

And people did talk. A crowd of more than two hundred discussed the controversy with Donis at a special community meet-

Donis painted his improbable same-sex couples on light-up boxes like stained glass windows.

Left: "Jesus and Lord Rama" (from My Cathedral), Alex Donis,1997. Oil and enamel on plexi light box, 36" x 24". Non extant (destroyed during exhibition). Courtesy of the artist and Sherry Frumkin Gallery.

ing called for that purpose. It was a chance for dialogue about artistic and religious freedom, and also about homophobia in the Latino community. Sermons at neighborhood churches urged tolerance. *My Cathedral* became the best-attended show since the Galería was founded in 1970.

Some praised the show as brave and thought-provoking, but many were shocked and disgusted. Almost every group could find a reason to be offended by the multi-layered challenge of *My Cathedral*. The same-sex kisses dominated the debate, overpowering all other aspects of the work. For example, it was so shocking to see Cesar Chavez kissing a man, *any* man, that few stopped to ponder the meaning of a kiss between a peacemaker and a guerilla warrior.

The religious figures are even more complex because they are presumed to be asexual, never kissing anybody at all, especially not with the erotic tongue-kisses that Donis pictured. *Jesus and Lord Rama* raises a series of issues: Did Jesus kiss *anyone* like that? If so, would he kiss another man? If he did kiss a man, would it be Rama, also known as Ram, the Hindu embodiment of the ideal family man?!

Christians were not the only ones who felt insulted by such speculations. Like the other images, the interfaith kiss also works in reverse. Donis particularly recalled one Hindu man who sneered, "You don't understand the true nature of *Ram!*" The taboo homoerotic content also distracted viewers from Donis' skillful draftsmanship and his luscious, luminous colors.

Donis insisted that he meant no disrespect and, in fact, he was honoring Jesus' teachings on love. "This project embodies the various interpretations of what it means to 'love thy enemy' both in the physical and spiritual form," he explained.

He has gone on to other subjects, including a series of police and gang members doing hip-hop dances in same-sex couples. That exhibition was so inflammatory that it was cancelled before it even opened. Undaunted, Donis relocated the exhibit to another gallery, and his newest series puts pairs of enemy soldiers in ballet poses, including an Iraqi and a U.S. Marine.

"This project embodies the various interpretations of what it means to 'love thy enemy' both in the physical and spiritual form."

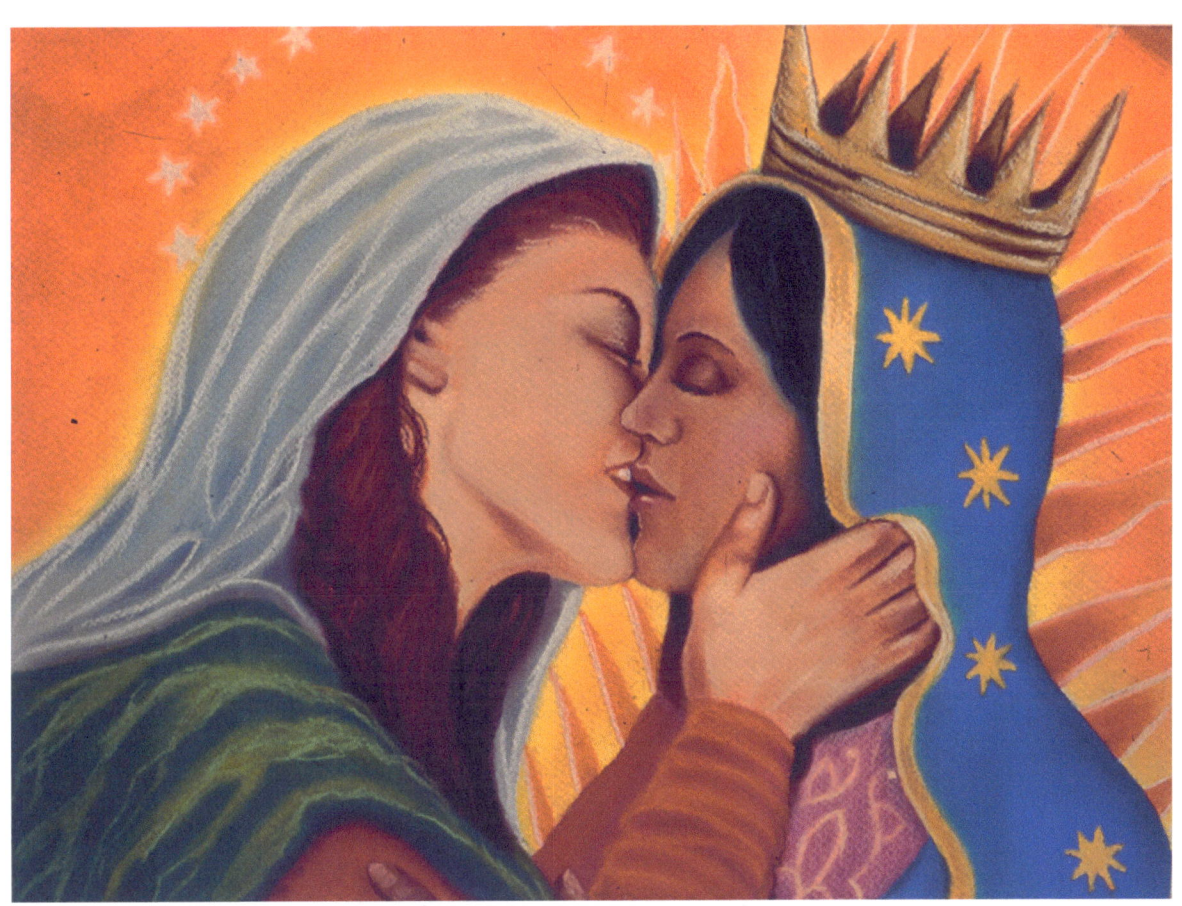

"Mary Magdalene and Virgen de Guadalupe"
(from My Cathedral), 1997. Pastel on paper, 17" x 23".
Private collection. Courtesy of the artist and Sherry Frumkin Gallery.

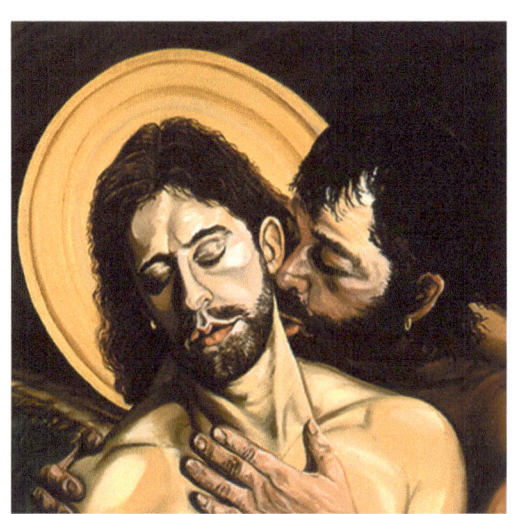

"Judas Kiss," detail

Becki Jayne Harrelson

b. 1954, Alton, IL

Becki Jayne Harrelson helped give birth to a new genre of art in 1993 when she painted Jesus in a homoerotic embrace. She and others would create many additional gay images of Christ in years to come. Political events combined with years of inner turmoil to lay the groundwork for Harrelson's landmark image, a life-sized oil painting titled *Judas Kiss*.

The Atlanta-based artist cared passionately about politics, and she painted *Judas Kiss* at the time when President Bill Clinton was backing down on his promise to allow gays in the military. He was being pressured by Christian conservatives, a type that Harrelson knew all too well. She grew up in a Christian fundamentalist family full of Baptist and Pentecostal ministers. When she came out to her mother as a lesbian in 1985, she was called "demon-possessed" and warned about going to hell.

She kept struggling with her family's homophobia and her own childhood abuse memories until she had a spiritual break-through in 1991. Her gay Christ images were conceived during that healing crisis, but she suppressed them, preferring the keep an uneasy peace with her family by painting pictures of people asleep. "What a metaphor!" she laughs now.

Anger over gays in the military was the catalyst that pushed Harrelson to start fighting fire with fire. "I said, Enough!" she

> Anger over gays in the military was the catalyst that pushed Harrelson to start fighting fire with fire.

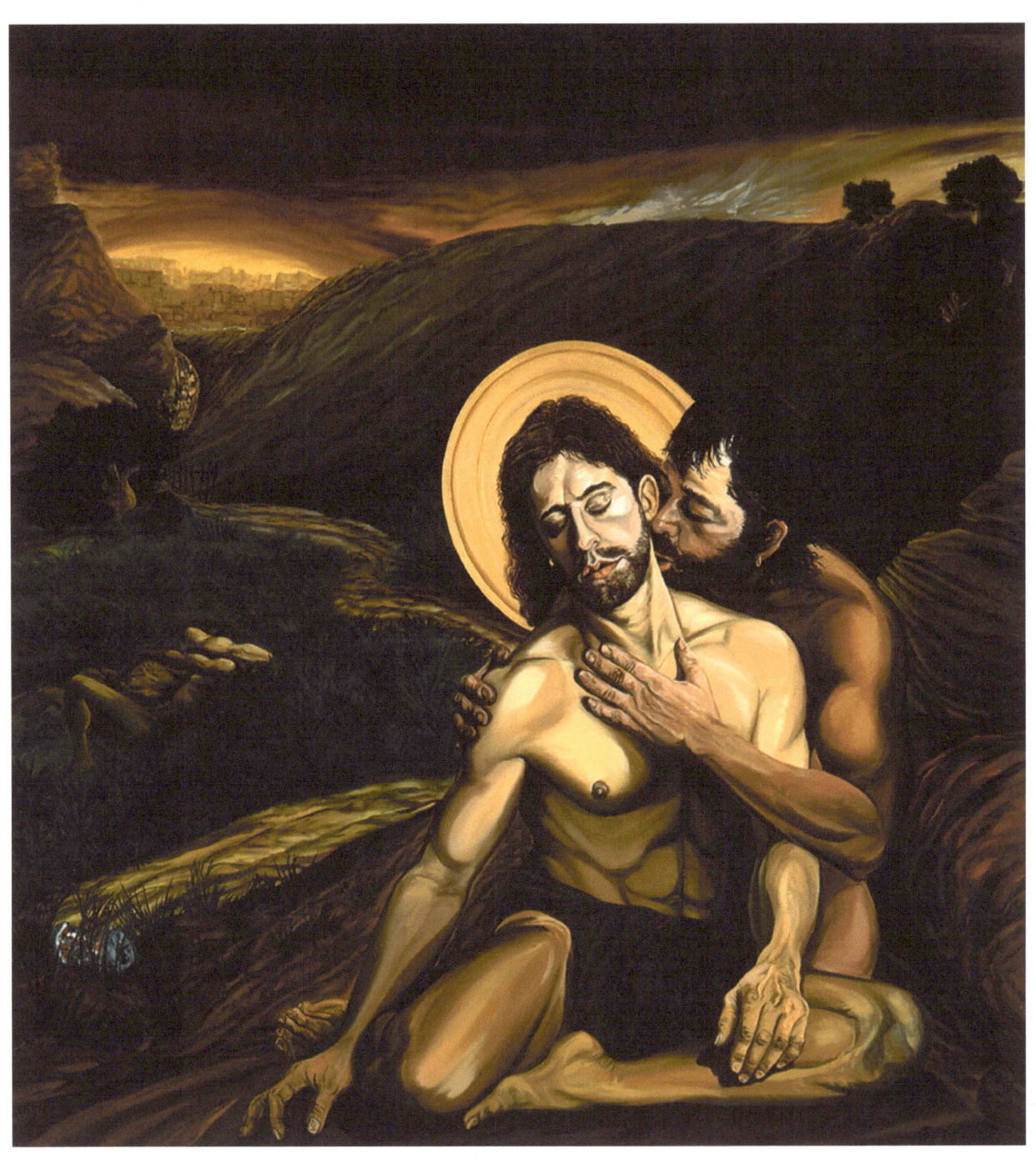

"Judas Kiss," Becki Jayne Harrelson, 1993.
Oil on canvas, 68" x 64". www.beckijayne.com

recalled. "I would address religion and transform the wealth of Christian knowledge I had received as a child, growing up in a family of preachers, into the message I thought was the true meaning, what had made sense to me as a child and as an adult. Jesus is for everyone. The Christ, the Buddha, God is within us all as we are and we are born in grace, not in original sin."

Harrelson's potent mix of rage, religion, memory, sex, and politics swirled together and brought forth stunning images: First came the sensual kiss between Jesus and Judas. She followed up with an ambitious series that re-envisions Bible stories from a lesbian feminist viewpoint. They include the Madonna with her female lover, Jesus rescuing a drag queen from stoning, and a female Holy Spirit raising Christ from the dead

Self-taught as an artist, Harrelson is also a versatile Renaissance woman who excels in many different fields: art, writing, marketing, advertising, graphic design, and web design and development. She speaks with quicksilver eloquence and a slight Southern drawl. A self-proclaimed "lipstick lesbian," she nonetheless usually runs around in "artist ragtag clothes" without makeup. She worked her way up to senior account manager for Mobil Chemical Company at an Atlanta ad agency, then left in 1991 to pursue art and writing. When she's not "art-ing," as she calls it, Harrelson relaxes by writing political commentary on her wickedly witty blog. All her models are lesbians and gay men in real life.

Perhaps her most blatant and therefore most controversial image is *The Crucifixion of Christ*. The sign on the cross usually reads "Jesus of Nazareth, King of the Jews." In Harrelson's crucifixion, the sign screams "Faggot."

"You miss the primary point if you think I'm saying Jesus was gay," she said. In her view, to take her literally would be to make the same mistake as taking the Bible literally.

"In Western civilization, Jesus is *the* ideal of holiness, of perfection in the flesh. My purpose is to de-shame our human sexual natures, especially gay sexuality, and present it as a sacred act," she said.

Harrelson's potent mix of rage, religion, memory, sex, and politics swirled together and brought forth stunning images.

Harrelson no longer calls herself Christian or puts any other label on her spirituality. She does connect to what she calls "the Source" by making art. She begins each painting with a sanctifying ritual that includes prayer, music, incense, and anointing the canvas with oil.

She painted the crucifixion through a steady stream of tears over human cruelty. "Look at the word 'faggot' on the cross. You could substitute the word 'nigger,' 'Jew boy,' 'honkie,' 'redneck' or 'bitch'—it all means the same. Anytime anyone rises up in condemnation, hatred, or violence against another, Christ is crucified," she said.

Plenty of people rose up to condemn the painting. "That is sick and disgusting," is a typical comment on conservative Christian websites where the "faggot crucifixion" has been viciously denounced. Harrelson's queer Christian art has been *de facto* censored in her hometown of Atlanta. Even gay gallery owners rejected it for fear of broken windows or worse.

Attacks also came from inside the queer community. Many appreciated her art, but some considered all Christian imagery to be inherently homophobic. Some said slurs like "faggot" should never be used. Some lesbians complained that she shouldn't paint men.

Her work has received critical acclaim, too, especially when it was exhibited in 1995 and 1998 by the Leslie-Lohman Gay Art Foundation in New York City. "The size, the color palette, and the skilled execution of the paintings demand that they be treated with as much reverence as any painting hanging in a church," wrote Andrew Wikholm of Gayhistory.com.

Her paintings function on multiple levels. In *Judas Kiss,* Jesus and his betrayer embrace in a time warp that is both Gethsemane and a contemporary gay cruising ground strewn with a beer can and a naked couple. *The Last Supper* is a tribute to Da Vinci's masterpiece of the same name, with disciples that include a Bacchus-like drag queen based on the work of Caravaggio. Their excesses are balanced by love, represented by Jesus and his Beloved in the center.

She painted the crucifixion through a steady stream of tears over human cruelty.

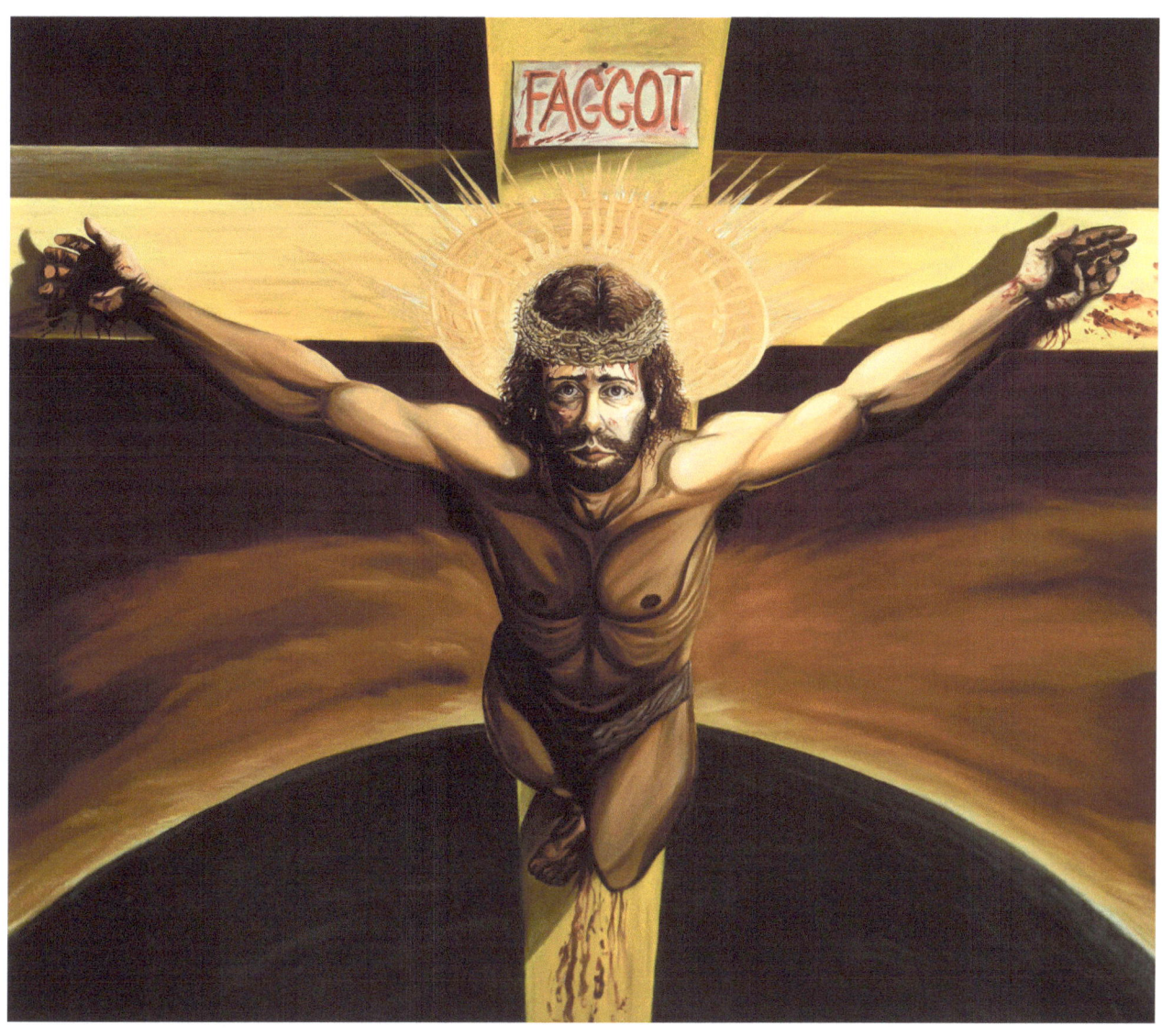

"The Crucifixion of Christ," Becki Jayne Harrelson, 1993.
Oil on canvas, 68" x 78". www.beckijayne.com

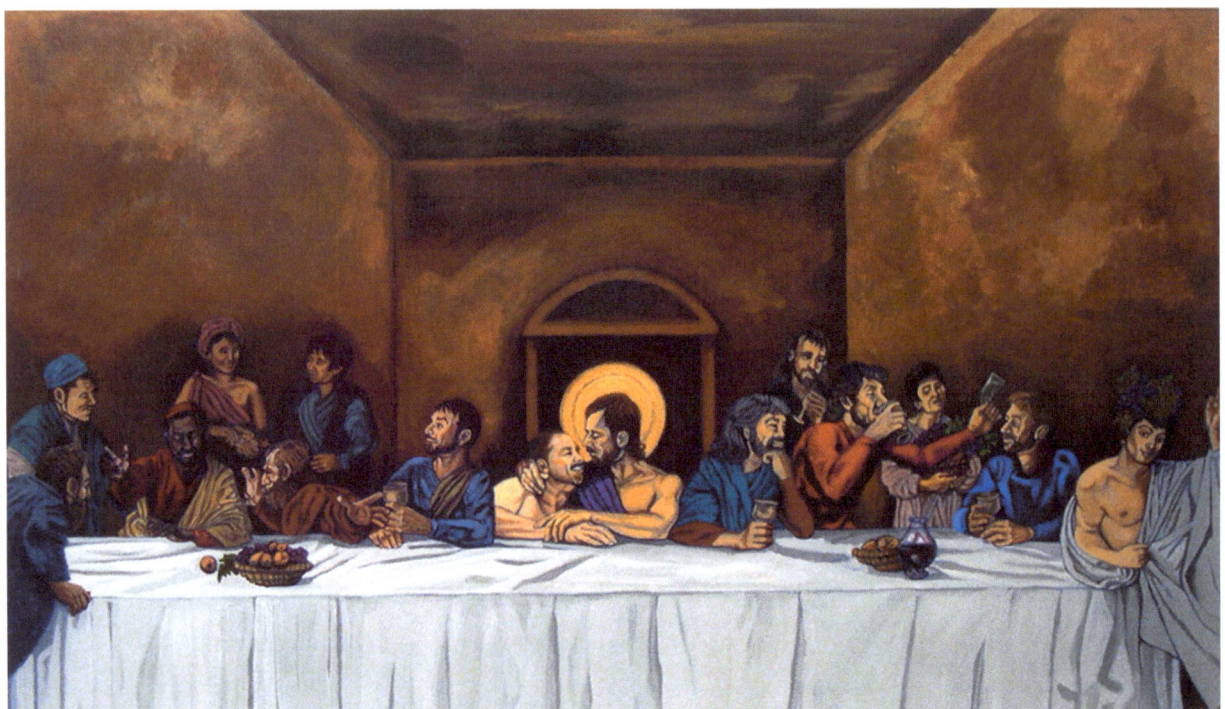

"Study for The Last Supper," Becki Jayne Harrelson, 2003. Acrylic on paper, 12" x 20". www.beckijayne.com

Each painting is packed with buried treasures for those who stay to study the details. For example, *Madonna, Lover and Son* is set in the same landscape as Da Vinci's *Madonna of the Rocks.* In Harrelson's version, the Madonna has a classic stylized halo while the landscape forms a natural sunlit halo around her blonde lover (based on the woman who has been Harrelson's partner since 1995). The contrasting halos are Harrelson's way of saying that lesbians are a natural part of creation, as opposed to the roles of wife and mother imposed by patriarchal religion.

"You'll also find, um, labia and vaginas if you look hard, usually in folds of clothing," Harrelson noted. A turkey baster is concealed in the bushes, a play on artificial insemination and virgin birth. "I think God has a sense of humor—where I get mine I like to think," Harrelson laughed.

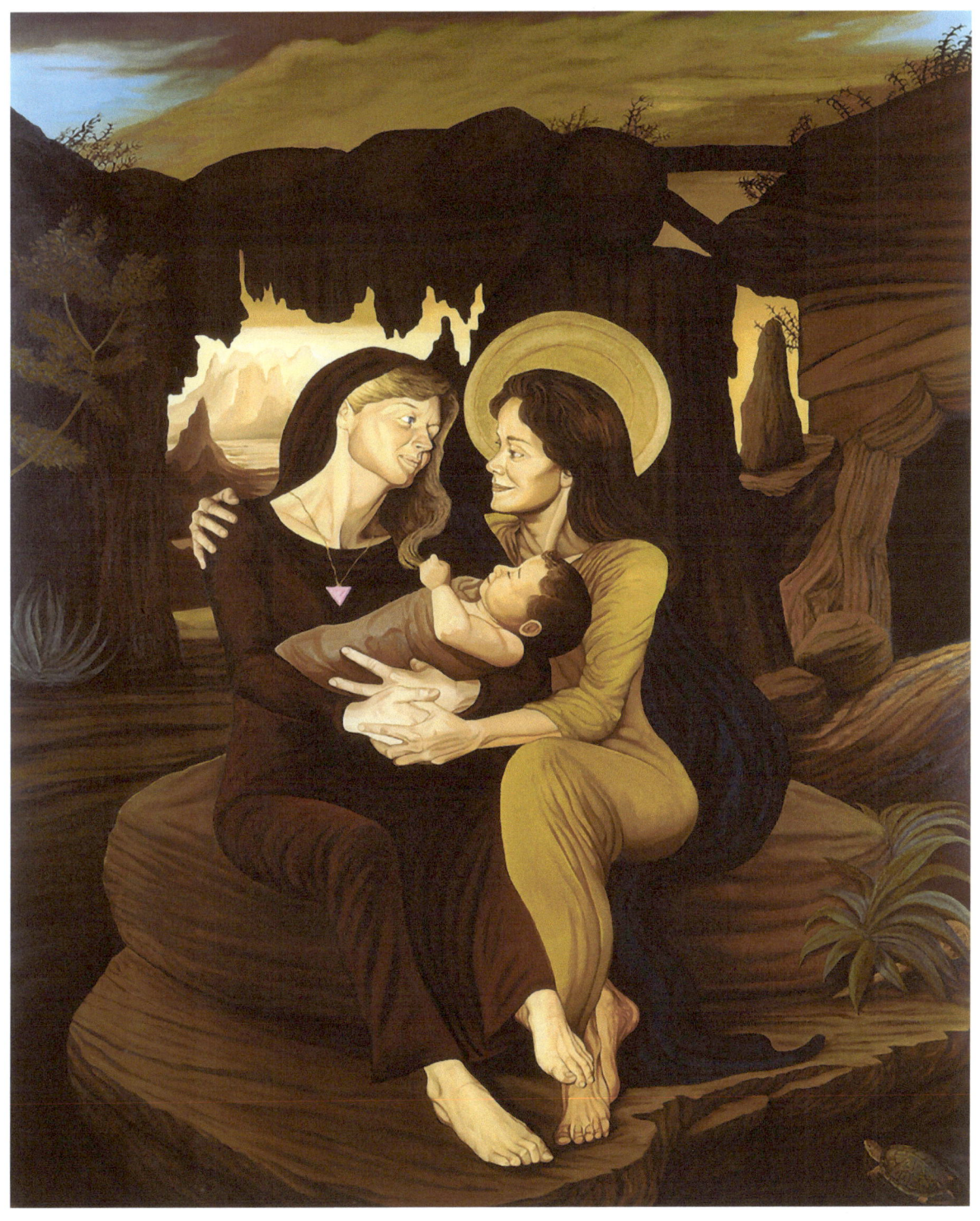

"Madonna, Lover and Son," Becki Jayne Harrelson, 1996.
Oil on canvas, 80" x 68". www.beckijayne.com

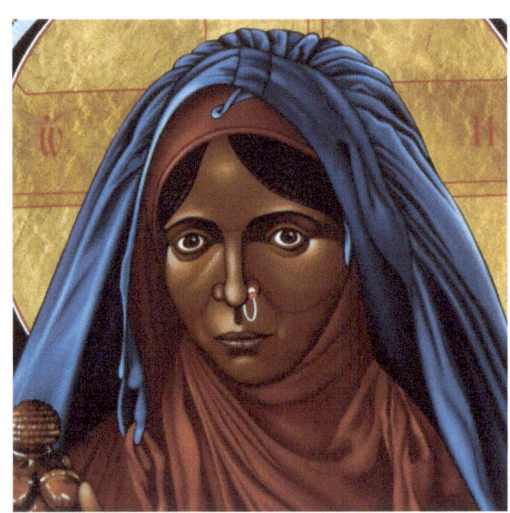

"Christ Sophia," detail

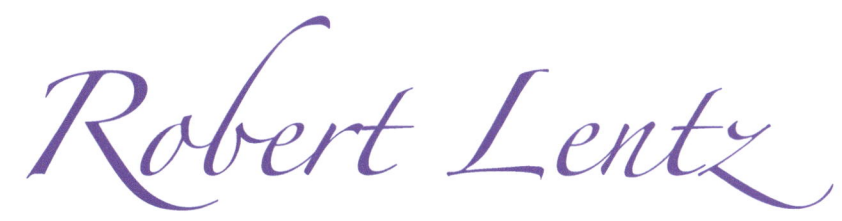

Robert Lentz

b. 1946, rural Colorado

Author-priest Henri Nouwen, famous but struggling with a secret gay identity, came to Brother Robert Lentz in 1983 with a special request: Make me an icon that symbolizes offering my own sexuality and affection to Christ. The project was a natural for Lentz, a world-class iconographer who was creating innovative icons in San Francisco after leaving monastic life. Research and reflection led Lentz to paint Christ being embraced by his beloved disciple John. He called it *Christ the Bridegroom.*

"Henri used it to come to grips with his own homosexuality," said Lentz, who rejoined the Franciscans as a friar in 2003 after a twenty-year absence. "I was told he carried it with him everywhere and it was one of the most precious things in his life." Nouwen's goal was celibacy and he did not come out publicly as gay before his death in 1996. Then biographer Michael Ford wrote about Nouwen's homosexuality—and how he kept *Christ the Bridegroom* opposite his bed to look at before sleep and as soon as he woke up.

The icon takes the Biblical theme of Christ as bridegroom and joins it to the medieval motif of Christ with St. John. The resulting image expresses their intimate friendship with exquisite subtlety. Lentz said he based his work on an icon from medieval Crete. Artists of the period also did several sculpture

> Lentz created innovative icons in San Francisco after leaving monastic life, but rejoined the Franciscans in 2003 after a twenty-year absence.

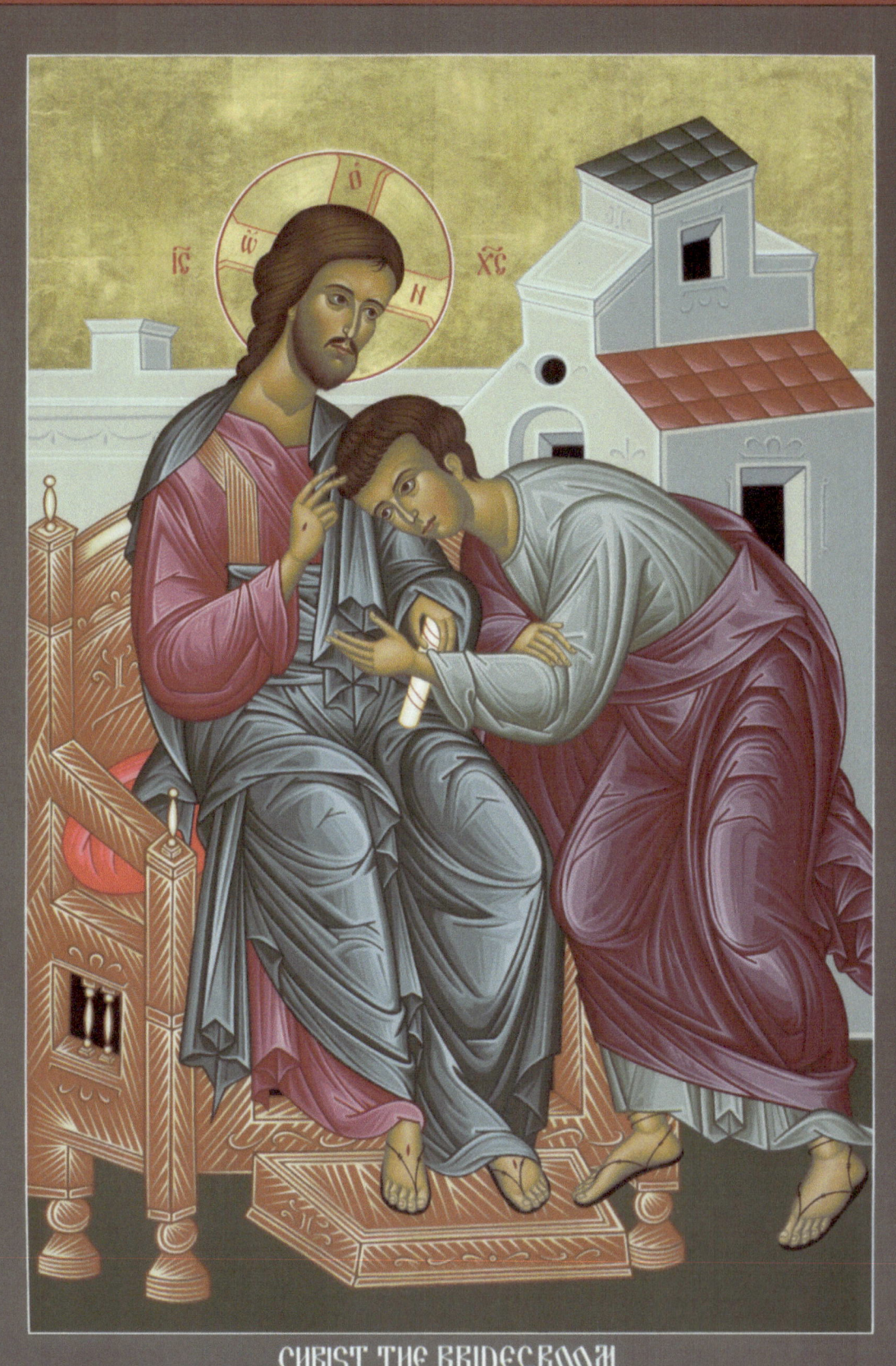

CHRIST THE BRIDEGROOM

groups of John resting on Jesus' chest. A notable example is the life-sized version done by Master Heinrich of Konstanz in the early fourteenth century for a convent in Switzerland. In that work, the two men hold hands while Jesus wraps a loving arm around John's shoulder.

If *Christ the Bridegroom* seems flat, it's because icons are a stylized art form designed to lead the viewer into the spiritual dimension. They are often called "windows to heaven." Lentz is a central figure in the worldwide revival of icons in the last half of the twentieth century.

Lentz made an ancient art form relevant—and sometimes controversial—by applying it to modern "saints" such as Gandhi, Martin Luther King, Jr., and Harvey Milk, the first openly gay elected official. Lentz's icons offer revolutionary visions of Christ and put official saints into historically accurate same-sex pairings, such as David and Jonathan.

"Window to heaven or road to hell?" trumpeted a conservative Catholic newsletter in February 2005. The article accused Lentz and his protégé Father William Hart McNichols of using icons to distort facts and glorify sin. Critics caused such a stir that in order to keep the peace between his Franciscan province and the Archbishop of Santa Fe, New Mexico, Lentz gave away the copyright for ten controversial images to his distributor, Trinity Stores. He had his name removed from those images on the Trinity website, but here he is reclaiming authorship.

"The fact that I painted them is history. Acknowledging them is acknowledging history," said Lentz, who speaks slowly in measured tones. "You can't turn history back. No matter how the bishops disagree with what I did in the past, they can't disagree with the fact that I'm no longer doing it. If it makes them uncomfortable, they're going to have to be uncomfortable."

His personal history begins with childhood in an immigrant family. His grandparents came to America from tsarist Russia.

Left: "Christ the Bridegroom," Br. Robert Lentz, OFM
© 1985; acrylic and gold leaf, 18" x 12".
Courtesy of www.trinitystores.com; 800.699.4482.

Lentz made an ancient art form relevant—and sometimes controversial—by applying it to modern "saints" such as Gandhi, Martin Luther King, Jr., and Harvey Milk.

Lentz grew up on stories of saints and labor unions instead of fairy tales, and icons covered the living room walls in his Russian grandmother's home. When he was old enough, he studied Byzantine iconography by apprenticing himself to a master painter in a Greek Orthodox monastery founded from Mount Athos. He spent the first eighteen years of his adult life in Orthodox and Roman Catholic monasteries.

Lentz left the monastery in 1982 and began painting icons full-time in San Francisco. At first he was shocked to meet openly gay men and lesbian women, feminists, anarchists, undocumented immigrants, and many others unlike the people he knew in cloistered life. Within a few months, he was making icons that expressed the holy passion for justice that he discovered on the streets of San Francisco.

His relatively traditional *Christ the Bridegroom*, done near the start of Lentz's explorations, was not on the list of ten unacceptable icons. The list does include four pairs of gay male saints, a female Celtic trinity, three people whom the institutional church deems unworthy of sainthood (Merlin, Harvey Milk, and Native American transgender We-Wha of Zuni), and two images of Christ. One of the taboo Christ figures is female and the other is joyously nude.

Christ sits naked, his crossed legs barely hiding his genitals, in *Lord of the Dance*. He has a halo—and horns—as he beats a drum in a cave marked with Stone-Age pictures of the horned god. This tawny, mustachioed fellow doesn't look like the usual Jesus, but he bears Christ's wounds and the initials above his head announce his identity.

The startling icon was commissioned by a gay art collector who gave Lentz the freedom to choose whatever subject he wanted.

"He asked me what I wanted to do. I was interested in Celtic spirituality and the horned god," Lentz said.

> Lentz found a happier solution by envisioning a horned Christ who wasn't ashamed of his body.
>
> "His confident nakedness emphasizes that what God has made is good."

Right: "Lord of the Dance," Br. Robert Lentz, OFM
©1991; acrylic and gold leaf, 20" x 16".
Courtesy of www.trinitystores.com; 800.699.4482.

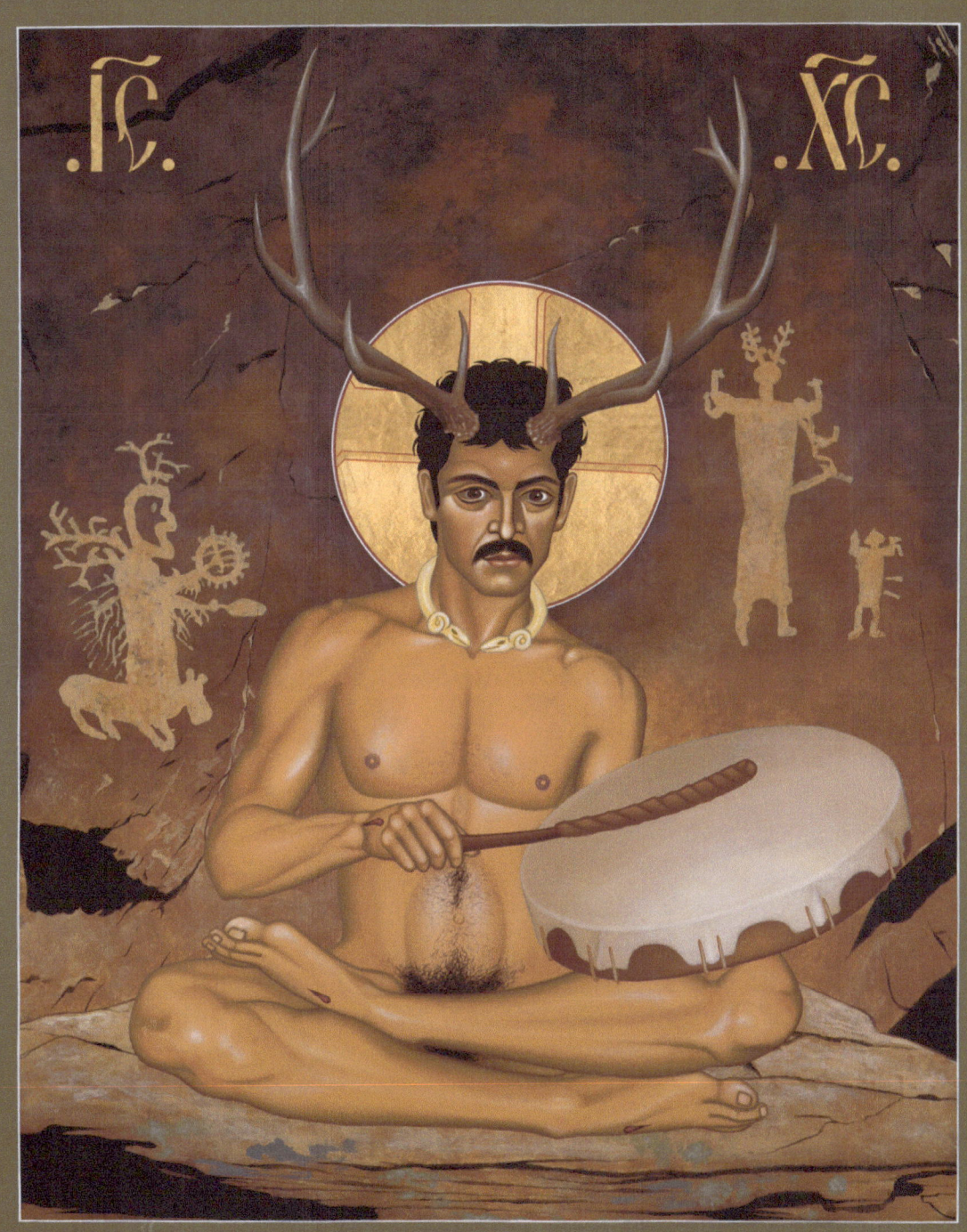

LORD of the DANCE

In the text he wrote to accompany the image, Lentz explained that "a benign antlered figure" is one of the most ancient masculine images of God in Europe. The horned god protects animals and guides souls to their destination after death. He embodies male sexuality and fertility. Christian missionaries tried to stamp out the horned god by turning him into a demonic figure.

Lentz found a happier solution by envisioning a horned Christ who wasn't ashamed of his body. "His confident nakedness emphasizes that what God has made is good," his text states. Throughout art history the nakedness of Christ has usually represented his vulnerability, but there are exceptions, such as the full frontal nudity of Michelangelo's triumphant *Risen Christ.*

Lentz's *Lord of the Dance* turns out to have broad appeal. "It's actually had a far better reception among straight men and married women than gay men. A lot of gay men have already dealt with their bodies in a way straight men haven't," he said.

A psychologist told him that men would be better companions if they were in touch with their bodies in the same way as the horned Christ in *Lord of the Dance.* Lentz still recalls her pronouncement: "If more men would live with that image, more women would dance."

His other forbidden Christ icon uses prehistoric imagery to affirm women's sexuality and the sacred feminine. *Christ Sophia* shows a female Christ in an egg-shaped mandala holding the *Venus of Willendorf,* a 25,000-year-old fertility goddess figurine. One of the common names for God throughout the Bible is the grammatically feminine term for Wisdom (*Sophia* in Greek and *Hokhmah* in Hebrew). Scholars say that Wisdom was prefigured by the Egyptian goddess Isis. In the Bible, Wisdom is a divine savior who creates the world and hosts feasts.

Like all artists who tackle the subject, Lentz faced the challenge of how to make Christ female, but still recognizable. He chose to paint Sophia as a dark-skinned Middle Eastern woman. She can only be identified as Christ by the inscriptions around her, and perhaps by her ineffable, magnetic gaze.

His other forbidden Christ icon uses prehistoric imagery to affirm women's sexuality and the sacred feminine.

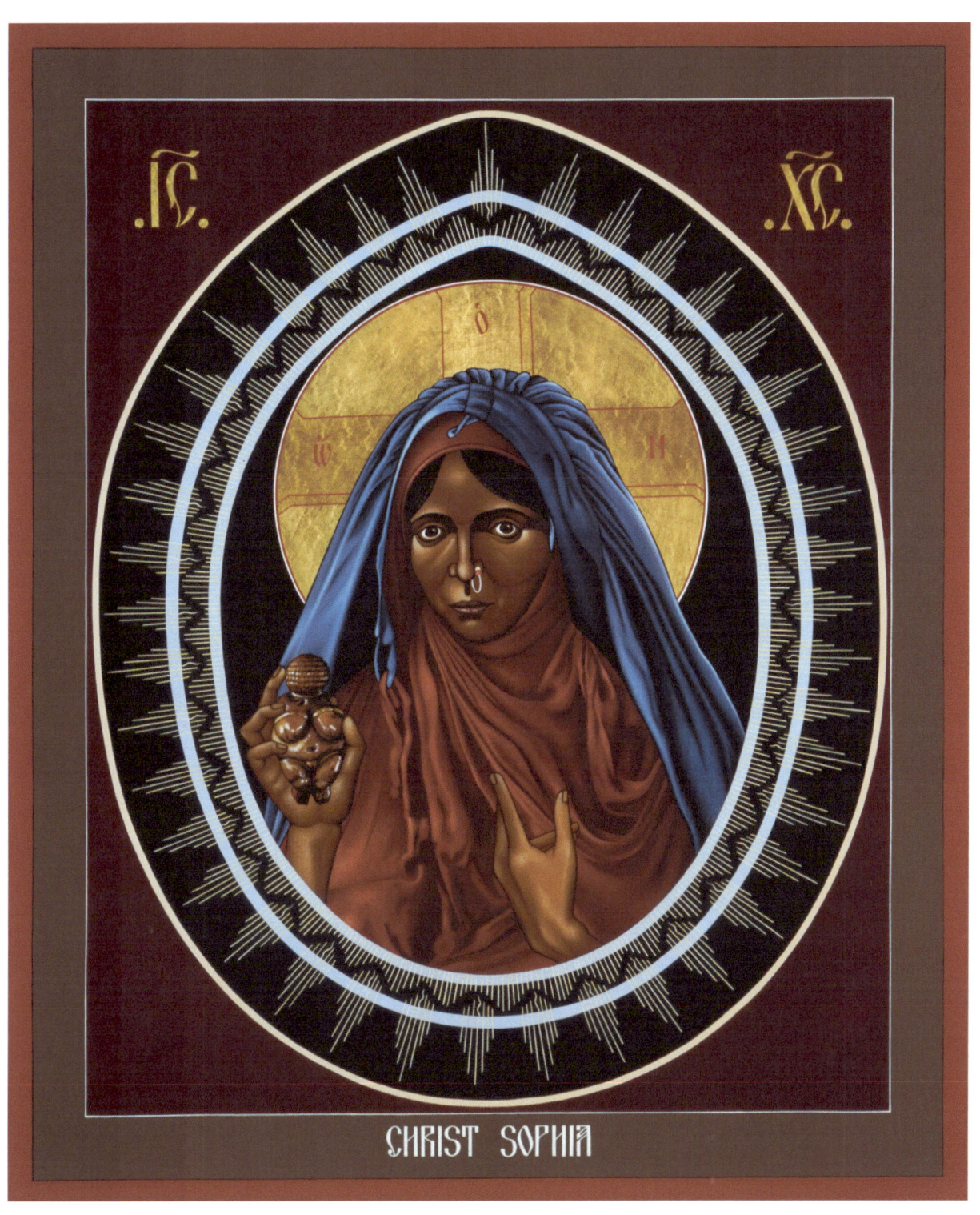

CHRIST SOPHIA

"Christ Sophia," Br. Robert Lentz, OFM © 1989.
Acrylic and gold leaf, 15" x 12". Courtesy of www.trinitystores.com; 800.699.4482.

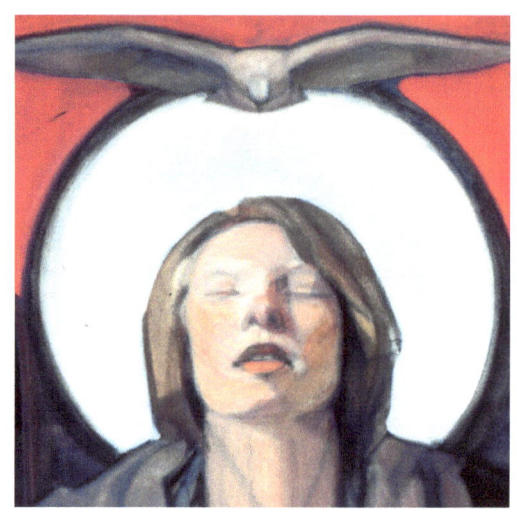

"Mary with the Midwives," detail

Janet McKenzie

b. 1948, Brooklyn, NY

An androgynous, dark-skinned figure came to mind when Janet McKenzie tried to envision how Jesus would look in the twenty-first century. The Vermont-based artist had built a successful career painting women who looked like herself, fair and blonde, but this time she wanted to create a truly inclusive image that would touch her nephew, an African American teenager.

"I felt it was time to include and pay homage to African Americans and women, two groups left out of imagery of Jesus," McKenzie explained. She thought of a graceful young African American woman who had started modeling for her in recent years. She picked up a brush and began to paint from memory.

"Jesus of the People simply came through me. I feel as though I am only a vehicle for its existence," McKenzie said. She considers herself "an unlikely being to have been used in this way." She had never even thought about painting the adult Jesus until a friend called to tell her that the *National Catholic Reporter* was sponsoring a contest to find an image of Christ for the new millennium.

Raised Episcopalian, McKenzie was a divorced mother with a spirituality that was "mercurial and evolving, and non-specific," drawing inspiration from many faith traditions. Her finished painting shows Jesus with an Asian yin-yang symbol and an

"I felt it was time to include and pay homage to African Americans and women, two groups left out of imagery of Jesus."

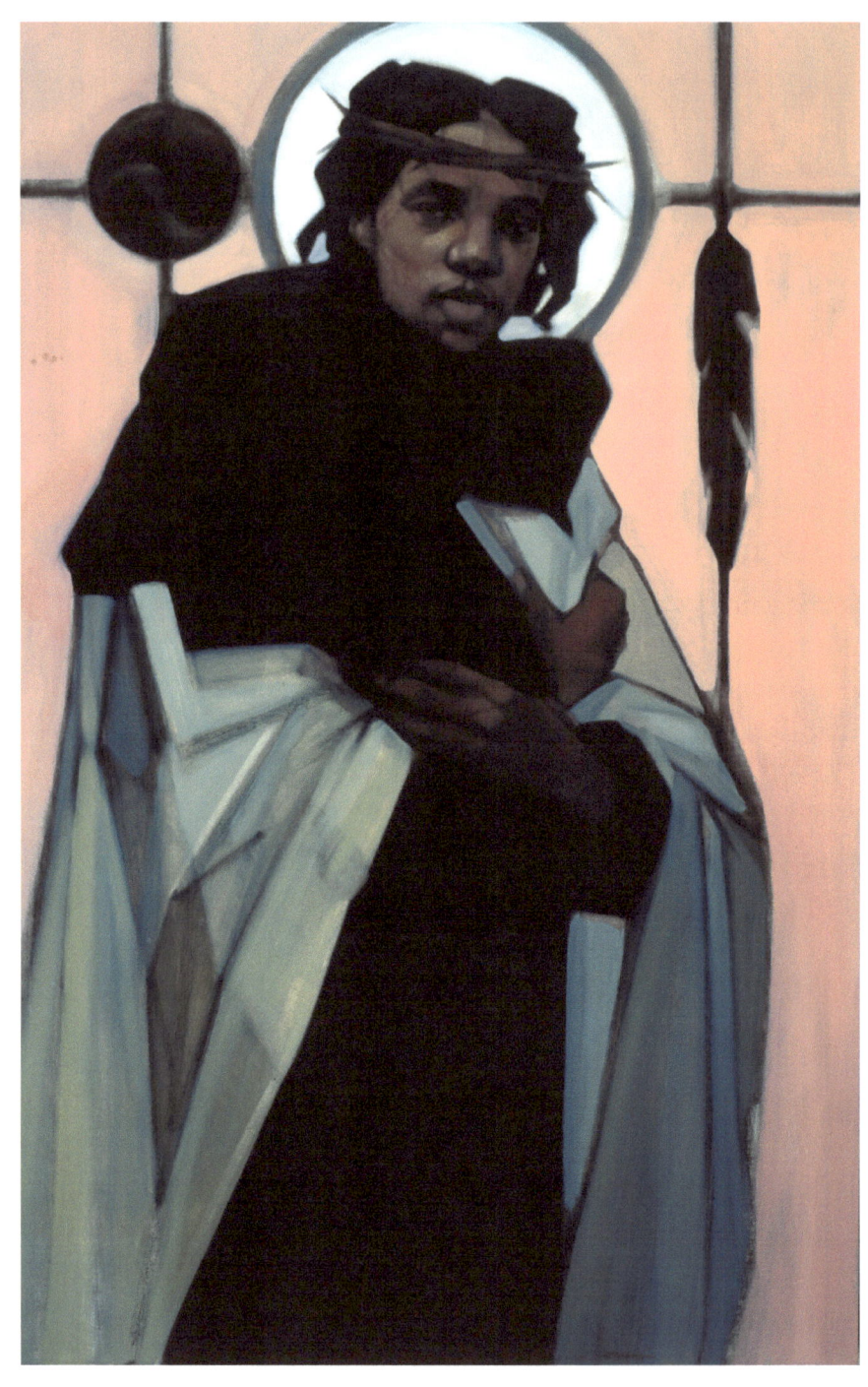

"Jesus of the People," Janet McKenzie ©1999.
Oil on canvas, 48" x 30". www.janetmckenzie.com

eagle feather that refers to the Great Spirit in Native American cultures.

McKenzie submitted it to the Jesus 2000 competition, which received nearly 1,700 other entries from nineteen countries on six continents. The judge was Sister Wendy Beckett, a former nun widely known for her BBC/PBS television series on great world art.

Sister Wendy's first choice was *Jesus of the People*. In her words, "This is a haunting image of a peasant Jesus—dark, thick-lipped, looking out on us with ineffable dignity, with sadness but with confidence."

McKenzie had won many scholarships and awards back when she was an art student at New York City's Fashion Institute of Technology and Art Students League. Still she was stunned when *Jesus of the People* took first place, and even more surprised by the intense opposition that began as soon as the winner was announced in December 1999.

People attacked every aspect of the painting, but the critics seemed most upset that McKenzie had painted a Jesus who was female or at least had a feminine aspect. "Jesus doesn't look like that," was the most common complaint.

McKenzie was swamped by negative e-mail accusing her of blasphemy, racism, and political correctness, and ordering her to read the Bible. People called and screamed obscenities at her. A hate group threatened to picket in front of her studio in a remote Vermont village. The local Post Office began separating her mail for fear of a letter bomb. The news media quoted people who called the work "garbage," "utter stupidity," and "patently false feminist ideology."

Jesus of the People also received a lot of heartfelt praise. People rejoiced at finding themselves celebrated. Men and women of every race all over the world said that it opened their eyes to new ways of perceiving Jesus. Some wept and others begged to buy the painting. McKenzie's African American nephew, the one whom McKenzie aimed to reach, happily filled his school locker with magnets and cards bearing the image.

> People attacked every aspect of the painting, but the critics seemed most upset that McKenzie had painted a Jesus who was female or at least had a feminine aspect.

Debate continued wherever *Jesus of the People* went during its three-year tour of the United States from 2000 to 2003. McKenzie's schedule was filled with television appearances and media interviews. Meanwhile *Jesus of the People* had to be displayed in a Plexiglas case for its own protection.

Over the years the criticism has quieted, while McKenzie continues to get countless requests to exhibit or reproduce the work. "I am only the guardian now," she said. Someday she hopes the painting will have its own chapel in a large church, "where many people of color can have long-term, loving access to it."

McKenzie's experience with *Jesus of the People* gave new directions to her art. African American women are now a favorite subject, especially Maria Hill Barnes, the inspiration for her Jesus painting. McKenzie has re-envisioned more of Jesus' life, including a gender-bending series for The Nativity Project.

Liturgy expert Barbara Marian founded The Nativity Project to revisit and revitalize the Gospel with new images of women. McKenzie's paintings for the project include *Epiphany,* which transforms the traditional three wise men into a multiracial trio of women, and *Mary with the Midwives.* The Bible doesn't mention midwives at Jesus' birth, but people in first-century Palestine would have assumed their presence. *Mary with the Midwives* pictures a flesh-and-blood Madonna in an unguarded moment, eyes closed and exhaling as she surrenders to the labor pain that leads to Jesus' birth. Her private act of courage and creation is witnessed by a pair of midwives seated solidly on the earth.

Jesus of the People freed McKenzie to paint an indisputably female Christ—an image so challenging that it has been censored by the gatekeepers who decide what gets exhibited. Called *Christ Mother,* it is a towering, gritty, and majestic painting of a nude woman bound in a crucifixion pose. McKenzie generally works smaller, incorporating drawing and line into oils to build luminous images, but *Christ Mother* is big and rough. McKenzie gave it texture with soft, crumbly lumber crayon and even exposed bare canvas to highlight Christ's breasts in stark white.

"She is the feminine aspect of Jesus, mother to us all, and to my mind, she is undeniable," McKenzie said. "*Christ Mother* is in the act of being crucified, yet she stands with strength, in acceptance, although bound. Her body glows with life but also reflects the coming hereafter."

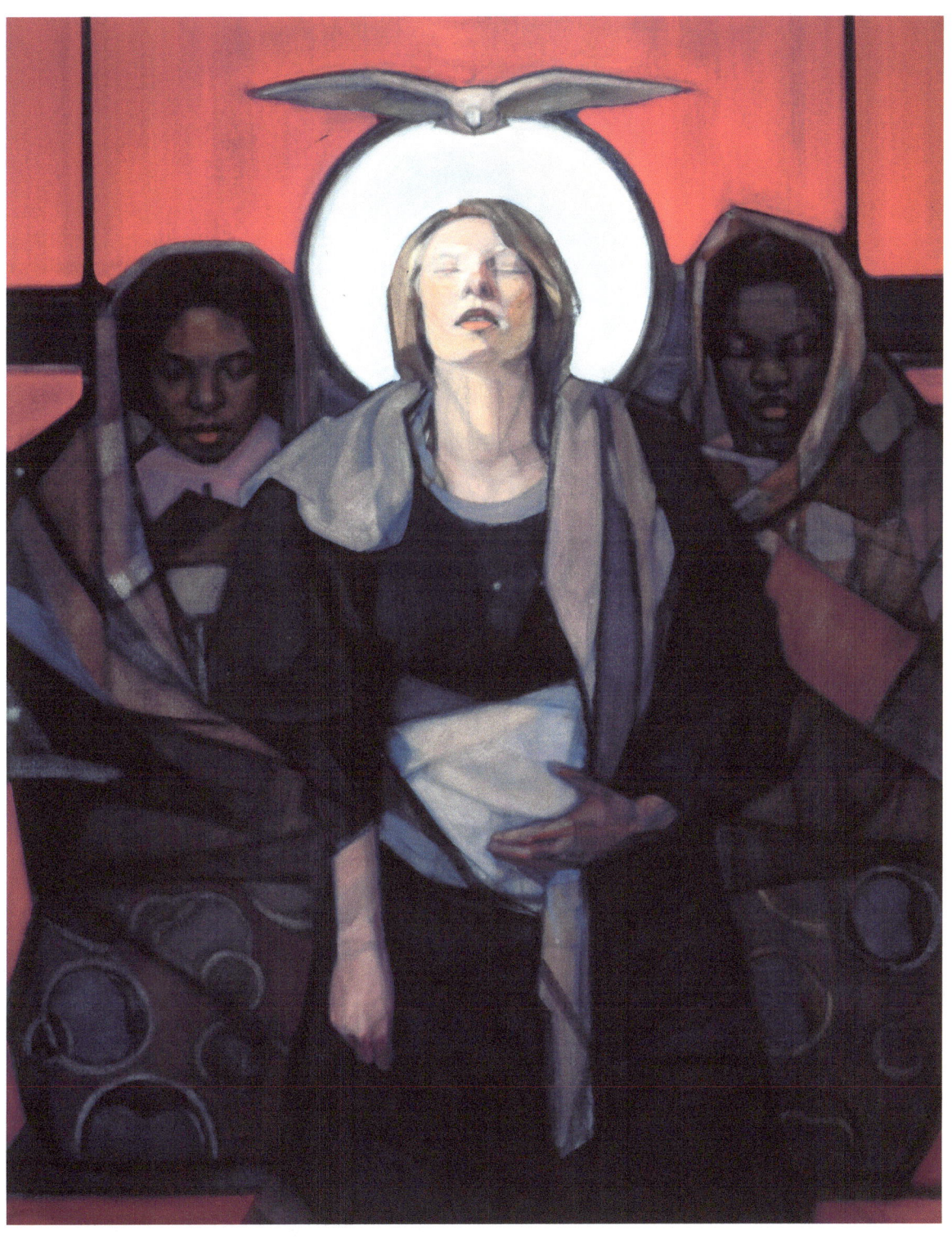

"Mary with the Midwives," Janet McKenzie © 2003. Oil on canvas, 54" x 42".
Collection of Barbara Marian, Harvard, IL. www.janetmckenzie.com

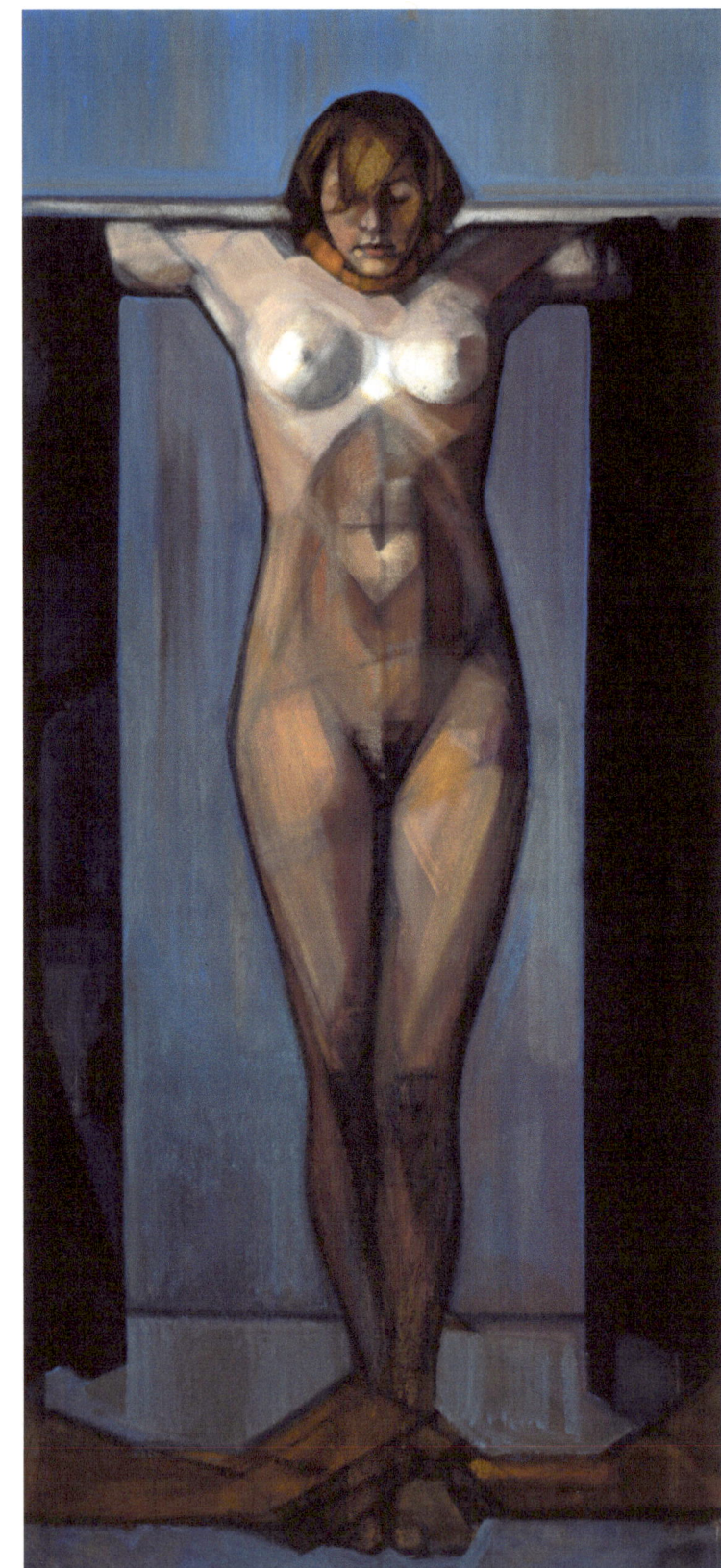

"Christ Mother,"
Janet McKenzie
© 2002.
Oil on canvas with
lumber crayon,
72" x 32".
www.janet
mckenzie.com

The idea for *Christ Mother* came to her in 2002 when a regional art center in Vermont invited her for a solo show featuring *Jesus of the People*. McKenzie wanted to paint something special for a prominent vertical wall at the entrance. "*Christ Mother* emerged and once she began to reveal herself I couldn't stop the work from moving into existence on its own, with its special voice," McKenzie recalled. "Sometimes 'controversial' art simply comes forward, like it or not. It is like a scream; you are doing it before you realize you are."

When three women from the art center visited McKenzie's studio to preview the exhibit, they turned their backs on *Christ Mother*, pretending that they didn't see the enormous masterpiece as they discussed the rest of the show. "Finally I asked them if they saw *Christ Mother?* When I said that, it was as if I burst an emotional balloon. They all said YES! And they could NOT show it because it would cause too much trouble (for them and potentially for their future funding expectations)," McKenzie said.

She was surprised to find herself feeling compassion for the women as they eagerly shared the docents' discomfort with "genitalia-specific art," avoiding the larger issues of crucifixion and the sacred feminine. "After years of confronting other peoples' rage and threats over *Jesus of the People,* I recognized a similar ring to their response and it only confirmed back to me that the work reached its mark," she said.

McKenzie chose not to fight the censorship directly, and *Christ Mother* made its debut in 2003 at the Episcopal Cathedral in Burlington, Vermont. Since then it has been invited for exhibition only rarely, and mostly in sacred spaces. The censorship launched McKenzie on a whole new series. All of the paintings in her *Woman Offered* series are female crucifixions, but unlike *Christ Mother,* their bodies are veiled and their identity is cloaked by the more generic title. *Christ Mother* stands alone in McKenzie's work as the only full-figure nude to bear Christ's name.

"I knew inherently as a little girl that I was made in *God's* image just as the boys were," she said. She emphasized that making sacred images of women and their suffering is important—and unstoppable. "Art that hits a nerve and confronts inequity is the art that sincerely contributes to change, and censorship cannot hold it back," McKenzie said.

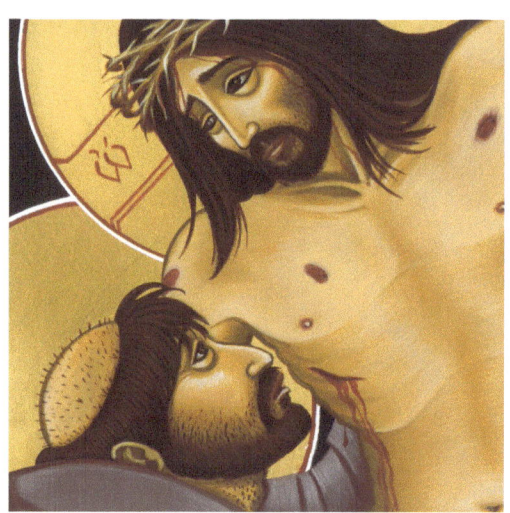

"St. Francis 'Neath the
Bitter Tree," detail

William Hart McNichols

b. 1949, Denver, CO

When Father William Hart McNichols worked in an AIDS hospice, he experienced firsthand the truth of Jesus' words: "What you did for the least of these, you did for me." McNichols met Christ in the faces and voices of people dying of AIDS, many of them young gay men. The Roman Catholic priest found strength amid the suffering by remembering saints such as St. Francis of Assisi, whose spiritual awakening began when he hugged a man who was a leper and an outcast.

McNichols spent seven intense years illustrating books while working with the AIDS hospice team at St. Vincent's Hospital in Manhattan. Then in 1990 he left for New Mexico to study the art of icons. He gave visual form to his hospice experiences in *St. Francis 'Neath the Bitter Tree,* first as a drawing in 1983 and then in 1991 as an icon commissioned by a New Jersey doctor treating people with AIDS.

The image shows Jesus covered with Kaposi's sarcoma lesions, a sure sign of AIDS before more effective drugs were developed in the mid-1990s. Words on the cross proclaim that Christ is an "AIDS leper" as well as a "drug user" and "homosexual," outcast groups at high risk for getting AIDS. The two men gaze intently at each other with unspeakable love as St. Francis

> McNichols met Christ in the faces and voices of people dying of AIDS, many of them young gay men.

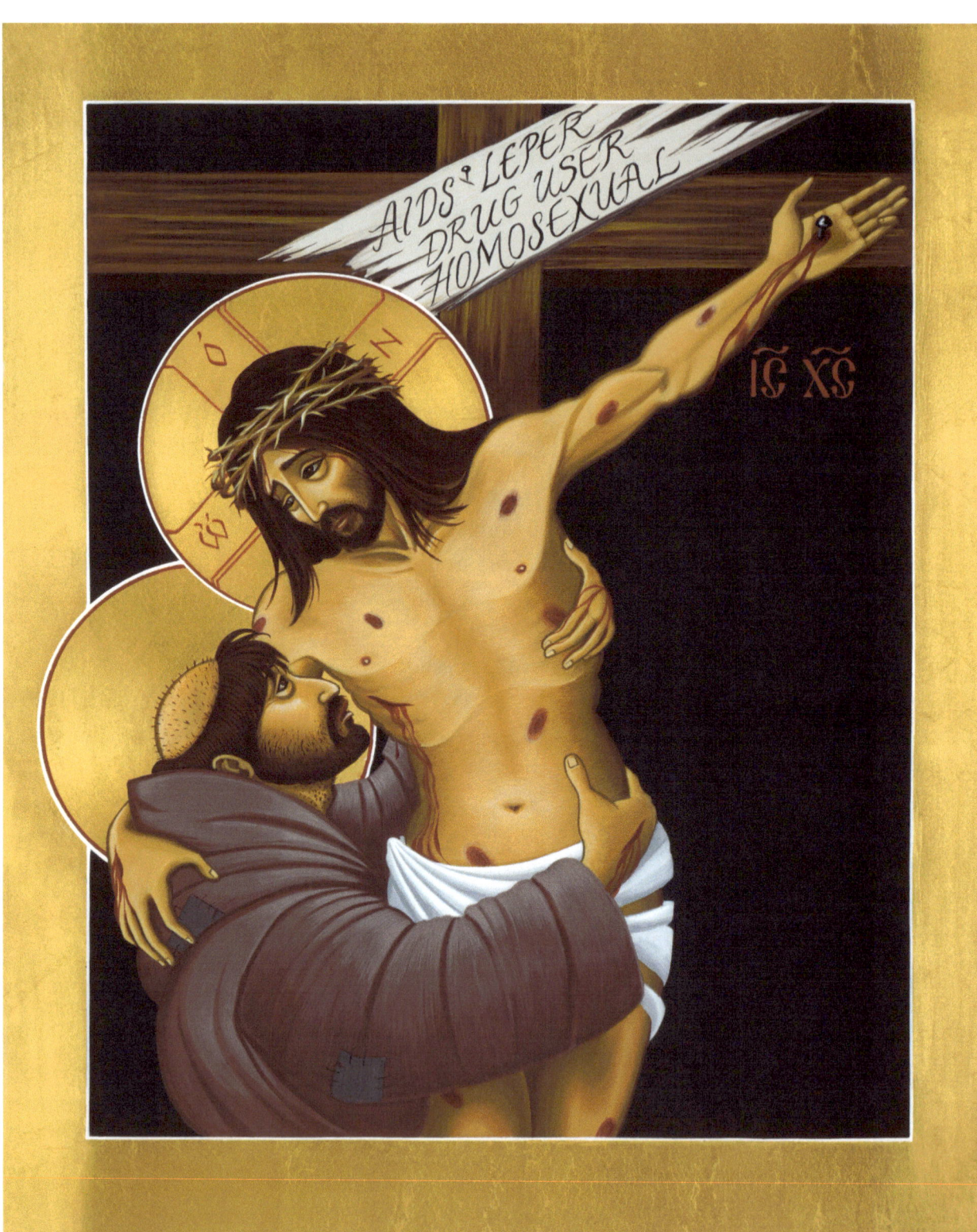

embraces the wounded Christ. McNichols has referred to St. Francis in this icon as the *Alter Christus,* Latin for the "other Christ." Thus the image reveals intimacy between two Christ figures, or between Christ and a Christ-to-be. Every priest is said to be an *Alter Christus.*

McNichols created the icon in his own gracefully elegant style based on a 1668 painting by Spanish painter Bartolome Esteban Murillo, which was surely inspired by the more passionate 1620 version of fellow Spaniard Francisco Ribalta. In Ribalta's work, Christ responds to St. Francis' ecstatic kiss by giving the saint his crown of thorns, a symbol of suffering that leads to divine union.

As a priest, McNichols has struggled to embrace social outcasts—and also the socially unacceptable parts of himself. He realized that he was gay in childhood. He joined the Jesuits in 1968 and a year later, willing to become straight, he began electroshock therapy. He stopped after several weeks on the advice of an older gay priest who assured him, "God made you the way you are."

He served as a Jesuit for thirty-five years with ordination in 1979 and a master of fine arts degree from the Pratt Institute in Brooklyn, New York, in 1983. Since the 1980s he has come out as a gay priest in various publications, including *Time* and the *Advocate* magazines in 2002. Not long after those interviews were published, he was forced to leave the Jesuits when "a very few in 'power'" said he was too open about his gay orientation. McNichols emphasizes that he does not blame all Jesuits, and in many ways his relationship with the Jesuits has never been better.

> As a priest, McNichols has struggled to embrace social outcasts—and also the socially unacceptable parts of himself.

Left: "St. Francis 'Neath the Bitter Tree," Father William Hart McNichols © 1991. Acrylic and gold leaf, 15" x 12". Private collection, New Jersey.

He has faced repercussions for coming out, but McNichols still serves the church in Taos, New Mexico, by making icons of Christ and a vast array of saints both ancient and modern. Saints have been his friends through the tough and lonely times ever since he was a child being harassed in grade school.

His relationship with the saints entered a new phase in 1990 when he began studying with world-renowned iconographer Brother Robert Lentz in New Mexico. "The vocation of the iconographer is to call beyond to the holy ones and beg them to be present in the icon so that others might converse with them," McNichols explained.

At first even McNichols felt that icons were stiff and distant. "The icon appears as a rather shy, respectful friend who takes a long time to get to know," he said. Icons differ from other art forms because they are meant for contemplation in order to make a mystical connection. According to tradition, artists don't "create" or "paint" the icons, but "write" them because they are visual revelations of theology transcribed by the artist. For the sake of humility, they are usually unsigned.

One of McNichols' first and most intriguing icons is *Hagia Hesychia: Jesus Christ Redeemer Holy Silence,* based on an eighteenth-century Russian icon of Jesus as female. While most female Christ figures provoke debate, this one is so formal and inaccessible that critics have kept silent. The icon could easily be mistaken for an angelic woman. Her identity is revealed to those who understand the initials at the top, "IC XC," a Greek abbreviation for "Jesus Christ." It was commissioned by a friend who told McNichols that it was "a picture of unconditional love."

"Originally I did not share my friend's enthusiasm for the image," McNichols admitted. He changed his mind while working on it. During the month it takes to write an icon, he is in constant conversation with his subject, almost as if the person in the picture was his houseguest. Sometimes as he paints, he feels like he actually touches the person behind the image. A month with Holy Silence left McNichols "aglow with the experience."

McNichols has been criticized for depicting "saints" not authorized by the church, including such gay martyrs as Matthew Shepard and an anonymous gay priest killed in a Nazi death camp. Whatever hardships he faces, McNichols continues to get energy from dialogue with the icons he creates. "We need to gaze at truly conversational, truly loving images…images that will return our love," he said.

Right: "Hagia Hesychia: Jesus Christ Redeemer Holy Silence,"
Father William Hart McNichols © 1991.
Acrylic and gold leaf, 14" x 12". Private collection, Amagansett, NY.

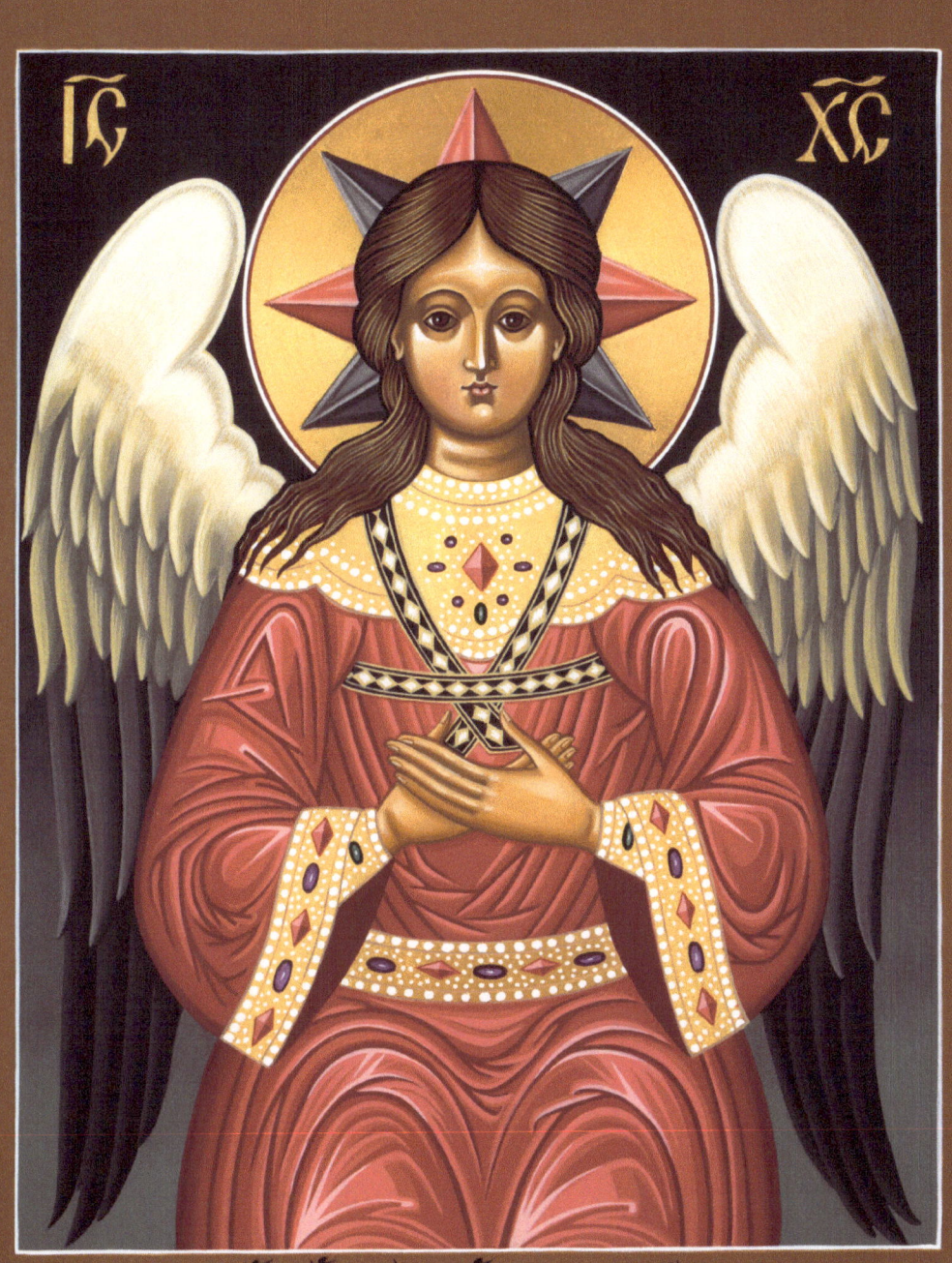

ΙͨϹ   ΧͨϹ

Ἡ ἁΓΙΑ ἩϹΥΧΙΑ

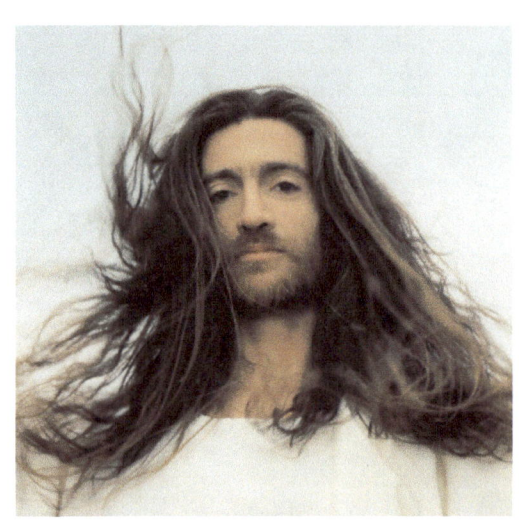

"Sermon on the Mount," detail

Elisabeth Ohlson Wallin

b. 1961, Skara, Sweden

Elisabeth Ohlson Wallin had lost many friends to AIDS, so she got mad when some Christians said that the disease was God's punishment for being gay. Ohlson Wallin, a Swedish photographer, remembered the Sunday school panels that had taught her about love when she was growing up. She tried to reconcile them with everything that she had learned about love as a young lesbian in Stockholm's lively subculture of LGBT people.

"I wanted to show that love is for everyone," Ohlson Wallin said. She combined the dual influences of Christianity and queer consciousness to create a groundbreaking series of twelve photos showing Jesus in a contemporary LGBT context. It became one of Europe's most noticed and notorious art exhibits, even arousing the disapproval of Pope John Paul II—who reacted by canceling his planned audience with the Swedish archbishop.

Ohlson Wallin called the series *Ecce Homo,* a pun meaning "See the human being" and "See the homosexual." The Latin phrase was used by the Roman governor when he showed Jesus to the crowd after scourging him. It was Ohlson Wallin's first photo exhibit. When she embarked on *Ecce Homo,* she was a self-taught photographer who had worked for several Swedish

Ohlson Wallin combined the dual influences of Christianity and queer consciousness to show Jesus in a contemporary LGBT context.

newspapers. She enlisted local LGBT folk to serve as models, and they spent three years meticulously recreating scenes from the life of Christ based on the artistic masterpieces of Michelangelo, Caravaggio, Rubens, and others.

"It's very important for me in my work that the picture have a documentary truth mixed with the way I arrange the story in the picture," Ohlson Wallin said. She and her models played with the contradictions. They transported themselves back into familiar tableaus such as Da Vinci's *Last Supper*. They brought Jesus forward in time to join them in classic queer situations such as a gay pride march that doubles as a Palm Sunday procession.

"These were my grownup Sunday school panels," Ohlson Wallin explained. "I wanted Jesus for me and my own sexual sense. I wanted to be able to identify with Jesus. There are millions and billions of Jesus pictures for heterosexuals to identify with. In Africa they have black Jesus. In China they have Chinese Jesus. Lots of different countries each have a different Jesus."

The exhibition opened in Stockholm during gay pride week 1998. Ohlson Wallin's huge photos were hung in chronological order in a cold, dark cave that had been used as a bomb shelter. It reminded Ohlson Wallin of the catacombs where the early church met secretly to avoid persecution. Under each photo was an appropriate Bible passage.

"I was very naïve when I made my pictures," Ohlson Wallin said. "I had my childlike way of believing in God. I thought all the Christian people were kind. I didn't understand how dangerous the pictures were when I made them. I didn't understand what was going to happen."

The exhibit provoked intense debate and even bomb threats. Those who welcomed Ohlson Wallin's vision arranged for *Ecce Homo* to tour Sweden, mostly in congregations of the state Lutheran Church. Its leader, Archbishop K. G. Hammar, angered the Pope by giving permission for a slide show of *Ecce Homo* during meditation services at Uppsala's National Cathedral, considered the holiest place in Sweden.

The exhibit went on to tour Scandinavia and continental Europe from 1998 to 2000, winning awards and breaking several attendance records. More than 250,000

Right: "Annunciation" (from Ecce Homo),
Elisabeth Ohlson Wallin, 1998. Photograph, 79" x 60".

The angel said to her, "Do not be afraid, Mary,
for you have found favor with God. And now, you will conceive
in your womb and bear a son, and you will name him Jesus."
—Luke 1:30-31

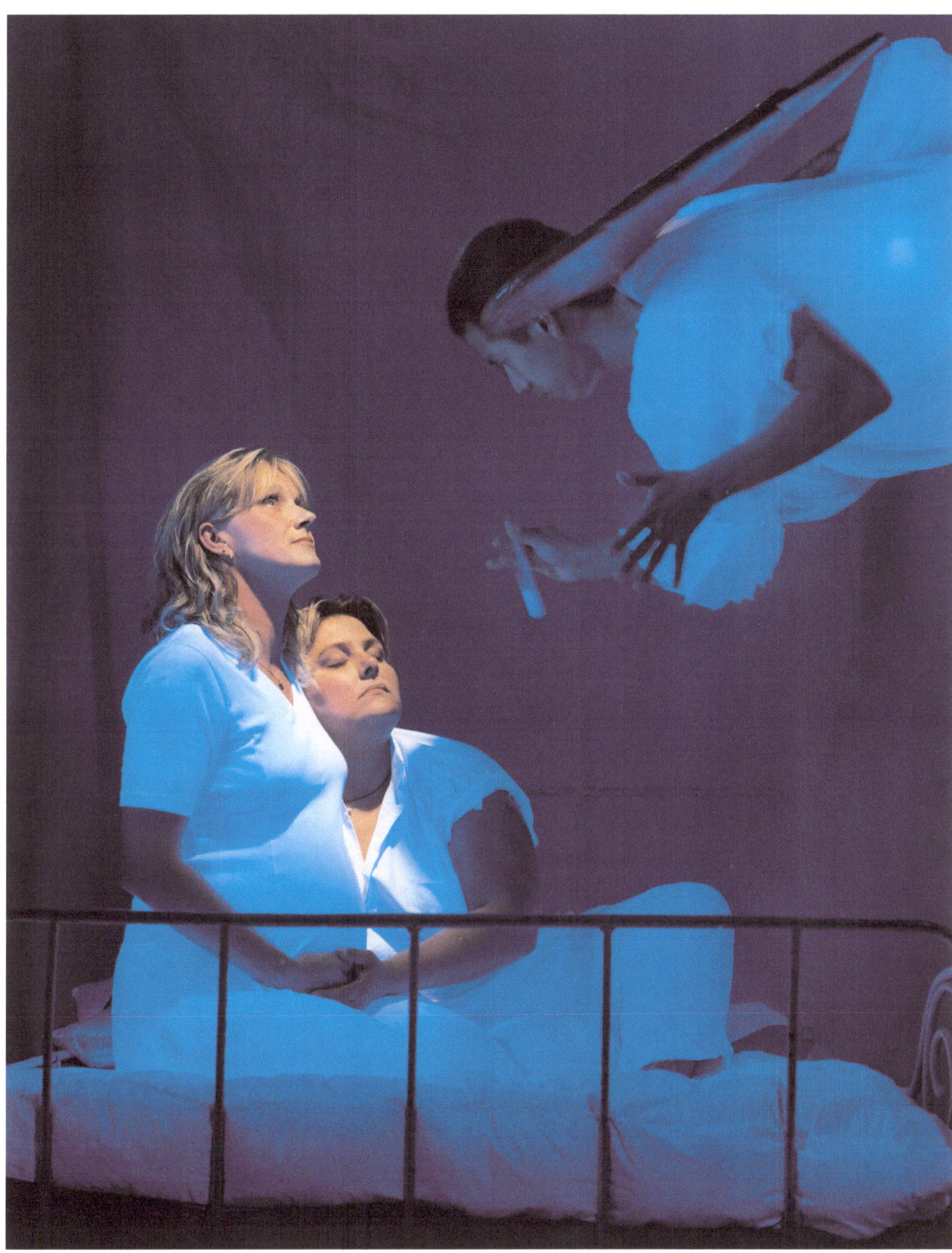

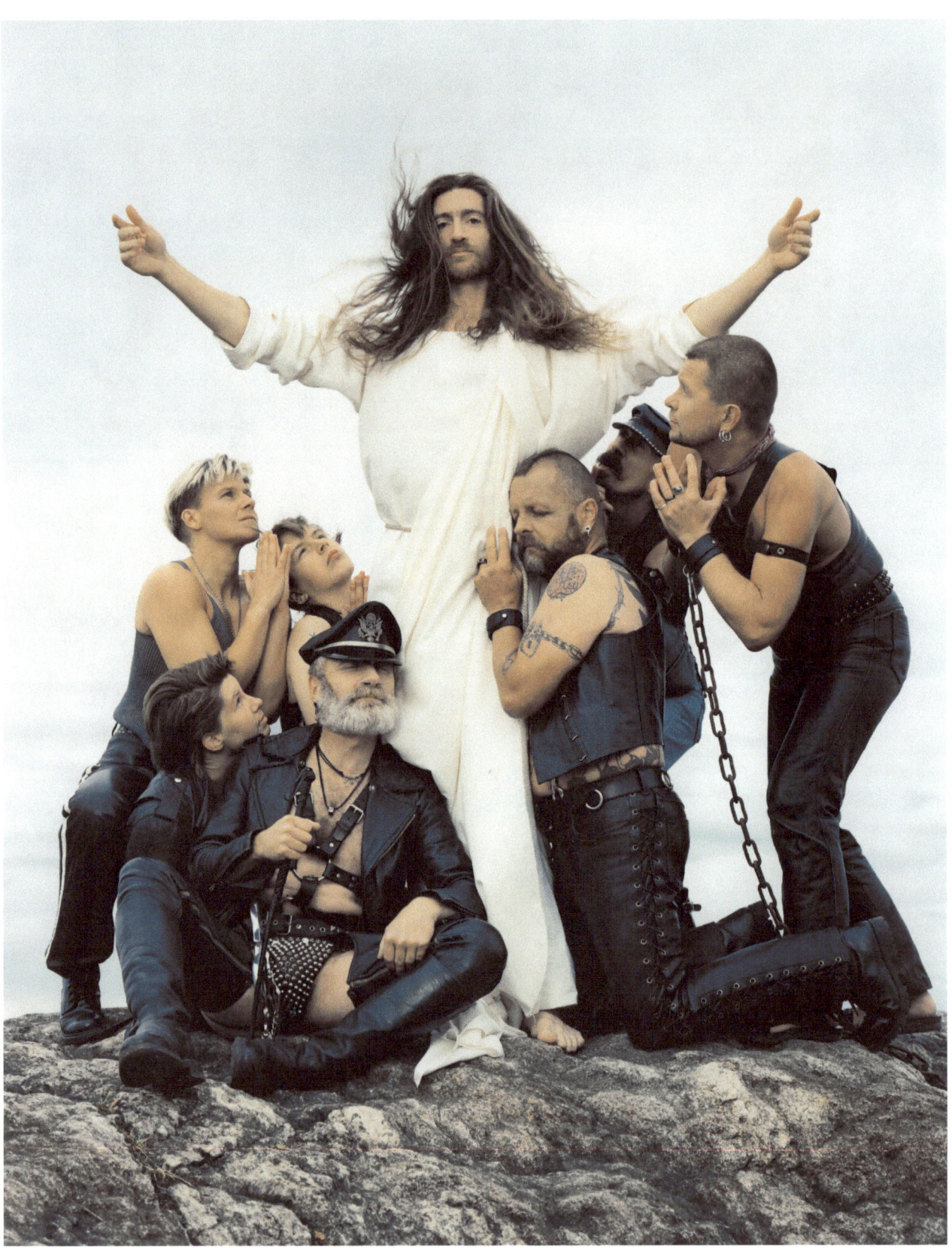

people viewed it. Not everyone liked what they saw. A man with an ax destroyed two of the photos. People threw stones at Ohlson Wallin and she needed police protection after receiving death threats.

Some Christians saw *Ecce Homo* as a deeply sacred expression of Christ's love for society's outcasts, while others considered it a disgrace and "a satanic trick." The diverse reactions were compiled into a book by Sweden's largest publisher. Eventually the European Parliament in Strasbourg reversed its decision to host the exhibition. A North American tour was planned, but never happened because nobody was willing to sponsor the controversial show.

The public frenzy was a far cry from the simple faith that originally motivated Ohlson Wallin. She remembers the joy of taking the first photo, *Sermon on the Mount*. She enlisted gays and lesbians from Stockholm's leather clubs to recreate Carl Bloch's *Christ the Consoler.* "It was fantastic to walk with 'Jesus' to the photo spot," Ohlson Wallin recalled. "People were looking and a little shocked. The picture is taken on the hill in a famous cruising park in Stockholm."

As in all the *Ecce Homo* images, the models spent a long time posing, paying close attention to the emotions they were trying to convey. Ohlson Wallin used a large-format camera to enhance the feeling of choreographed, carefully orchestrated scenarios. Each image is haunting and sharply beautiful, with a fashion-photo clarity that makes the familiar story become acutely real.

Ohlson Wallin recorded the whole span of Jesus' life, death, and resurrection, beginning with the announcement of his coming birth. In her version, the Madonna and her female lover are portrayed by a lesbian couple, seven months' pregnant through artificial insemination. The angel Gabriel comes in the form of their gay male friend, who floats in with a message from God—and a test tube for insemination.

Ohlson Wallin's most controversial image is Jesus' baptism. It crosses several boundaries by showing Jesus enjoying a homoerotic moment with full frontal nudity.

Left: "Sermon on the Mount" (from Ecce Homo), Elisabeth Ohlson Wallin, 1998. Photograph, 79" x 60".

But woe to you, scribes and Pharisees, hypocrites!
For you lock people out of the kingdom of heaven.
For you do not go in yourselves, and when others are going in, you stop them.
—Matthew 23:13

He is gloriously at ease in his own skin as he receives a sensual baptism from another man in a gay bathhouse

Each "Jesus" got to pick which scene he wanted to play. A gay man who was about to die of AIDS chose the *Pieta,* resulting in a poignant image that sheds new light on Michelangelo's prototype sculpture of the Madonna cradling her dead son. Ohlson Wallin let "Jesus" choose who would be his grieving mother, and he picked a female leather bar employee who was well known in Stockholm for mothering gay men. The mood was quiet and somber as they posed at the door to the AIDS ward of a Stockholm hospital. Behind that door Ohlson Wallin said goodbye to three friends.

The man in Ohlson Wallin's *Pieta* said he hoped that people would remember him by the picture after his death—but this "Jesus" experienced his own personal resurrection. Shortly after the photo shoot, he began taking the new AIDS drug cocktail. "The Jesus is still alive!" Ohlson Wallin marveled a decade later. And the AIDS ward no longer exists.

Much more has changed since Ohlson Wallin shot *Ecce Homo.* Back then she was known as Elisabeth Ohlson, but she has gotten legally married to a woman and added Wallin to her name. The image of Jesus is no longer visible in her work, but Ohlson Wallin says his spirit remains in the photos she takes of female prostitutes, blind women, South Africans with AIDS, and other outcasts. The *Ecce Homo* controversy has permanently transformed her relationship to the institutional church.

"It changed me a lot when I realized the connection between religion and politics," Ohlson Wallin said. "I've had a harder time going to church after that. I'd rather go to other places to find the spirit world. I still believe in God, but it looks a little different."

Each "Jesus" got to pick which scene he wanted to play. A gay man who was about to die of AIDS chose the *Pieta.*

Right: "Pieta" (from Ecce Homo), Elisabeth Ohlson Wallin, 1998. Photograph, 79" x 60".

Woman, here is your son.
—John 19:26

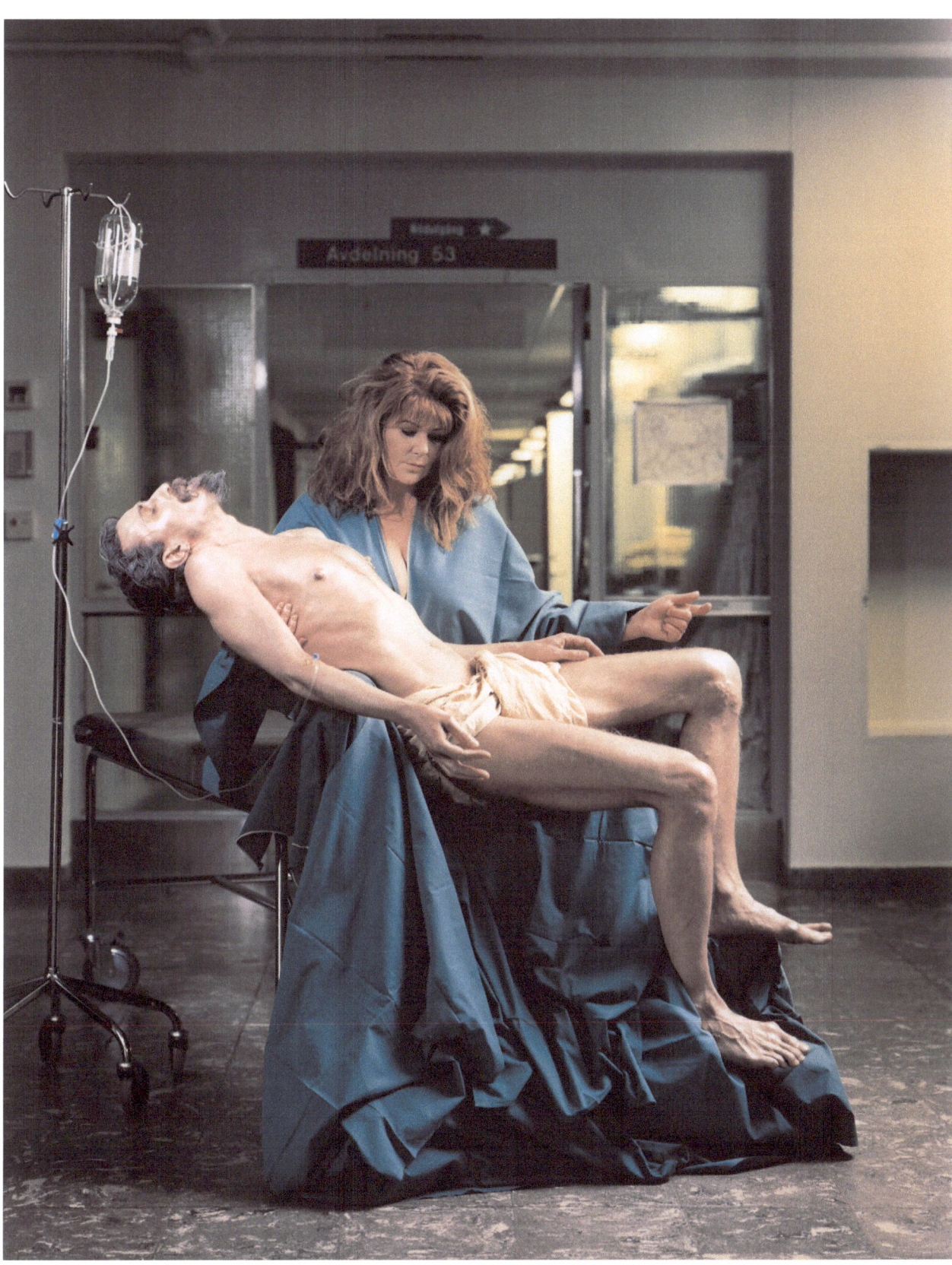

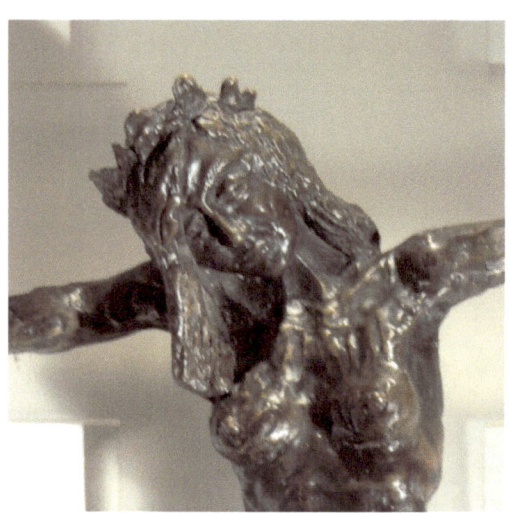

"Christa," detail

Edwina Sandys

b. 1938, London, England

Christa is the first and most famous artwork of a female Christ. The magnificent bronze crucifix has graced the pages of the *London Times, Time, Newsweek, Life,* and other major publications. It has appeared at respected galleries and churches throughout Europe and North America over the last thirty years. Wherever *Christa* goes, the sculpture triggers debate about the nature of God and the role of women.

The most prominent church to display *Christa* was the Episcopal Cathedral of St. John the Divine in New York City. Its tradition of artistic enlightenment dates back at least to 1914, when it scandalized people by showing the first female angels in church art. The ten-day *Christa* exhibit began on Maundy Thursday 1984 and continued over Easter, stirring arguments that spilled onto the pages of the *New York Times.*

"This symbol is theologically and historically indefensible," one bishop contended, while the dean of the cathedral declared, "Theologically, it's very important for this kind of thing to be done." People who were comfortable seeing a man on the cross found the image pornographic when the Christ figure was a woman. Supporters praised the work for expressing that God's incarnation is for all people, male and female, and that nobody is exempt from the sufferings of the cross.

> Supporters praised the work for expressing that God's incarnation is for all people, male and female.

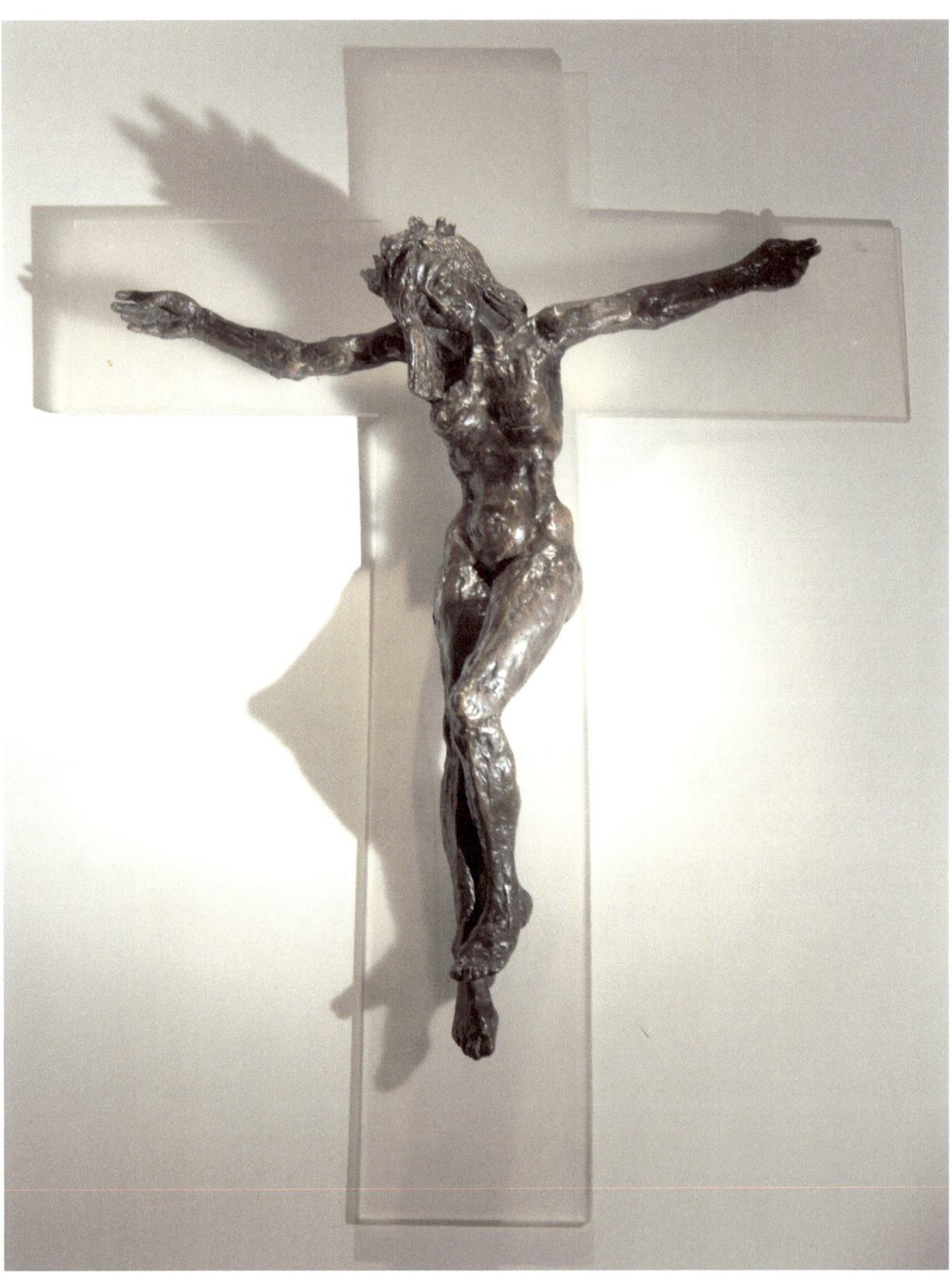

The sculpture was created by Edwina Sandys (pronounced "sands"), the granddaughter of Winston Churchill. Now based in New York, she is married to architect Richard Kaplan. Sandys has gained international acclaim for her art, including the sculptures she made for United Nations Centers in Geneva, Vienna, New York, and Rio de Janeiro. She sculpted *Christa* in London in 1975. Her female Christ wears the beaten-down expression of a battered woman resigned to pain, and yet her posture suggests that she is about to step off her cross and start dancing. Sandys' expressive technique and the natural heft of bronze raise Christa's all-too-common suffering to the level of the finest art.

"People constantly asked me: Why Christa? The short answer is: I don't know. I didn't think it through or consider at the time the implications of such a piece. It was largely an unconscious or subconscious act on my part," Sandys explained in a 1984 speech.

She noted the influence of the women's liberation movement and the U.N. Decade for Women. "Christ on the cross symbolizes sacrifice. Christa symbolizes the sacrifice of women. That is what she means to me. She will mean other things to others," she concluded.

The sculpture still had the power to shock more than three decades after its creation. In 2006 controversy forced organizers to cancel an exhibit with a photo of *Christa* at Alaska Pacific University in Anchorage.

"Christa symbolizes the sacrifice of women. That is what she means to me. She will mean other things to others."

Left: "Christa," © Edwina Sandys, 1975.
Bronze figure on resin/Lucite cross, 55" x 45" x 10". ＼

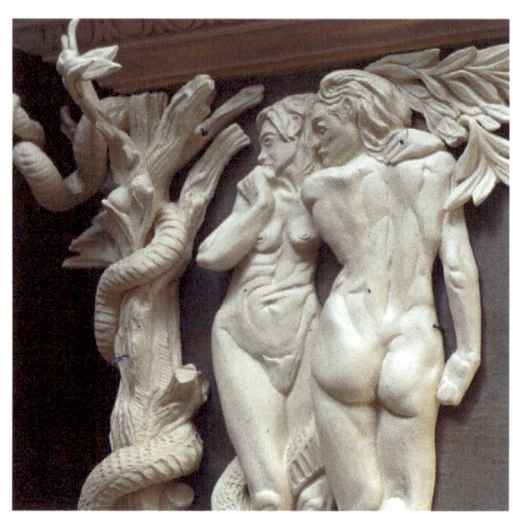

"Eve and the New Eve" (from Cripia),
Gary Speziale, work in progress.
Bisque porcelain and wood, 18" x 19" x 18".

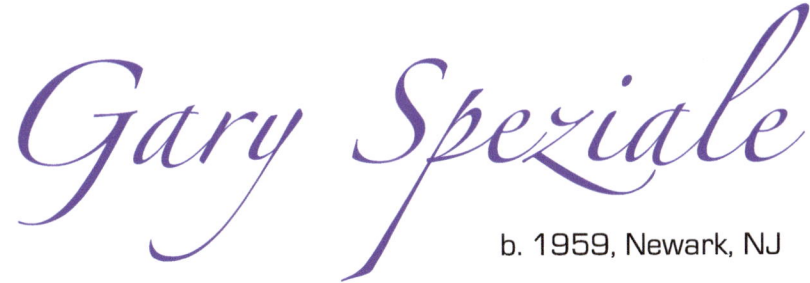

Gary Speziale

b. 1959, Newark, NJ

Gary Speziale doesn't self-consciously try to unite sexuality and spirituality in his art. Speziale is an openly gay New York artist whose art flows naturally from his full-bodied Roman Catholicism and who experiences life as one holy, homoerotic whole. "We're living in a world where religion is being used in the most dangerous ways. Maybe we need a bunch of gay people who are very concerned with the flesh and blood of it," he said. "If the stereotype is that we're preoccupied with the flesh, then so be it at this time. That is probably why I'm still Catholic. It is the emphasis on the incarnational aspect."

Speziale's colleagues think he's "hopelessly and incurably Catholic." His art and conversation are peppered with references that make standard Catholic theology feel deliciously gay-positive. Speziale rejoices in Jesus as "mankind's bridegroom" and the Eucharist as a sensual experience in which he takes the flesh of Christ into his mouth. "It *is* the tradition! It's not like we're injecting this stuff!" he exclaims with typical exuberance.

He has done a variety of murals and exhibitions while working in a library and pursuing a master's degree at New York University. He tries to make gay-positive art without reinventing Christianity. "It takes a long time for mythology to happen, so I

"We're living in a world where religion is being used in the most dangerous ways. Maybe we need a bunch of gay people who are very concerned with the flesh and blood of it."

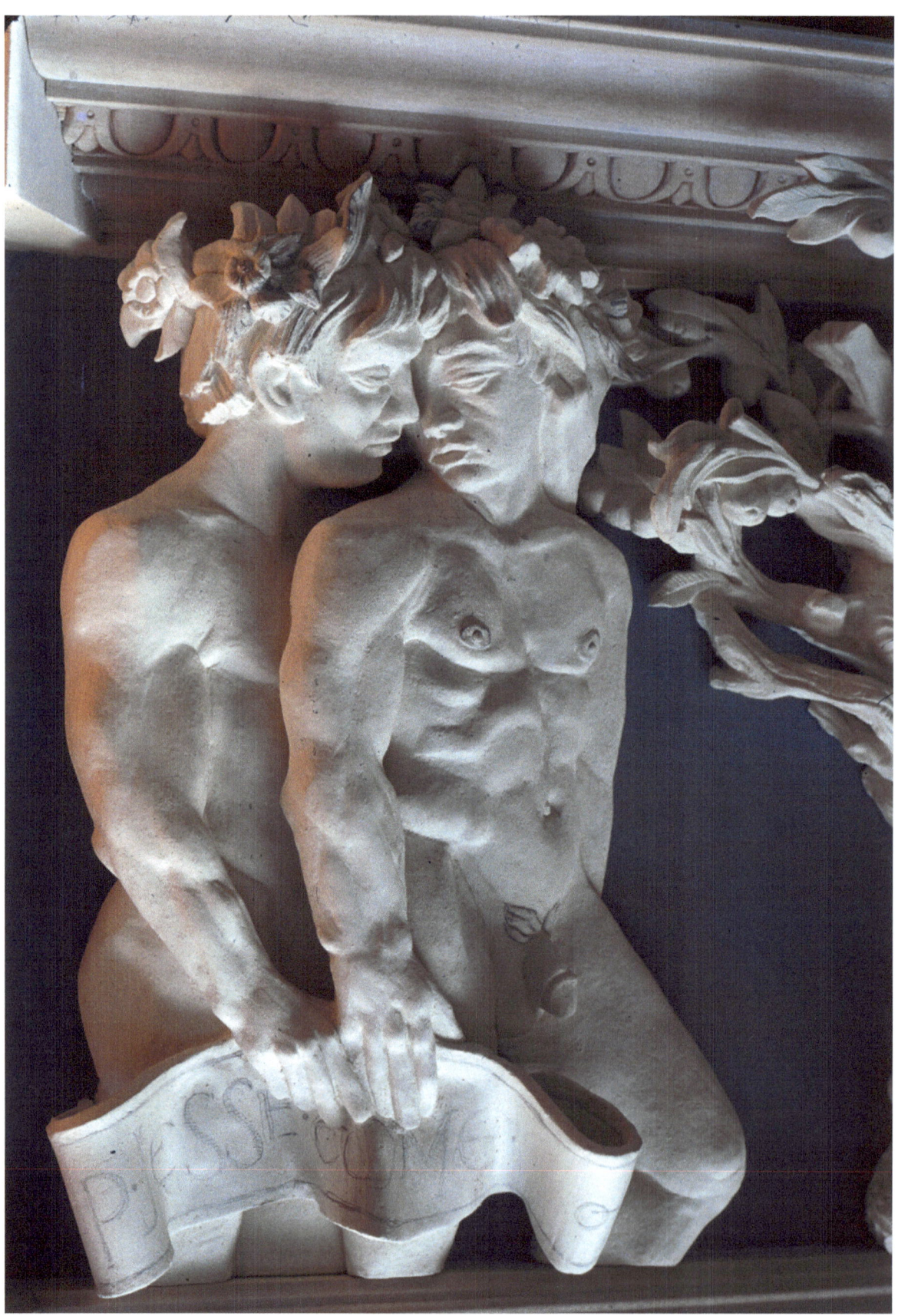

like to go to places that are already fertile," he said. Speziale explores the interplay between Adam, Christ, and homoeroticism in two major works in progress: *Cripia,* a star-shaped Christmas tree stand with a frieze around the perimeter, and *Felix Culpa,* the basis of his master's thesis. Both display Speziale's awesome virtuosity at depicting the human figure.

Cripia recasts the creation myth in a queer light by separating Adam and Eve and giving each a same-sex partner. A snake-entwined tree divides the two men from the female pair. Differences in scale also encourage viewers to read each same-sex couple separately.

Speziale's *Adam and the New Adam* pairs Adam with Christ, who has been called "the last Adam" by theologians starting with the Apostle Paul in the Bible. The men stand close together in primeval nakedness. Christ as the New Adam places the crown of betrothal on Adam's head and breathes new life into him.

Mary is likewise referred to as the Last Eve because she redeemed Eve's sin of accepting forbidden fruit from a serpent. In *Eve and the New Eve,* Mary supports Eve, who is caught in the serpent's coils. Mary as the New Eve raises her heel over the snake's head.

When the work is complete, the accompanying text will be rhyming lyrics from Christmas carols: for the men, "God rest ye merry gentlemen, let nothing you dismay…" and for the women, "O sisters too, how may we do, for to preserve this day?"

Speziale uses these sculptures and much more to elevate his annual Christmas tree into a work of installation art. He began his Christmas tree project in high school to mark his youngest brother's birth and later added a crèche (*Cripia* in Latin) in homage to the *Angel Tree* at the Metropolitan Museum of Art.

Christ as the New Adam places the crown of betrothal on Adam's head and breathes new life into him.

Left: "Adam and the New Adam" (from Cripia), Gary Speziale, work in progress. Bisque porcelain and wood, 18" x 19" x 18".

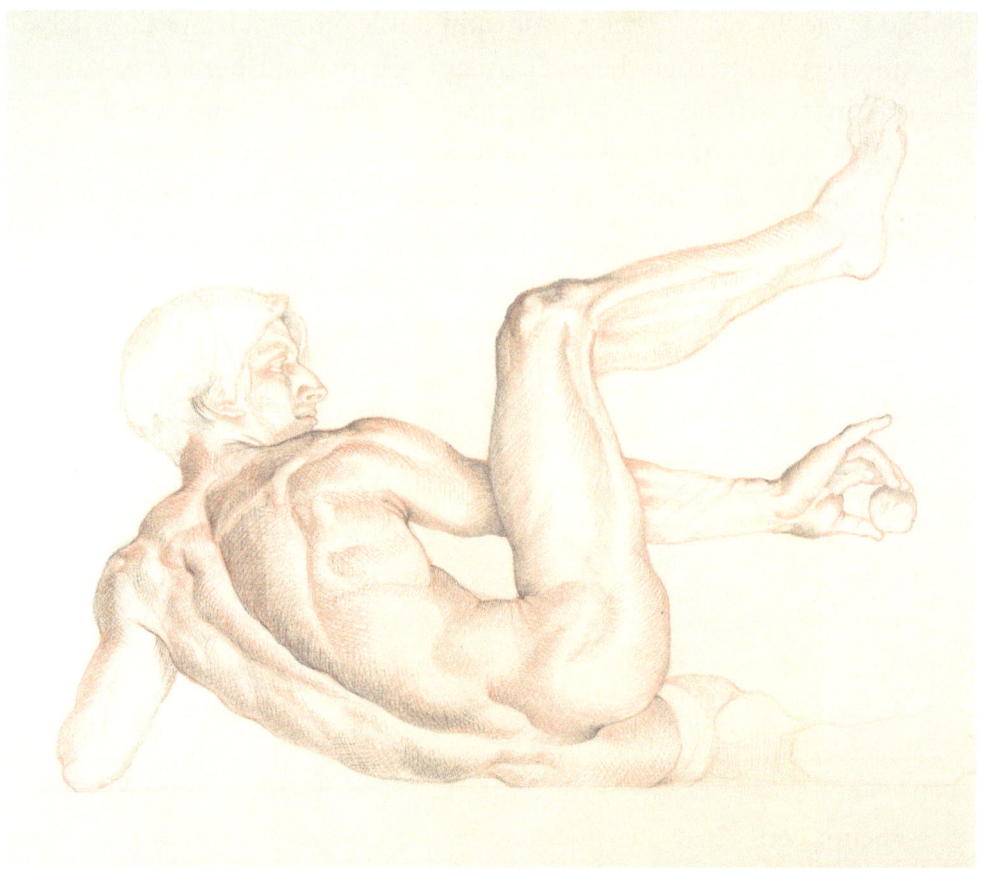

In 1988 Speziale came across figurines of St. Michael and the devil in Florence, Italy. "My friend said, 'You can't put the devil on the tree...' But I bought him anyway," Speziale recalled. "From that Christmas on, most gifts of ornaments that I received were for this section of the tree, which has developed into a full-blown hell section."

Speziale, a self-professed "mystical kid" who grew up with nonreligious parents, says some of his relatives were disturbed to see hell lit up in red on his Christmas tree. "The older generation, the Rosary-praying Italian aunts totally get it," he added. "If someone says it's sacrilegious, they say, 'Jesus came to save you, but from *WHAT?!*'"

His attitude toward sin is also revealed in *Felix Culpa* (Latin for "happy fault.") "This Adam is kind of faulty because he's gay," Speziale chuckled. The title comes from the Easter Vigil liturgy: "O happy fault

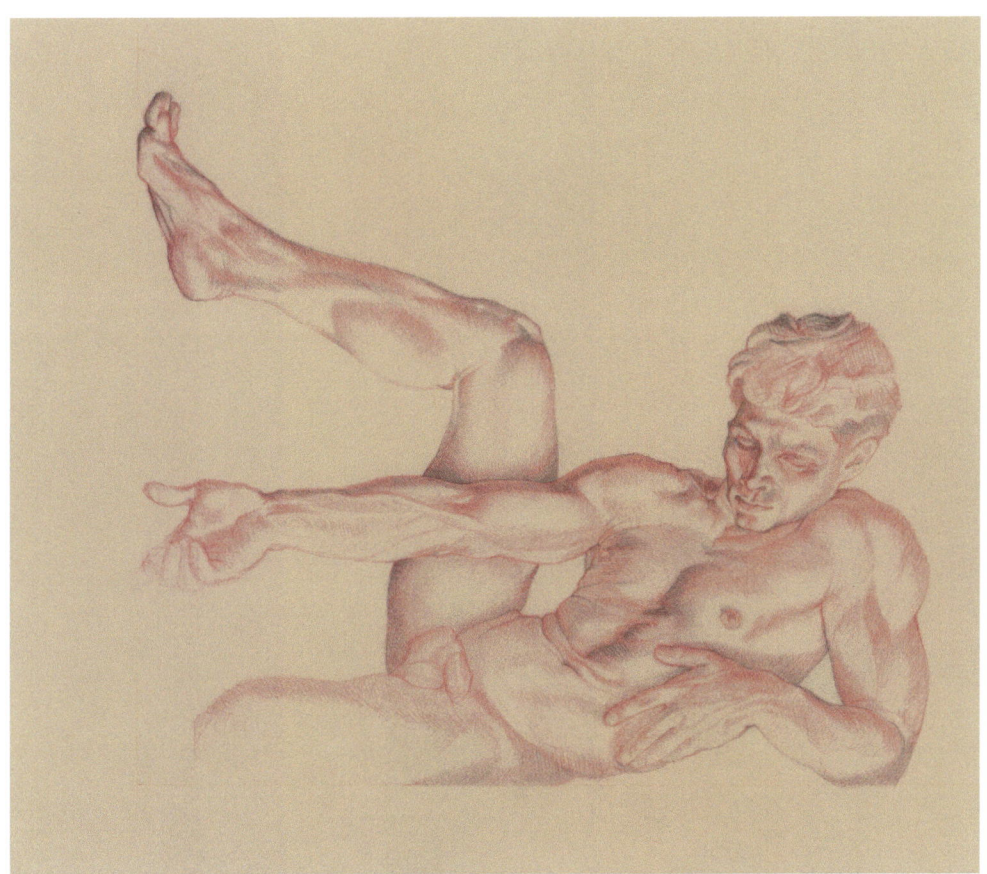

of Adam which gained for us so great a Redeemer." When complete, *Felix Culpa* will be a huge crucifix with St. John nursing from Jesus as Adam and Steve, the original gay couple, flirt at the foot of the cross.

Felix Culpa is homoerotic without taking a stand on whether homosexuality is a sin. "It's not something we have to figure out in this life," Speziale said. "A lot of religious folk think it is their job to keep sinners out of the church. I think my job is to send invitations to everyone I can think of."

Left: "Steve"; above: "Adam" (Studies for "Felix Culpa")
Gary Speziale, work in progress. Colored pencil on paper, 20" x 21".

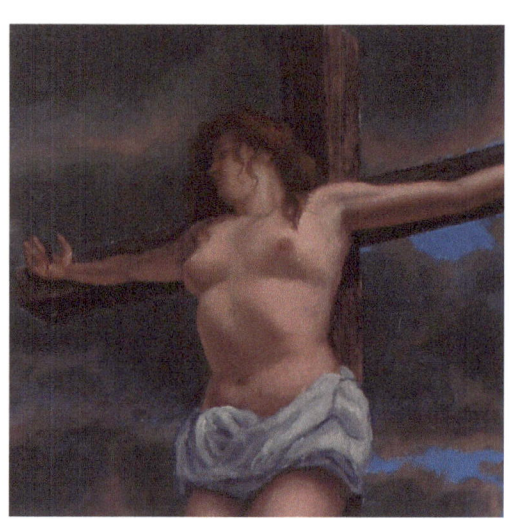

"Crucifixion," detail

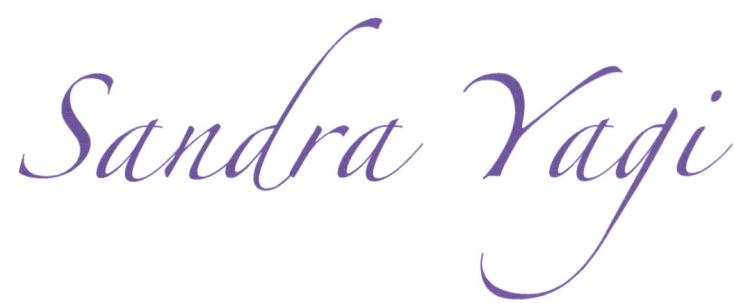

Sandra Yagi

b. 1955, Long Beach, CA

Sandra Yagi is fascinated by big questions, such as why a religion based on love is used to exclude women and suppress love. "It mystifies me that Christianity is so down on homosexuality," the San Francisco artist said. "Why are those righteous people trying to discourage two people who love each other from building a life together with legal protections?"

Her paintings are pretty little gems encoded with nightmarish, subversive twists that prick the conscience and provoke more questions. Yagi, a lesbian in a twenty-year relationship, has painted a female crucifixion and a series of Nativity scenes in which the baby Jesus is deformed—because "the *message* has been mutated."

In her *Crucifixion,* a woman Christ hangs on the cross while three twenty-first century men loot her purse: an Islamic militant counts her money, a businessman fingers her tampon, and a Pope watches, doing nothing to stop the crime. "Christ treated women with much more equality than today's church does," the San Francisco artist explained. "To say I can't reach the same spirituality as a man is bunk!"

Unlike most crucifixions, female or otherwise, Yagi's version raises the issue of who is responsible for killing Jesus. "The *Crucifixion* is a comment about how many organized religions

"Christ treated women with much more equality than today's church does. To say I can't reach the same spirituality as a man is bunk!"

and society treat women," she said. "It's not something limited only to Christianity."

Yagi's art also includes dancing skeletons, unicorns, minotaurs, and other figures from classical mythology. Her quirky sensibility came out recently when she was asked why she ignores symbols from her own religion, Buddhism. "Buddhist images are so peaceful," she replied with distaste. "Christian imagery is so much more interesting!"

Raised in suburban Denver, Yagi has been drawing since childhood, when she used to sketch in her mother's Buddhist prayer book. Her parents valued financial stability as a result of their internment with other Japanese Americans during World War II, and they urged her to pursue a "practical" career. With characteristic wry humor, Yagi said that she got her "evil MBA" from the University of Colorado at Denver and became "a corporate slave." After a few years she returned to art while keeping her day job. She developed an award-winning style influenced by such masters as Titian, Goya, Delacroix, Michelangelo, and Masami Teraoka, and her work has been widely exhibited.

"Through my art, I have realized that there are some questions that can really matter—such as, 'What is evil?' 'Is it an inherent part of the human condition?' Art is my vehicle to explore those questions, even if the likelihood of a concrete answer is very remote," Yagi said.

> Unlike most crucifixions, female or otherwise, Yagi's version raises the issue of who is responsible for killing Jesus.

Right: "Crucifixion," Sandra Yagi, 2003.
Oil on panel, 36" x 24."
Collection of Salvatore J. Giambanco.

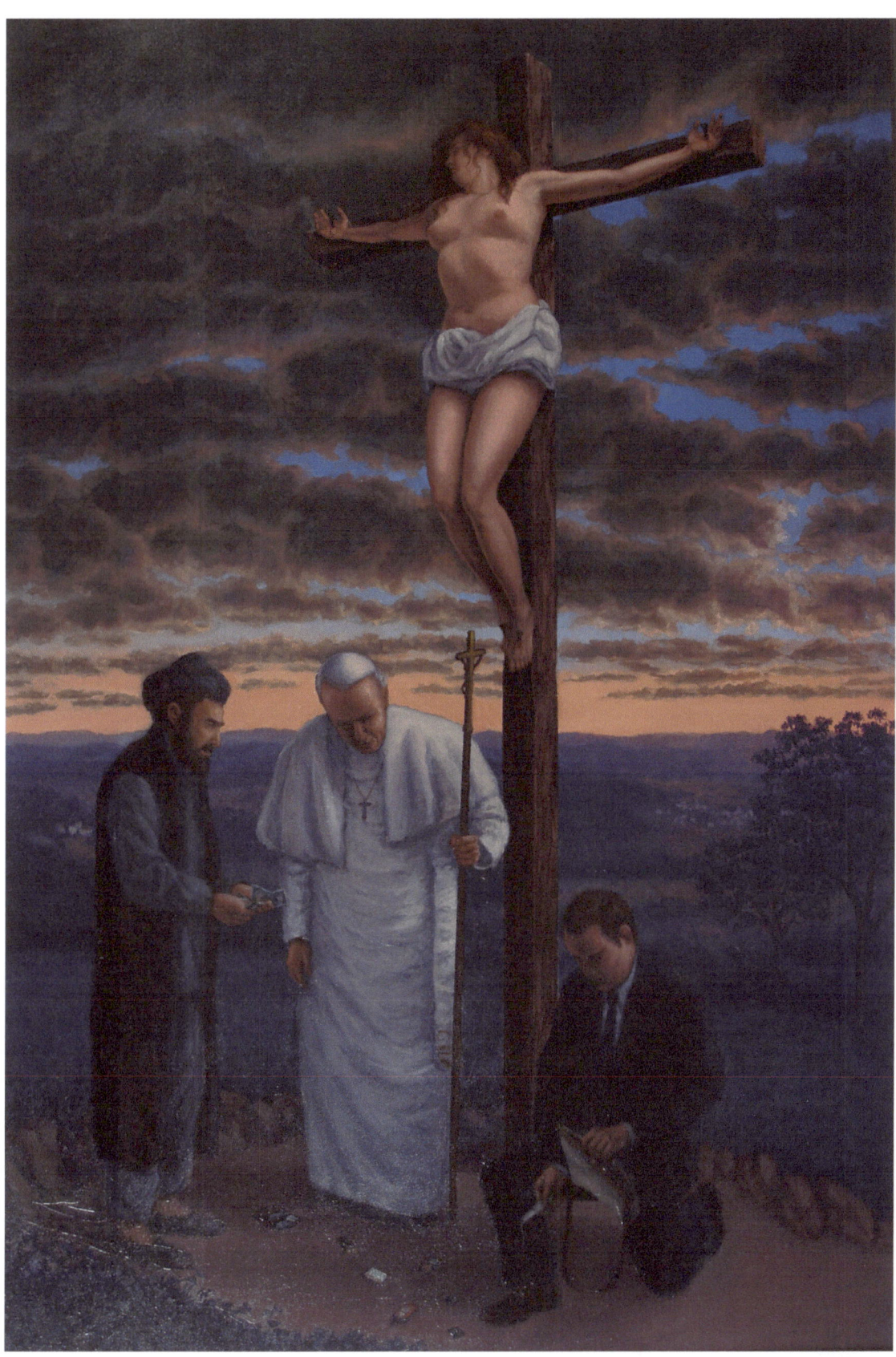

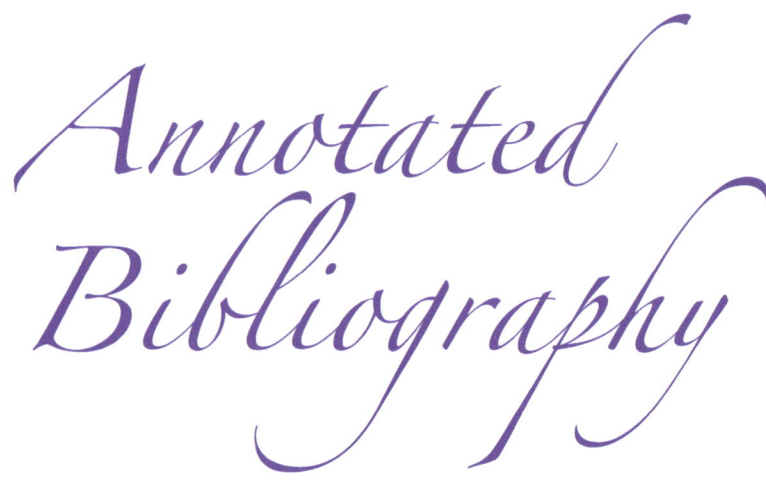

Annotated Bibliography

Gay Jesus

Carlson, Stephen C. *The Gospel Hoax: Morton Smith's Invention of Secret Mark*. Waco, TX: Baylor University Press, 2005. Hopes ran high that the historical Jesus' homosexuality could be proven by the Secret Gospel of Mark. Here an attorney attempts to debunk the document.

Cherry, Kittredge. *Jesus in Love: A Novel*. Berkeley, CA: AndroGyne Press, 2006. A queer Christ has today's emotional sophistication as he lives out the Christian myth in first-century Palestine.

Goss, Robert E. *Queering Christ: Beyond Jesus Acted Up*. Cleveland, OH: Pilgrim Press, 2002. This scholarly study has aphrodisiac qualities. It covers such fun topics as erotic contemplatives, the heart-genital connection, and who's doing what in the queer-Christ field.

Jennings, Theodore W., Jr. *The Man Jesus Loved: Homoerotic Narratives from the New Testament*. Cleveland, OH: Pilgrim Press, 2003. Jesus defied gender roles, supported same-sex relationships—and probably had a male lover himself. A seminary professor tells all.

McCleary, Rollan. *Signs for a Messiah: The First and Last Evidence for Jesus*. Christchurch, New Zealand: Hazard Press, 2003. An Australian theologian finds evidence of Jesus' homosexuality in the Bible and astrology.

McNally, Terrence. *Corpus Christi*. New York: Grove Press, 1998. Bomb threats almost prevented the off-Broadway opening of this bittersweet play about Jesus as a gay teen in 1950s-era Texas.

Roscoe, Will. *Jesus and the Shamanic Tradition of Same-Sex Love*. San Francisco: Suspect Thoughts Press, 2004. Did Jesus do a naked baptism rite with the man he loved? An anthropologist seeks answers in the Secret Gospel of Mark, tribal cultures, and his own life.

Worsnip, Michael. *Gay Ideas about God in Post-Apartheid South Africa: A Comparative Study of the Views Articulated by Selected Gay and Lesbian Christians and Some Mainline Church Theologies*. Ph.D. thesis (in progress), University of Kwazulu-Natal, Pietermaritzburg. An Anglican priest in South Africa looks at queer imaging of Christ.

Woman Christ and the Sacred Feminine

Ronan, Susan, Marian Taussig and Hal Cole. *Wisdom's Feast: Sophia in Study and Celebration*. Lanham, MD: Sheed & Ward, 1996. Christ is celebrated in female form by the rituals in this user-friendly book.

Davis, Elizabeth Gould. *The First Sex*. New York: Putnam, 1971. People either love or hate this bold description of an ancient, goddess-worshipping era when women ran everything. My college friend refused to marry her fiancé until he read it. Enough said.

Eisler, Riane. *The Chalice and the Blade: Our History, Our Future*. San Francisco: Harper & Row, 1988. A sociologist re-envisions human history, tracing a global shift from egalitarian to patriarchal cultures. Some compare its impact to Darwin's *Origin of the Species*.

O'Neill, Dennis. *Passionate Holiness: Marginalized Christian Devotions for Distinctive People*. Victoria, BC, Canada: Trafford Publishing, 2005. A pastor provides a thorough history of Christ Sophia and many queer saints. Color illustrations of contemporary icons bring it alive.

Stone, Merlin. *When God was a Woman*. San Diego: Harcourt, Harvest Books, 1976. Here is the Biblical patriarchs' worst nightmare: a revelation of the goddess-happy matriarchies of the Near and Middle East that were suppressed by Judaism and Christianity.

Sexuality and Spirituality

Gafni, Marc. *The Mystery of Love*. New York: Simon & Schuster, Atria Books, 2003. An Israeli rabbi writes a readable guide to eros in the Hebrew mystical tradition. Perhaps Jesus himself studied these ideas.

Helminiak, Daniel A. *Sex and the Sacred: Gay Identity and Spiritual Growth.* Binghamton, NY: Haworth Press, Harrington Park Press, 2006. A psychology professor surveys this popular topic—and even dares to address the gay community's last taboo: sexual ethics.

Heyward, Carter. *Touching Our Strength: The Erotic as Power and the Love of God.* HarperSanFrancisco, 1989; AndroGyne Press, 2007. Heyward led the pack as an openly lesbian Episcopal priest, and it's worth slogging through the theological jargon to see how she unites sexuality and spirituality.

Steinberg, Leo. *The Sexuality of Christ in Renaissance Art and in Modern Oblivion,* 2nd ed. University of Chicago Press, 1996. This is the definitive work on the subject, with 300 illustrations. A must-see!

Blasphemy and Art

Meyer, Richard. *Outlaw Representation: Censorship and Homosexuality in Twentieth-Century American Art.* Oxford University Press (USA), 2002. An art historian examines censorship of gay artists, particularly Paul Cadmus, Andy Warhol, and Robert Mapplethorpe.

Plate, S. Brent. *Blasphemy: Art That Offends.* London, UK: Black Dog Publishing, 2006. A theorist considers all things blasphemous, from Hieronymus Bosch to Andre Serrano's *Piss Christ* and beyond.

Saslow, James M. *Pictures and Passions: A History of Homosexuality in the Visual Arts.* New York: Viking Press, Penguin Group, 1999. This tasty art history survey starts in the Stone Age and ends post-Stonewall.

Acknowledgments

Writing *Art That Dares* has been like joining a delightful dance in progress, and I am grateful to those who led the way, those who participated with me, and those who will come after publication. Most of all I thank the artists who share their work and their lives in this book. I received invaluable assistance from their various agents, assistants, and galleries, including Debra De La Torre of Taos Traditions Gallery, Sherry Frumkin of Frumkin Gallery, Mary Holmes-Smith, Jesse and Barry of Barry Norris Studio, John O'Brien of Trinity Stores, and Jodi Simmons and Michael Roberts of JHS Gallery.

A special configuration of people set this book in motion. My life partner Audrey Lockwood and spiritual director Jim Curtan introduced me to my first gay Jesus image. Web-design genius Franklin Odel at Oversight Design asked me to find images for my website, JesusInLove.org, and started an avalanche of art. When *Art That Dares* was still just a dream, Becki Jayne Harrelson became the first artist to jump on board and her unflagging enthusiasm helped propel it into reality.

More allies emerged to bring *Art That Dares* into being. Judith Finlay and Lissa Dirrim gave their incisive commentary and the loving support that only long-term friends can provide. Linda Drake escorted me on many merry fact-finding missions to the library. The brave folks at AndroGyne Press stepped forward at just the right moment to design and produce this book with care and consummate artistry.

Art historian and art educator Ron Steen and author-priest Dennis O'Neill each supplied background information with a smile. Author-activist Toby Johnson was always ready with words of wisdom. Research assistance also came from Michele Shigoka in Los Angeles, California; Rollan McCleary in Australia; Guido Hermans in Antwerp, Belgium; and Michael Worsnip in Johannesburg, South Africa. My mother, Margaret Humphries, endowed me with an innate love of art and then allowed me the freedom to follow where it led. Those who helped indirectly are too numerous for me to name or even to comprehend.

Audrey Lockwood is not only my life partner, but also my guiding light. As we discussed this book, we had brainstorms daily—sometimes hourly! We celebrated the discovery of each artist. The readers of this book will be blessed if they find even a fraction of the joy that Audrey and I had in the development of *Art That Dares*.

Kittredge Cherry

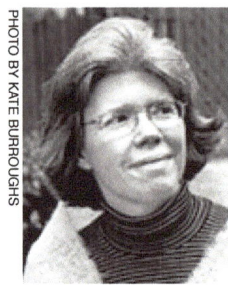

PHOTO BY KATE BURROUGHS

Kittredge Cherry is a lesbian Christian author whose ministry put her on the cutting edge of the international debate on sexuality and spirituality. She offers spiritual resources through JesusInLove.org., the first website devoted to the queer Christ.

Cherry was ordained by Metropolitan Community Churches and served as clergy in the lesbian, gay, bisexual, and transgender community for seven years until health issues forced her into a more contemplative life. One of her primary duties was promoting dialogue on homosexuality at the National Council of Churches (USA) and the World Council of Churches.

A native of Iowa, Cherry has degrees in journalism and art history from the University of Iowa, and a master of divinity degree from Pacific School of Religion in Berkeley, California. Her books include *Jesus in Love: A Novel, Hide and Speak: A Coming Out Guide, Equal Rites: Lesbian and Gay Worship, Ceremonies, and Celebrations,* and *Womansword: What Japanese Words Say About Women.*

The New York Times Book Review praised her "very graceful, erudite" writing style and her poetry has won several awards. She has also written for *Newsweek* and the *Wall Street Journal.* Cherry and her partner, Audrey Lockwood, live in Los Angeles.

Reconocimientos

Muchos individuos e instituciones me dieron un extraordinario acceso a sus colecciones. Desde uno, "La Certidumbre del Cambio", en Blanco, Texas, a algunos en Austin, Texas y San Miguel de Allende, Gto. Mx. A lo ancho, en el Museo Nacional de Máscaras, San Luis Potosi, S.L.P., Mx y el Museo de Máscaras Rafael Coronel, Zacatecas, Zac. Mx. Se me permitió fotografiar la colección Donald Cordry en el departamento de Estudios Latinos, Universidad de Texas en Austin y la colección de la Galeria MexicArte, Austin, Tx.

Lamentablemente, he perdido el rastro de aquellos que amablemente me dejaron llevar sus preciadas posesiones, confiando en que se las devolvería enteras. Les agradezco a todos. Danna Yarrell me llevó a al mercado de Lagunilla en la ciudad de Mexico, donde compré mis primeras máscaras. George O. Jackson Jr. Compartió sus fotografías y conocimientos de las máscaras y su uso. A mis bellas modelos: Kristin, Metis, Lourdes, Sheri y Zifa les agradezco su paciencia y participación.

Jonathan Cole, Isabel Rico, Adrian Gonzalez y varios otros traductores incluyendo a Jeanne Croes Nadal. Adrian, con sus amplios conocimientos de informática, ayudo a recopilar el material, enlazando todos los hilos de gente y objetos y conocimiento y amabilidad y buena fe hasta finalizar este libro. Gracias.

Y, por último, me gustaría dar las gracias a Emma Suttie, para el diseño de este libro.

Michael P. Earney
Port Aransas, TX 2011

www.MichaelEarney.com
https://fineartamerica.com/profiles/michael-earney.html
themichaelearney@yahoo.com
© Michael P. Earney 2012

Magic Faces
Caras Magicas

Paintings by
Michael P. Earney

ISBN-13: 978-1-941345-66-5 HB

Second Edition

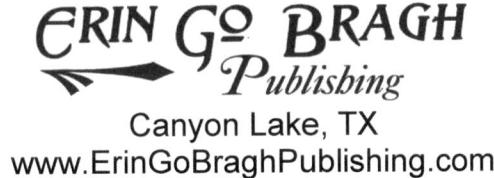

Canyon Lake, TX

www.ErinGoBraghPublishing.com

MAGIC
FACES

CARAS
MAGICAS

Acknowledgements

Many individuals and institutions gave me extraordinary access to their collections; from one mask in Blanco, Texas, a few in Austin, Texas and San Miguel de Allende, Mexico, to many at the National Mask Museum in San Luis Potosi, S.L.P., Mexico, and the Rafael Coronel Mask Museum, Zacatecas, Zac. Mexico. I was permitted to photograph the Donald Cordry collection at the department of Latin Studies, University of Texas at Austin and the collection at MexicArte Gallery, Austin, Texas.

Regrettably, I have lost track of some of those individuals kind enough to let me make off with their prized possessions, trusting I would return them in one piece. I thank them all. Donna Yarrell took me to Lagunilla market in Mexico City where I purchased my first masks. George O. Jackson Jr. shared his photographs and his knowledge of the masks and their usage. My lovely models, Kristin, Metis, Lourdes, Sheri and Zifa I thank for their patience and participation.

Thanks to various translators, including Jonathan Cole, Isabel Rico, Jeanne Croes Nadal and Adrian Gonzalez. Adrian, with his considerable computer skills, helped to compile all the material, bringing all the threads of people and objects and knowledge and kindness and goodwill to completion in this book. Thank you.

And finally, I would like to thank Emma Suttie, for designing this book.

www.MichaelEarney.com
https://fineartamerica.com/profiles/michael-earney.html
themichaelearney@yahoo.com
© Michael P. Earney 2012

Prologo

Los Nativos americanos, con lo cual quiero decir todos los pueblos indígenas de todas las Américas, sufrieron, tal vez, un ataque mayor a sus bases culturales que la mayoría de los pueblos invadidos, con excepción de aquellos que fueron completamente aniquilados por sus conquistadores. Cuando una cultura es reprimida por un invasor dominante y extraño, se sumerge en la clandestinidad. Los ritos se llevan a cabo en secreto y continúan paralelamente con las nuevas prácticas de fe impuestas. Muchos de los pueblos indígenas continúan viviendo una vida aislada del resto de la nación. Esto es asi para la mayoría de los pueblos indígenas en todo el mundo. En parte para su preservación y en parte por su pobreza y una forma de vida que no adoptan los no-nativos, el conocimiento de este pasado importante y vital está rápidamente desapareciendo.

En Mexico aunque los pueblos nativos han sido cristianizados se han adaptado a la vida moderna con una inmensa poblacion mestiza, las costumbres del remoto pasado conviven con el sistema que prevalecen actualmente.

Los festivales que incluyen el uso de máscaras muestran esta mezcla de religión católica y pagana. Principalmente ejecutados por las poblaciónes rurales pobres, estos festivales son generalmente ignorados o vistos como entretenimiento. Es irónico que la continuación de tales tradiciones pueda depender de los folkloristas y conservadores. Afortunadamente, nuevas generaciones de nativos Americanos y Latinos interesados en su herencia cultural están encontrando dignidad y un sentido de orgullo al adoptar formas de arte, música, vestimenta y puntos de vista mundiales que reflejan más ampliamente la realidad de sus vidas.

El propósito de este libro es presentar mis pinturas a una audiencia que pueda no conocer las máscaras mejicanas y su importante lugar en la historia y cultura de Mexico.

Foreword

Native Americans, by which I mean all the indigenous people of all the Americas, suffered, perhaps, a greater attack on their cultural foundations than most invaded people, except for those who were completely annihilated by their conquerors. When a culture is suppressed by an invader, it goes underground. Rites are performed in secret and continue in parallel with the newly imposed beliefs and practices. Much of the indigenous population continues to live in isolation from the rest of the nation. This is true for most indigenous people throughout the world. In part because of their own conservatism and in part because of their poverty and a way of life that non-natives do not embrace, knowledge of this important and vital past is rapidly disappearing.

In Mexico, where the native peoples are Christianized and used to modern ways, and with its huge mestizo population, customs from the ancient past have been co-opted or surreptitiously attached to the prevailing system.

Festivals that include the use of masks exhibit this blending of pagan and catholic religion. Mostly performed by the rural poor, these festivals are generally ignored or viewed as mere entertainment. It is ironic that the continuation of such traditions may depend upon folklorists and preservationists. Happily though, new generations of native Americans and Latins interested in their cultural heritage are finding dignity and a sense of pride through the embrace of forms of art, music, dress and world views that more fully reflect the reality of their lives.

The aim of this book is to present my paintings to an audience that might be unaware of Mexican masks and their important place in the history and culture of Mexico.

"Ningún pueblo tiene un sistema de religión mas elaborado que nuestros aborígenes, y ninguno es mas devoto en la celebración de los deberes inherentes a ella. Son pocos los actos de la vida de los Indios que no involucre alguna representación ceremonial que sea por si misma un acto religioso, a veces tan complicado que conlleva mucho tiempo y estudio el captar aunque sea una parte de su real significado,"

Edward Sheriff Curtis

La observación de Edward Curtis es aplicable a todos los pueblos nativos en todas la Américas antes de la llegada de los europeos. Hoy en día, a pesar de los mejores esfuerzos de la Iglesia Católica y Romana, muchas antiguas tradiciones sobreviven entre los pueblos nativos así como las prácticas religiosas de la población mestiza dominante.

Estas llamadas tradiciones paganas pueden ser vistas en las celebraciones y festivales religiosos de Mexico. En los bailes que se ejecutan en estas ocasiones se han mantenido muchos motivos Pre-Conquista. Aún en eventos y personajes ostensiblemente cristianos, son evidentes los símbolos asociados con los viejos Dioses. Las familiares imágenes de animales de Dioses abundan en las máscaras usadas en los bailes. Originalmente, tanto los bailarines como la audiencia reconocía que estos símbolos, imágenes y atributos personificados no eran meramente adornos sino reales manifestaciones de los Dioses, mágicamente transformados. Son los Dioses haciéndose visibles y disponibles al pueblo. Las serpientes, ranas, lagartos, murciélagos y otras figuras representadas en máscaras indicaban cual aspecto del Dios o Diosa era representado. Los Dioses mismos bailaban sus responsabilidades. Los Dioses bailaban para asegurar la armoniosa progresión de las estaciones y el bienestar general del pueblo.

Sin importar que tan serio es el propósito de los bailes con máscaras, el entretenimiento era y sigue siendo un componente importante. Personajes cómicos como el bromista, cumplen una función social. La máscara libera al usuario de la conducta diaria y le permite dar rienda suelta a payasadas, humor vulgar y otras libertades. Los tabúes son violados con impunidad. Los bailadores toman el pelo a las tradiciones y costumbres de la sociedad. Es una válvula de escape a las preocupaciones de disputas y rivalidades en una atmósfera relajada.

Las mascaras durante mucho tiempo han jugado un papel en los esfuerzos del Hombre por influenciar al mundo visible e invisible. Personajes enmascarados, aparecen en arte rupestre en todo el mundo, pertenecen a las mas antiguas representaciones de humanos. La máscara ofrece anonimidad, provee el poder transformados de una personalidad asumida y un punto de vista diferente del mundo, donde es posible actuar en formas totalmente inusuales. La palabra en latín persona, para "máscara de actor", tiene ahora como significado la fachada social del individuo, es el rol que asumimos como resultado del previo entrenamiento, o el que asumimos, basados en nuestra percepción de las expectativas de la sociedad.

La identificación con una persona específica inhibe el desarrollo psicológico, mientras que una persona flexible alimenta un ego fuerte. Esto podría sugerir que todos podríamos beneficiarnos de un cambio de cara de vez en cuando.

Michael P. Earney

"No people have a more elaborate religious system than our aborigines, and none are more devout in the performance of the duties connected therein. There is scarcely an act in the Indian's life that does not involve some ceremonial performance or is not itself a religious act, sometimes so complicated that much time and study are required to grasp even a part of its real meaning."

Edward Sheriff Curtis

Edward Curtis' observations apply to all native peoples throughout the Americas prior to the arrival of Europeans. Despite the best efforts of the Roman Catholic Church, ancient traditions survive today among indigenous people and are also found in the religious observances of the dominant mestizo population.

These so-called pagan traditions are to be seen in Mexico's celebrations and religious festivals. In the dances that are performed on these occasions many Pre-Conquest motifs have been retained. Even in ostensibly Christian events and characters, symbols associated with the old Gods are evident. Images of the animal familiars of the Gods abound in the masks used in the dances. Originally, dancers and audience alike recognized that the symbols, images and attributes portrayed were not mere adornment but actual manifestations of the Gods, magically transformed. It is the Gods making themselves visible and available to the people. The snakes, frogs, lizards, bats and other figures depicted on masks indicated what aspect of the God or Goddess was being enacted. The Gods themselves were dancing out their responsibilities. The Gods danced to assure the harmonious progression of the seasons and the general well being of the people.

No matter how serious the purpose of masked dances, entertainment was and remains an important component. Comic characters such as the prankster, serve a social function. The mask exempts the wearer from everyday behavior and gives license to indulge in horseplay, vulgar humor and other liberties. Taboos are violated with impunity. The dancers poke fun at the mores and conventions of society. An outlet is provided to give vent to concerns over disputes and rivalries in a relaxed atmosphere.

Masks have long played a role in Man's efforts to influence the seen and unseen world. Masked figures appear in rock art throughout the world, being among the earliest depictions of humans. The mask offers anonymity; it provides the transformative power of an assumed personality and a different view of the world, where it is possible to act in totally unusual ways.

The Latin word persona, for "actors mask", has come to signify the individual's social façade. It is the role we adopt as the result of early training, or one we assume, based upon our perception of society's expectations. Identification with a specific persona inhibits psychological development, while a flexible persona nurtures a strong ego. This would suggest that we all might benefit from a change of face from time to time.

Michael P. Earney

"Je est un autre"

Arthur Rimbaud

1. Tigre

2000 Acrylic on canvas (36" x 36")

Lord of the Animals. The jaguar mask remains the most popular mask throughout Mexico. Unfortunately, due to hunting and loss of habitat, the jaguar has disappeared from most of its former range in Mexico and is so rare now that mask representations often resemble the Asian tiger rather than the jaguar of the Americas. Both animals are now threatened with extinction.

1. Tigre

2000 Acrilico en tela (91cm x 91cm)

El Señor de los Animales. La mascara del Jaguar recuerda la mas popular mascara de Mexico. Desafortunadamente debido a la caceria y a la perdida de su habitat, el Jaguar ha desaparecido de las anteriores areas donde habitaban en Mexico. Asi que es poco comun que en la actualidad la representacion de las mascaras a menudo se asocie a los Tigres de la Asia en lugar del Jaguar Americano. Ambos animales estan amenazados con su extincion.

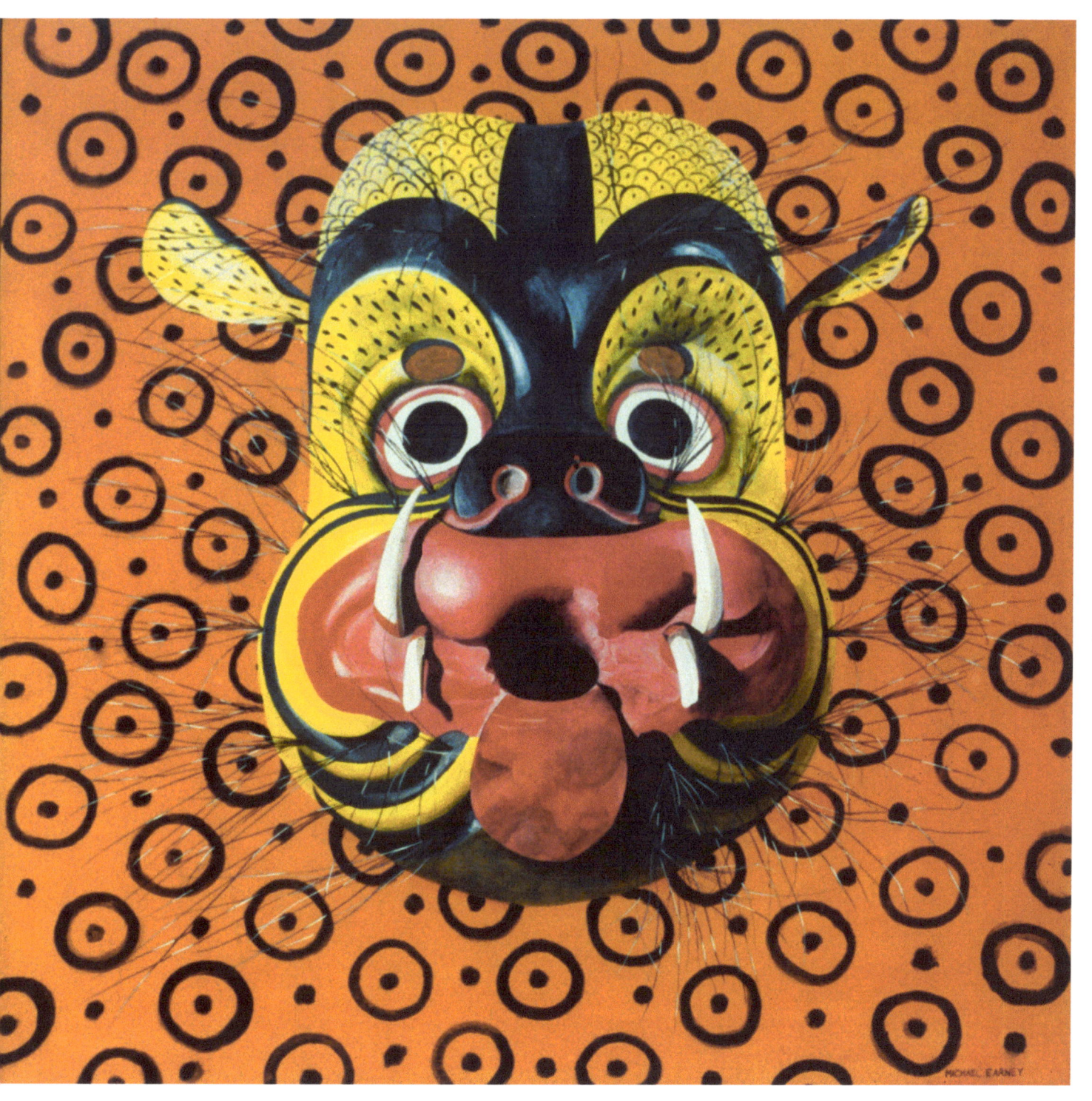

2. Smoking Negrito

2000 Acrylic on board (32" x 24")

The Dance of the Negritos can be comic in one region and serious in another. It is a crop fertility dance performed to rid the fields of snakes to make them safe for planting. Negritos also show up in other dances where they fill a sexual clowning/ fertility role, bringing levity to the proceedings.

2. Negrito fumando

2000 Acrílico en fibracel (81cm x 61cm)

El baile de los Negritos puede ser cómico en una región y serio en otra. Es un baile de fertilidad de la cosecha ejecutado para eliminar a las serpientes de los cultivos y prepararlos para su plantación. Los Negritos aparecen en otros bailes donde cumplen con un rol sensual de payaso/fertilidad aportando frivolidad a las reuniones.

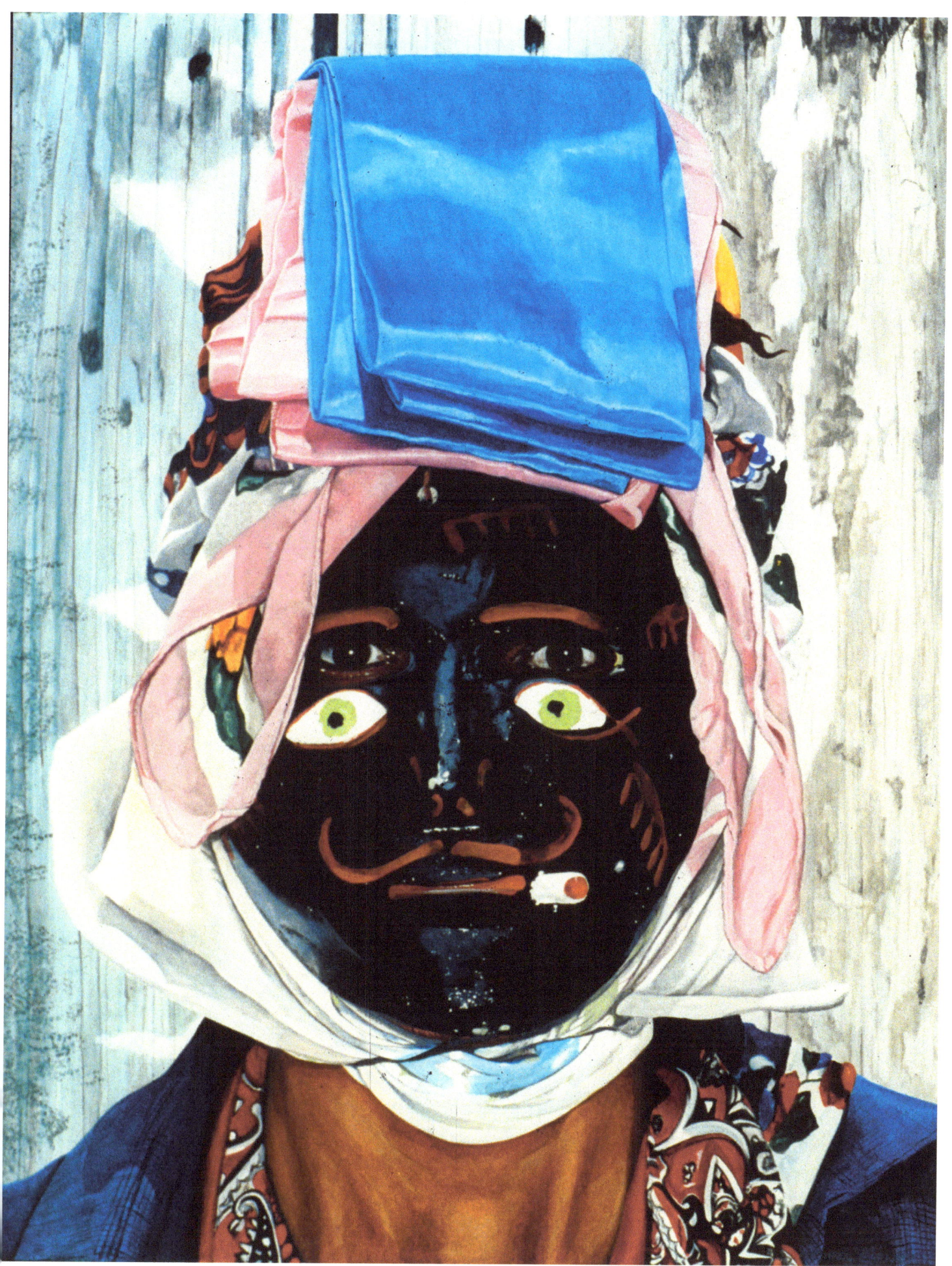

3. Yaqui Pascola

2000 Acrylic on board (32" x 24")

Pascola mask motifs come from face painting. The Pascolas clear the area and entertain the crowd before the Deer Dance, but their role is infinitely more important. The mask allows them to enter the world of the spirit and through ritual bring that sacred realm into Man's world. All participants recognize that the Pascolas make this difficult journey on their behalf. The word "Pascola" comes from "pahko'ola" meaning "Old Man of the Ceremony". The term comes from two words: pahko-ceremony and o'ola- an affectionate term for old man. The two words were shortened into pahko'ola and are pronounced pascola in Spanish.

"Pascolas are individuals who perform as a result of dreamed visions. Their knowledge is gained from animals of the woods, rather than from Christian supernaturals." (Fontana, Flaubert, Burn 1977).

3. Yaqui Pascola

2000 Acrílico en fibracel (81cm X 61cm)

Los motivos de las máscaras Pascola se originan en pinturas faciales. Los Pascola limpian el área y entretienen a la muchedumbre antes de la Danza del Venado, pero su papel es infinitivamente más importante. La máscara les permite entrar mediante rituales en el mundo de los espíritus y devolver ese mundo sagrado al mundo del Hombre. Todos los participantes reconocen que los Pascolas recorren este difícil camino en beneficio de ellos. La palabra "Pascola" viene de "pahko'ola que significa "Hombre Viejo de la Ceremonia". El término proviene de dos palabras: pahko o "ceremonia" y o'ola un término afectuoso de referirse al hombre viejo. Las dos palabras se acortaron a "pahko'ola" y se pronuncia "pascola" en español.

"Los Pascolas" son individuos que actúan a consecuencia de sus visiones soñadas. Sus conocimientos fueron aprendidos de los animales del bosque y no de los Cristianos sobrenaturales."(Fontana, Flaubert, Burn 1977)

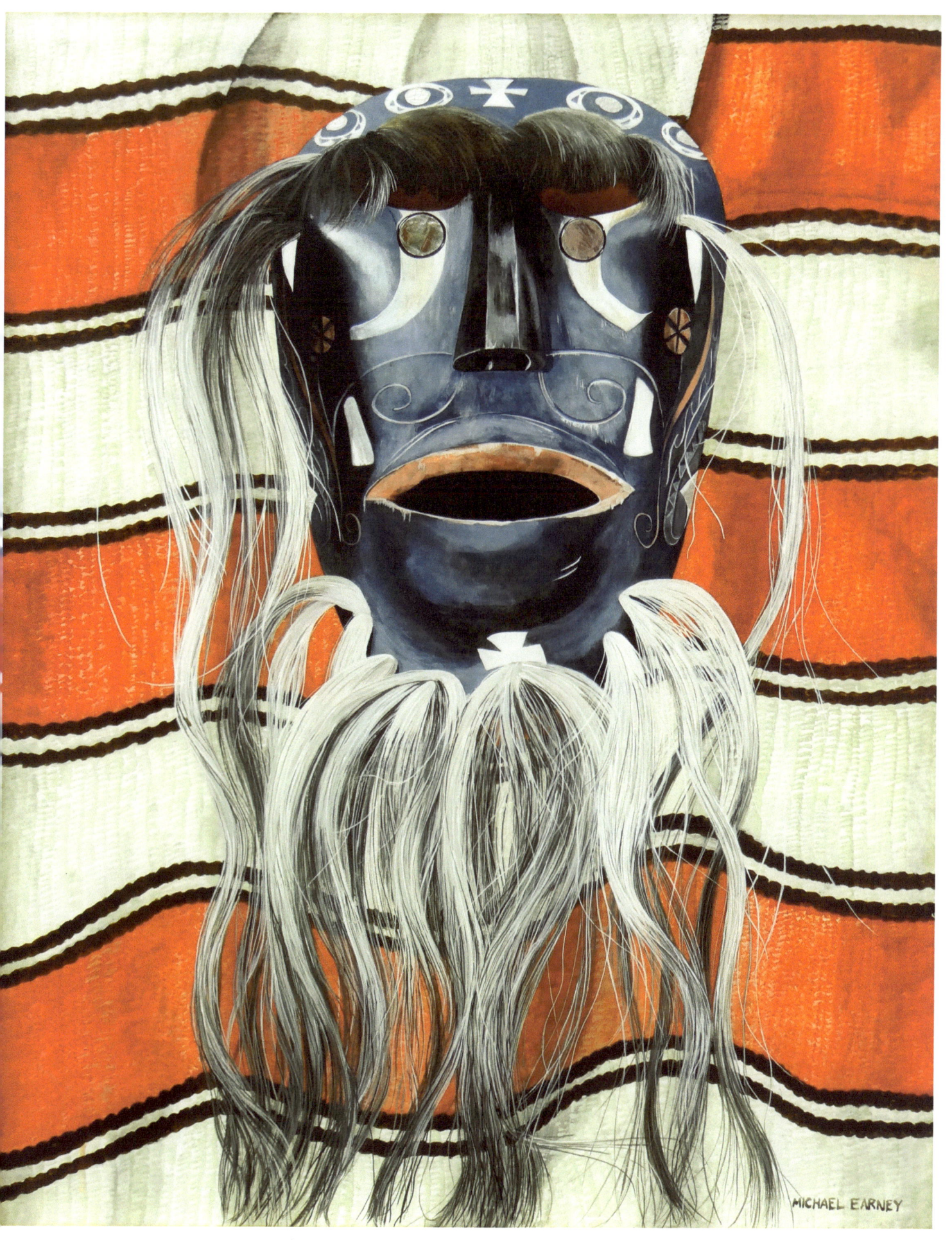

MICHAEL EARNEY

4. Jalisco Mask

2000 Acrylic on board (32" x 24")

This mask is said to come from Jalisco where hallucinogenic plants form part of the native rituals. The colors suggest some such influence. During certain ceremonies, under the influence of the hallucinogen, the Shaman sends lizards to obtain information. Upon their return the lizards whisper secrets to the masked Shaman.

4. Máscara de Jalisco

2000 Acrílico en fibracel (81cm X 61cm)

Se dice que esta mascara proviene de Jalisco donde las plantas alucinógenas forman parte de los rituales nativos. Los colores psicodélicos sugieren el efecto de su uso. En algunas ceremonias, bajo la influencia del alucinógeno el Chaman envía lagartos para que obtengan información. Al regresar los lagartos susurran secretos al Chaman que lleva la mascara.

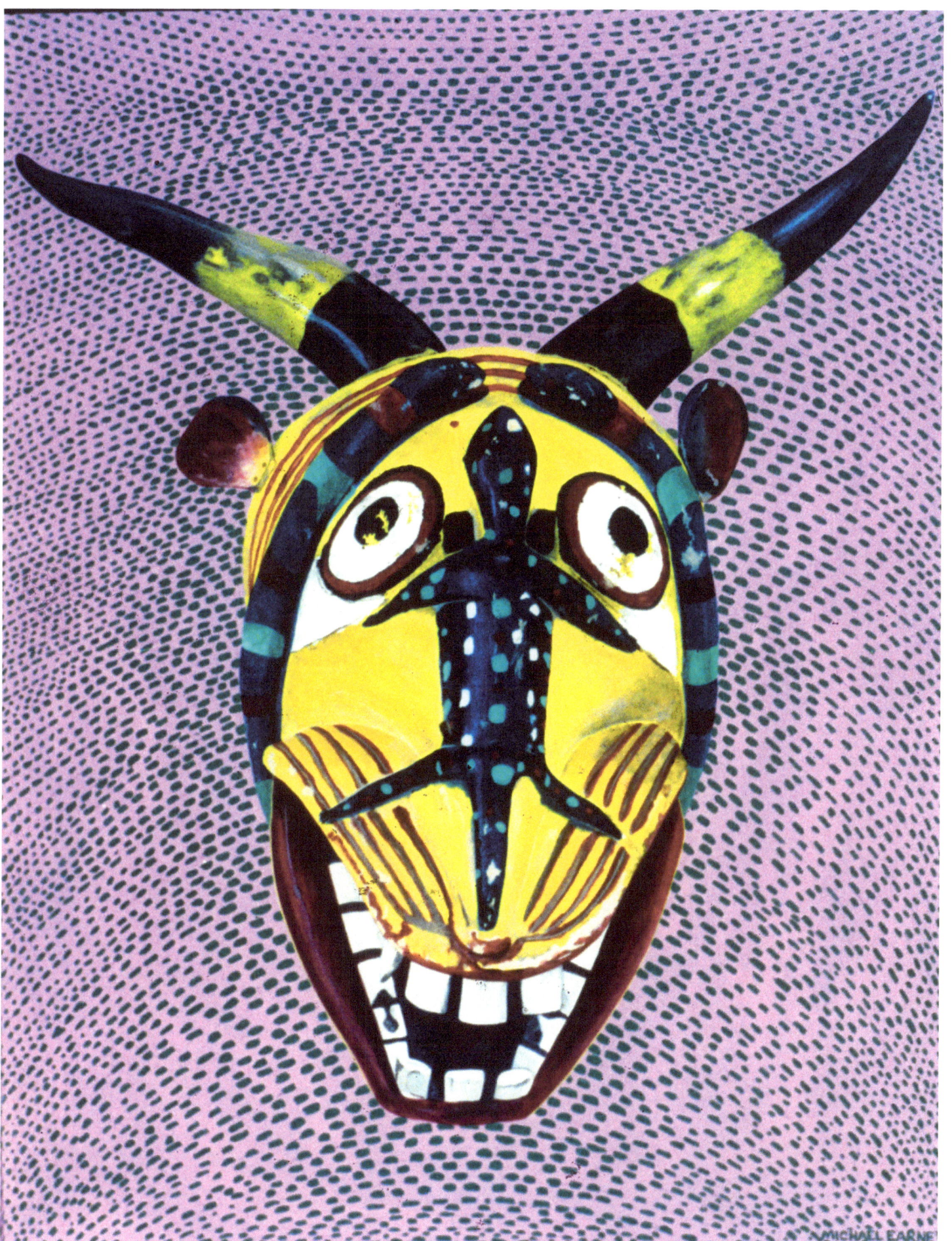

MICHAEL EARNE

5. Katy & Anna

2000 Acrylic on board (32"x 48")

Each sister chose the costume and mask she would wear for this double portrait. Though the masks are similar, anyone who knows the girls can tell which is which. It would appear that even the disguise we choose to hide our identity can also serve as a clue to who we are.

5. Katy y Ana

2000 Acrílico en fibracel (81cm x 122cm)

Cada hermana escogió el disfraz y la máscara usarian para este doble retrato. Aunque las máscaras son similares, cualquier persona que conozca a las niñas las puede distinguir. Parece que hasta el disfraz que escogimos para ocultar nuestra identidad también sirve como una pista para saber quienes somos.

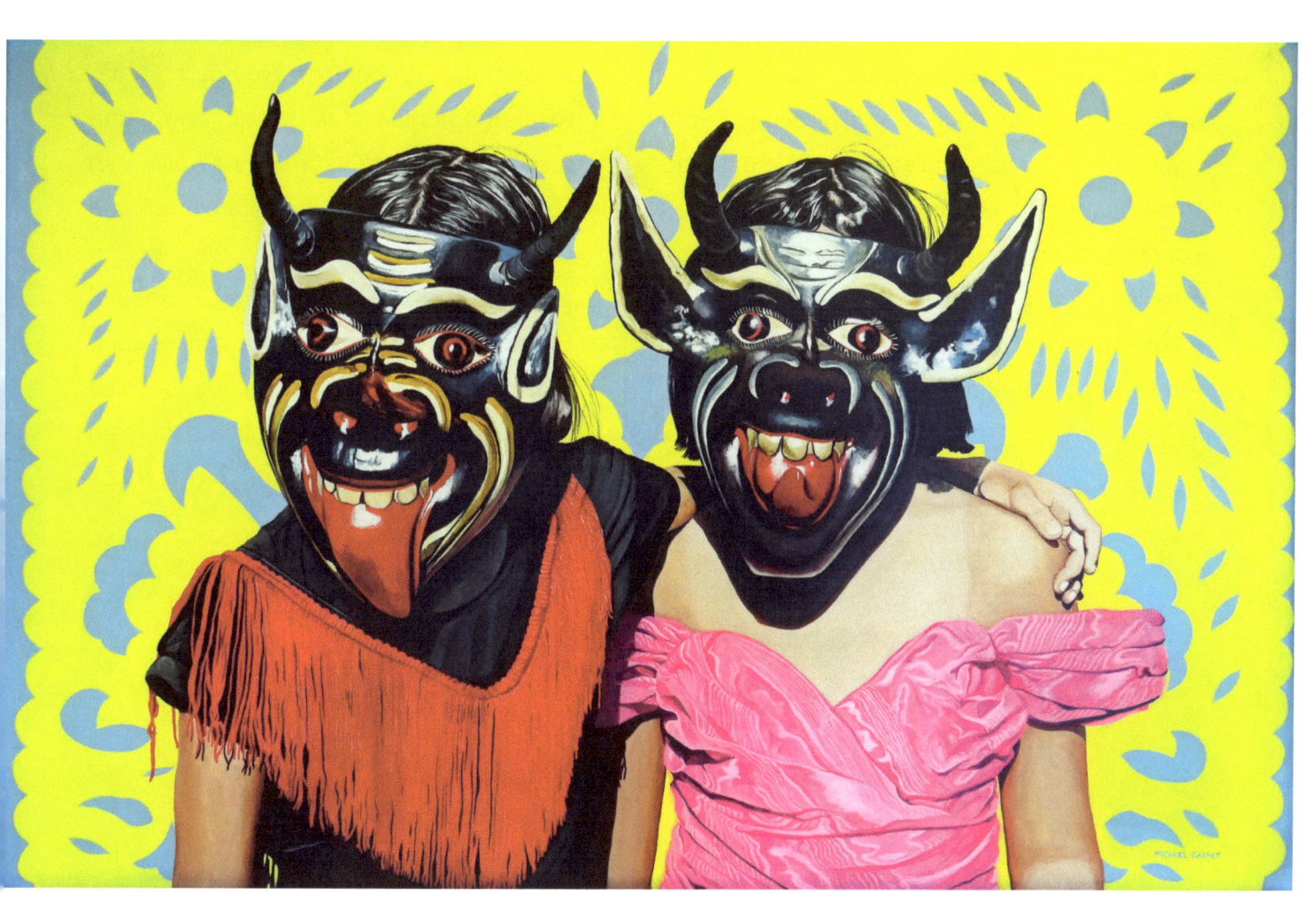

6. Laughing Calavera

2001 Acrylic on board (48" x 32")

Death is represented in multiple ways in Mexican masks, usually with a mocking smile to remind us of our fate. Ancestor worship, reverence for the remains of sacrificial victims and a fascination with the afterlife contributed to a proliferation of representations of skulls and skeletons in Pre-Columbian Mexico. These concerns continue today, especially among the native peoples, it's most overt expression being seen during the Dia de los Muertos (Day of the Dead) celebrations.

6. Calavera riendo

2001 Acrílico en fibracel (122cm X 81cm)

La muerte es representada en múltiples formas en las máscaras mejicanas, usualmente con una sonrisa burlona para recordarnos nuestro destino. Los cultos Ancestrales, presentan reverencia por los restos de las víctimas de sacrificio y una fascinación con la vida del mas allá, eso contribuyo a la proliferación de representaciones de cráneos y esqueletos en el México Pre-Colombino. Estas preocupaciones se mantienen todavía, en especial entre los pueblos nativos, siendo su más amplia expresión las celebraciones del Día de los Muertos.

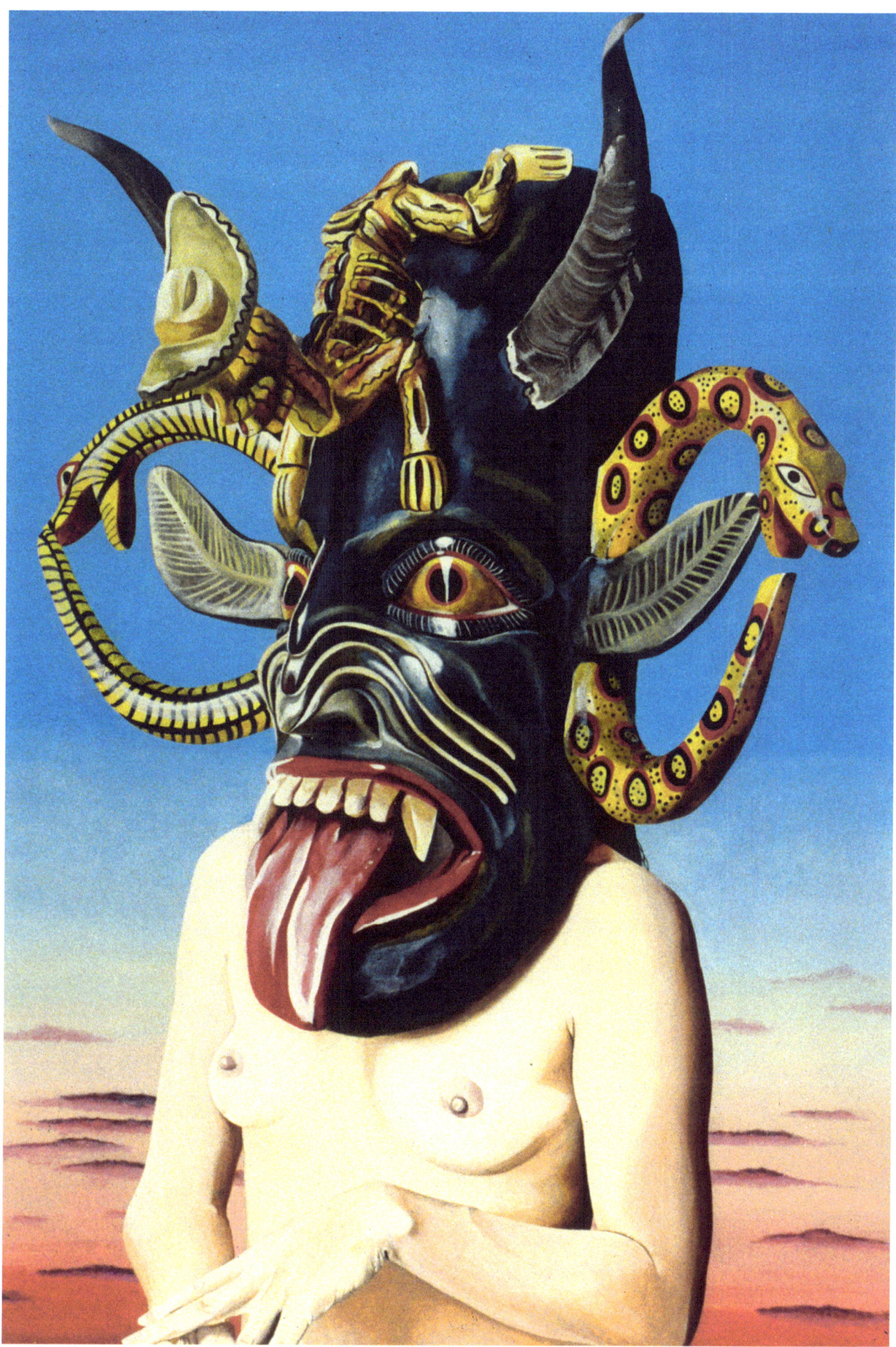

7. Tubular Ears

2001 Acrylic on board (32" x 32")

This crudely made and painted mask, missing its antlers, (notice the holes on the sides), still evokes the face painting of ancient ceremonies. Facial painting and scarification once identified the priests and other performers in the sacred rituals as actors dwelling in that state where man and god are one. The tire inner tube, used here to fabricate the mask's ears, has been an important material in mask making. The introduction of the radial tire will have a profound effect on the art.

7. Oídos tubulares

2001 Acrílico en fibracel (81cm X 81cm)

Aunque a esta máscara le faltan sus cuernos y está tallada y pintada de una forma primitiva, todavía trae recuerdos de las caras pintadas en las ceremonias antiguas. En las viejas épocas, las caras pintadas y los diseños hechos con cicatrices identificaron a los sacerdotes y a otros intérpretes de los rituales sagrados como actores que vivían en un estado donde el hombre y dios son lo mismo. El tubo que se encuentra dentro de la llanta de hule ha sido un importante material en la elaboración de máscaras. La introducción de la llanta radial tendrá un profundo efecto sobre este arte.

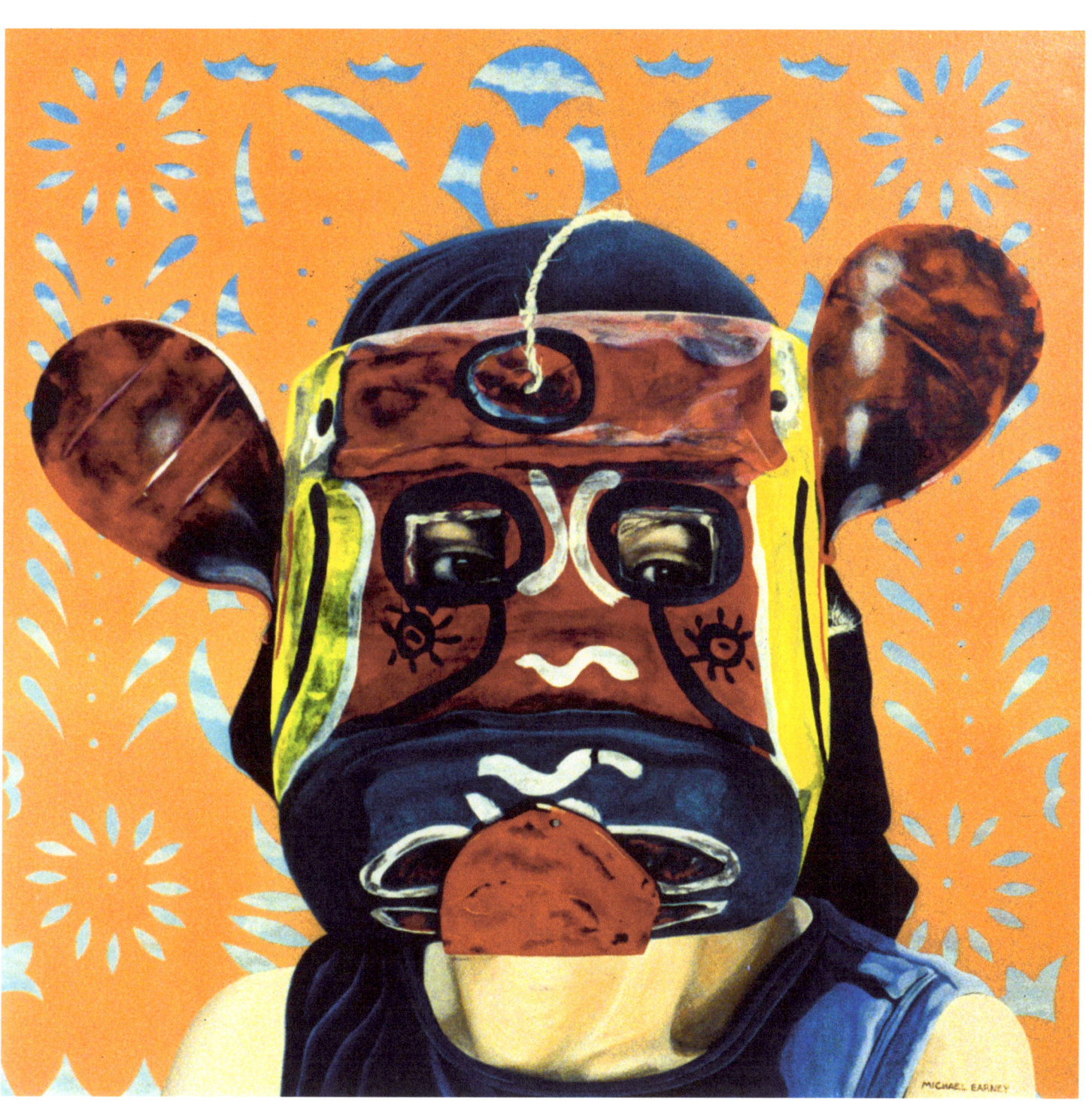

8. La Virgen Purisima

2001 Acrylic on board (32" x 32")

This variation of the negrito mask reveals the Pre-Columbian roots of this dance and shows the connection with gods such as Tezcatlipoca, Quetzalcoatl or Ehecatl among others, who were portrayed as black with fangs.

The "Milagro" in the background, is typical. Usually cut from tin and simply painted, they are hung in churches as thanks to whichever saint was perceived to have performed the "miracle" that the scene portrays.

8. La Virgen Purisima

2001 Acrílico en fibracel (81cm X 81cm)

Esta variación de la máscara del negrito revela las raíces pre-colombinas de esta danza y muestra la conexión con dioses como Tezcatlipoca, Quetzalcoatl o Ehecatl entre otros, a quienes retrataban como negros con colmillos.

"El Milagro" al fondo, es característico de los que se cuelgan en las iglesias como agradecimiento al santo que se creía le había "hecho el milagro" que retrata la escena. Normalmente se cortan en hojalata y pintan con simpleza.

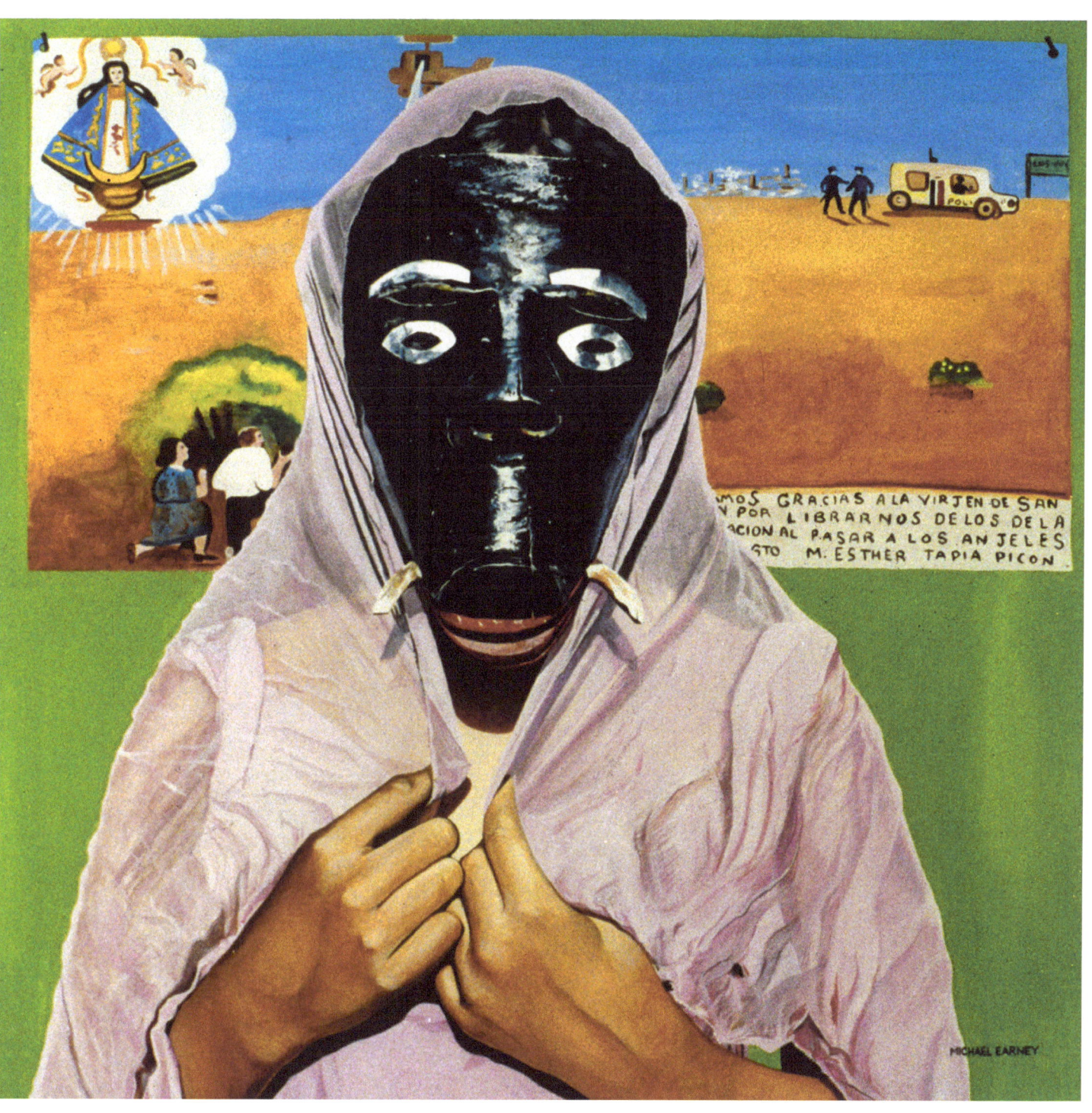

9. Tigre & Jaguar Warriors

2001 Acrylic on board (32" x 32")

A late Classic (7th century CE), polychrome vase, in the background, shows Maya warriors clad in jaguar skins. It provides the link to this modern tigre mask. Mirrored eyes appeared in pre-hispanic jaguar masks. Presumably, then too, jaguars were sacrificed to the gods to bring rain.

9. Guerreros Jaguar y Tigre

2001 Acrílico en fibracel (81cm X 81cm)

Una jarra policromada del período Clásico tardío, en el fondo, muestra guerreros Maya vestidos con pieles de jaguar, nos da la clave a esta moderna máscara de tigre. Ojos con reflejos, de obsidiana, mica u otro material brilloso son encontrados en máscaras pre-hispánicas de jaguar. Se asume, que también entonces, se sacrificaban jaguares a los dioses para traer lluvia.

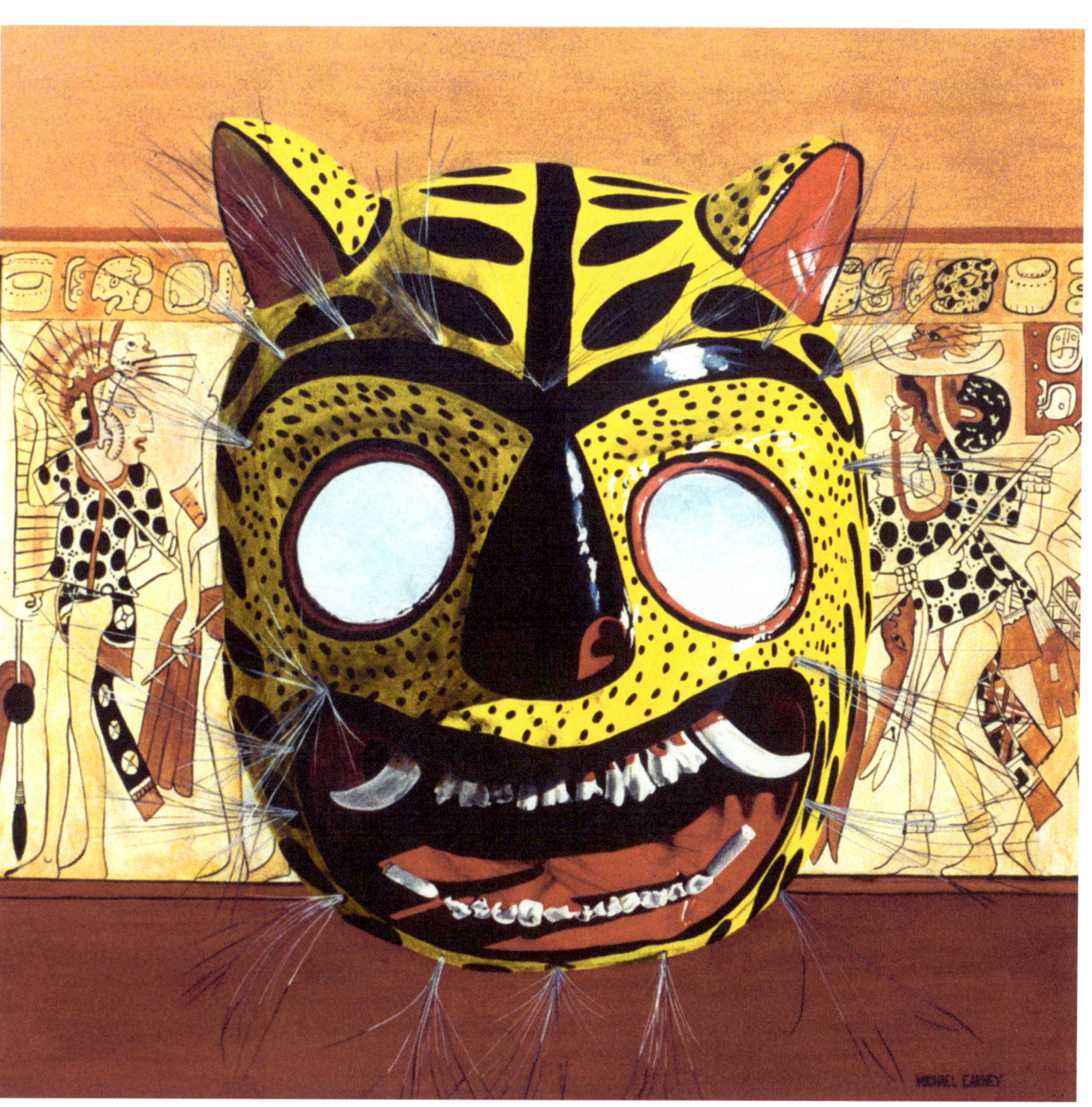

MICHAEL EARNEY

10. La Sirena

2001 Acrylic on board (48" x 32")

The Spanish probably introduced the mermaid to Mexico but traditional events such as The Fish Dance and The Caiman Dance, which use sympathetic magic to ensure a successful catch, incorporate anything with the requisite attributes that could help. The Mermaid fit right in.

10. La Sirena

2001 Acrilico en fibracel (122cm X 81cm)

Los españoles probablemente introdujeron la sirena al pueblo mexicano. Pero eventos tradicionales como la danza del pescado y la danza del caimán, las cuales usan una magia favorable para asegurar una buena captura, incorporan cualquier cosa que podría ser de ayuda. La Sirena fue una adición natural.

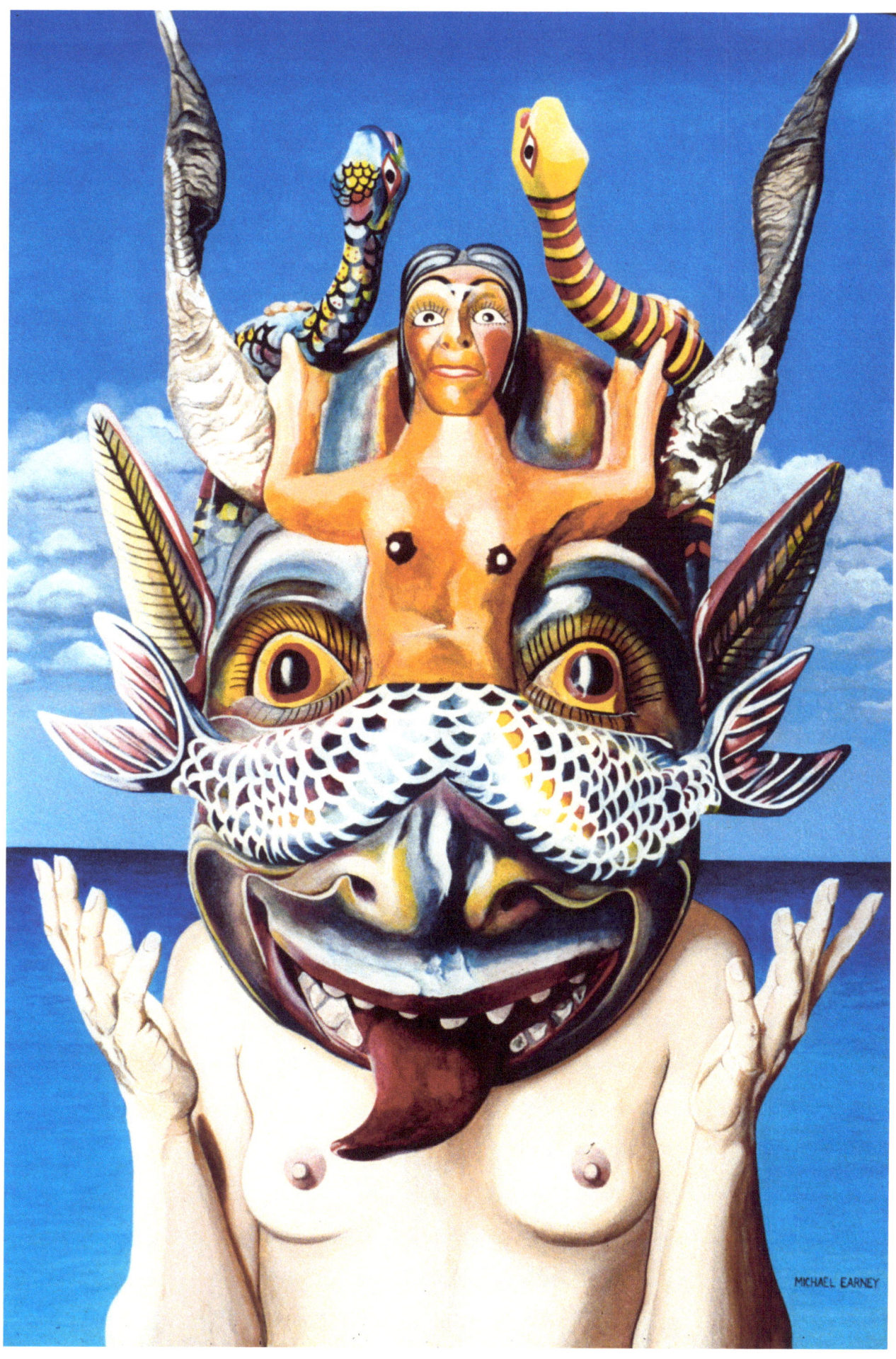

MICHAEL EARNEY

11. The Certainty of Change

2001 Acrylic on board (38" x 24")

The church fathers, unable to eradicate customs which they saw as inherently evil, affixed the horns of animals imported by the Spanish from Europe, to masks known to portray native gods. In so doing they created a new category, the Devil mask. It is a mask that has become very popular and takes many forms.

11. La Certeza del Cambio

2001 Acrílico en fibracel (96cm x 61cm)

Creyendo que eran de origen malvado, a los padres de la iglesia, incapaces de aniquilar las viejas costumbres, se les ocurrió la idea de ponerle cuernos de vacas, chivos y ovejas, animales todos importados de Europa por los Españoles, a las máscaras conocidas como retratos de dioses nativos. Al hacerlo crearon una nueva categoría, la máscara del Diablo. Es una máscara que se ha hecho muy popular y asume muchas formas.

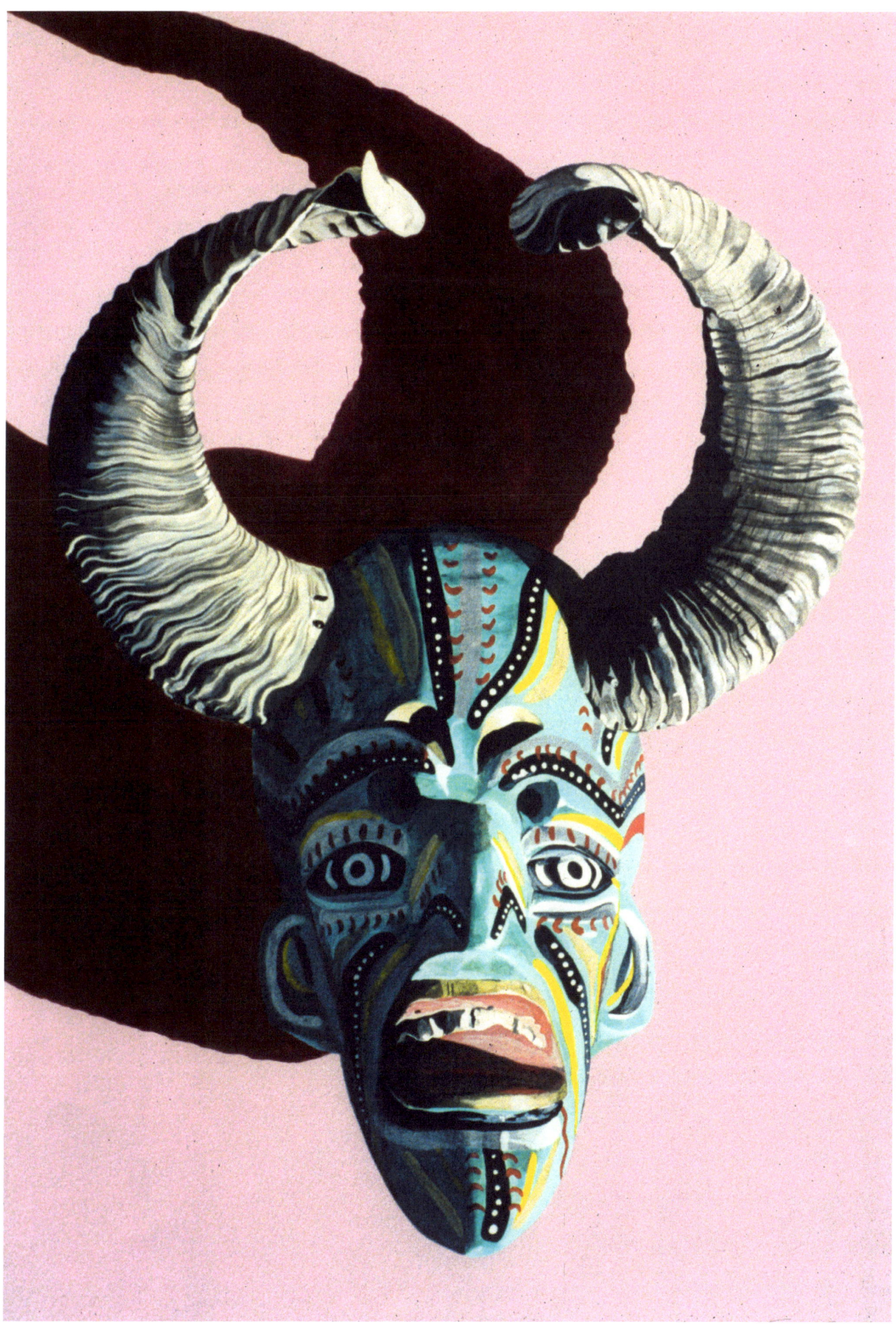

12. A la Posada

2001 Acrylic on board (24" x 32")

Jose Guadalupe Posada (1851-1913), a master of the art of engraving, is best known for his use of skeletons to mock authority and satirize social mores in penny sheets published before and during the Mexican revolution. This colorful skull reminds us of the theme's continued popularity.

12. A la Posada

2001 Acrílico en fibracel (61cm x 81cm)

José Guadalupe Posada (1851-1913) un maestro del arte del grabado, es mejor conocido por su uso de esqueletos para burlarse de las autoridades y satirizar costumbres sociales en paquines publicados antes y durante la revolución mejicana. Este colorido cráneo nos recuerda la prolongada popularidad del tema.

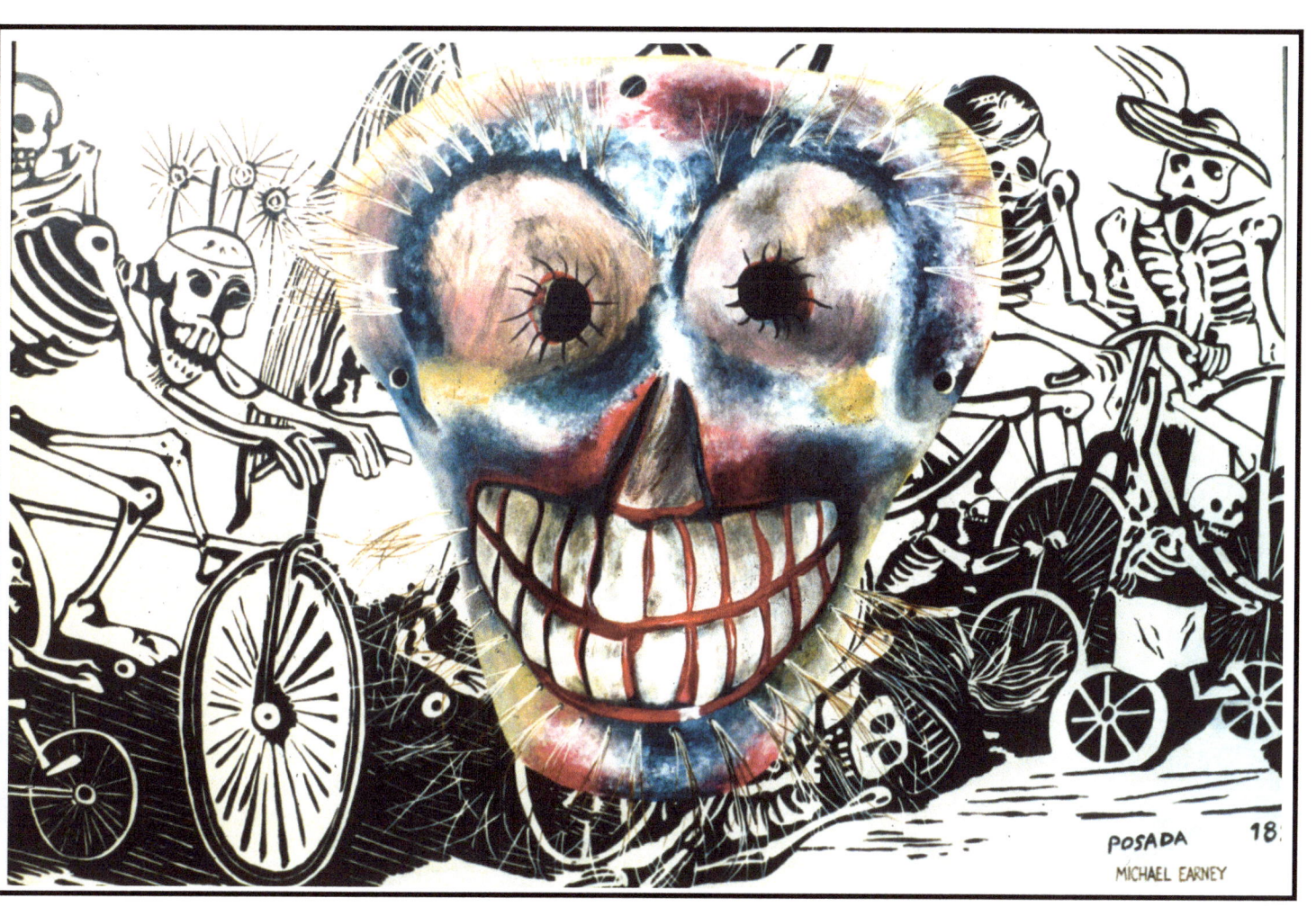

POSADA   18

MICHAEL EARNEY

13. Machisma

2001 Acrylic on board (48" x 48")

Adelita is the idealized symbol of revolutionary womanhood. She represents the women who broke down the barriers that had defined their roles in society, not only by serving as camp followers but by fighting alongside men during the revolution. The female wrestler could represent the invasion of that last bastion of macho, Lucha Libre (professional wrestling).

13. Machisma

2001 Acrílico en fibracel (122cm x 122cm)

Adelita es un simbolo idealizada de la mujer revolucionaria. Representa a las mujeres que rompieron las barrereas que limitaban su rol en la sociedad, no solo al acompañar a sus hombres en los campamentos, sino que tambien al pelear junto con ellos en los campos de batalla durante la revolución. Esta luchadora quizás represente la invasión del último refugio del machismo, la lucha libre profesional.

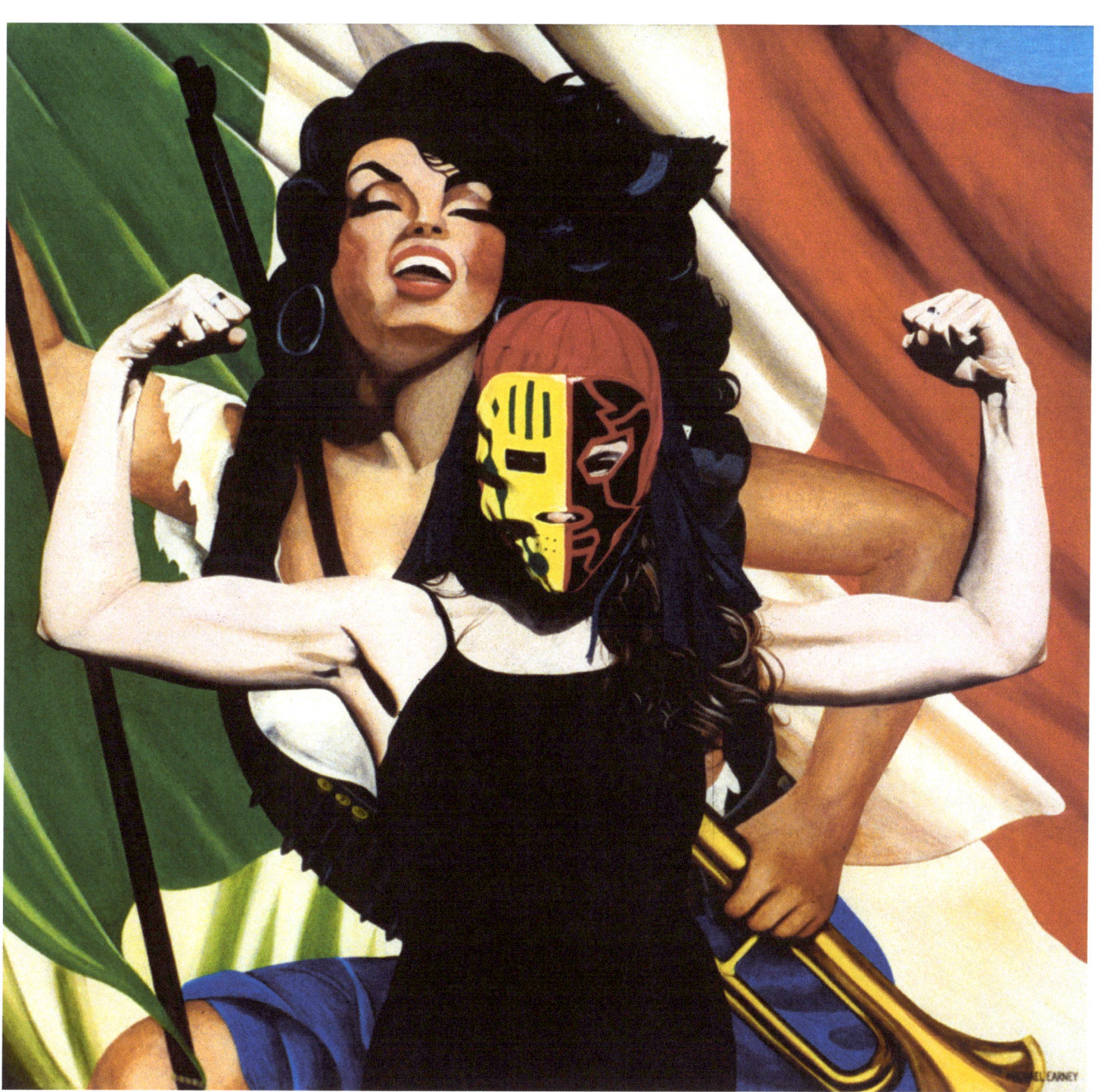

14. Mexicano

2001 Acrylic on board (32" x 24")

Clowning and irreverence are important elements of fiestas, occasions to poke fun at the establishment. Traditional dances are, for the most part, performed by indigenous or mestizo country folk who identify first with their ethnic group, town or state. The "Mexican" is almost a foreigner exemplified by the white, blue-eyed, five-o'clock-shadowed Charro portrayed in this mask.

14. Mexicano

2001 Acrilico en fibracel (81cm X 61cm)

Hacerse el payaso y ser irreverente son dos elementos importantes de las fiestas, cuando la gente puede burlarse del gobierno. Generalmente las danzas tradicionales las hacen los indígenas o la gente mestiza de los campos, quienes se identifican principalmente con su grupo étnico, su pueblo o su estado. El "mexicano" es casi siempre un extranjero, ejemplificado por el charro blanco, de ojos azules y con bigotes que está representado en esta máscara.

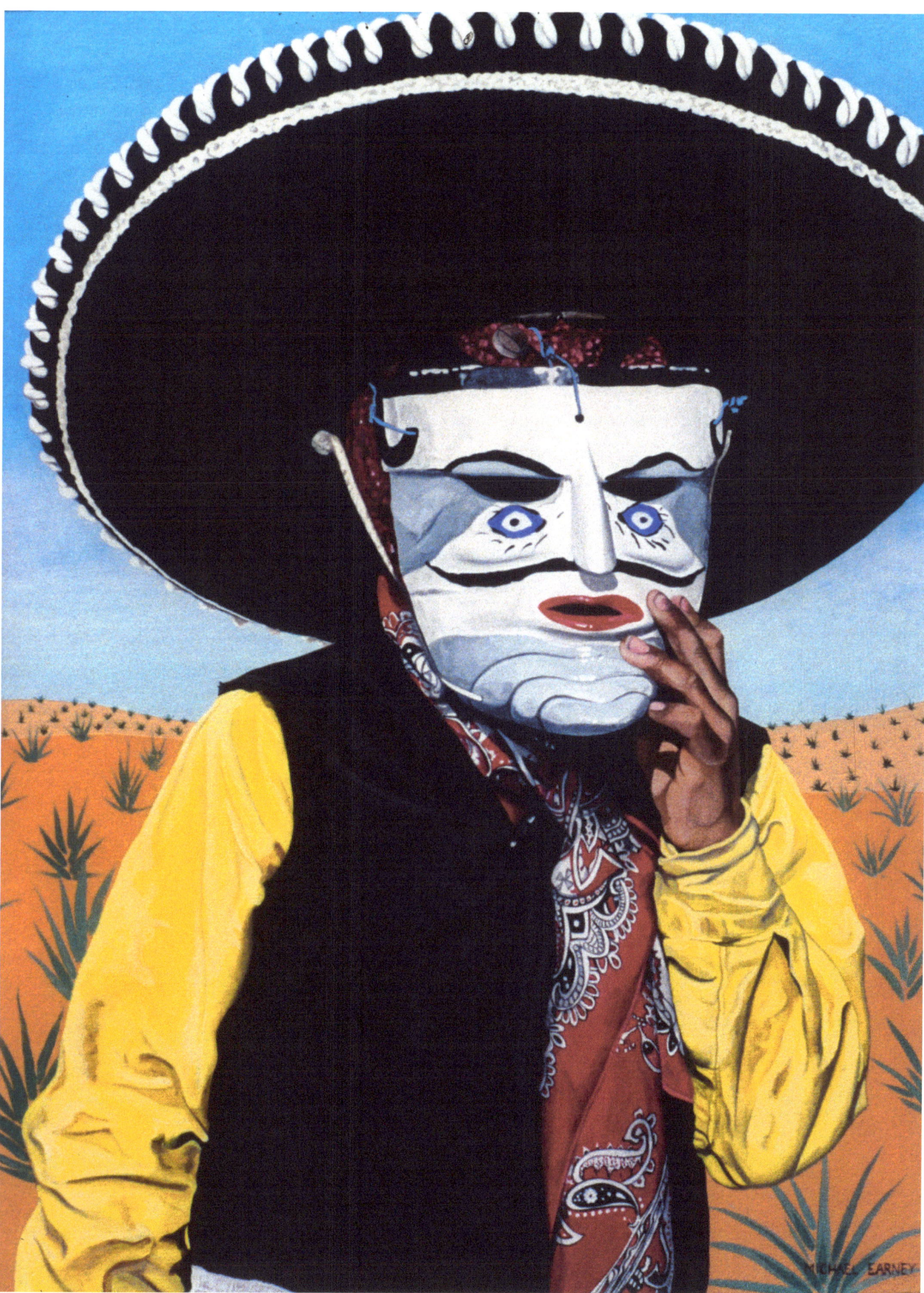

MICHAEL EARNEY

15. Clay Mask

2001 Acrylic on board (20"x 16")

Although this unique unglazed clay mask may not have been used by a dancer, black & white paint and little snakes on a rose colored face are characteristics of Maringuilla (Little Mary). This character is usually played by a man wearing women's clothes who is part of the Negrito dances. In some states, "Little Mary" loses the snakes and may even be played by unmasked women and girls.

15. Máscara de Barro

2001 Acrilico en fibracel (51cm x 41cm)

Esta singular máscara de barro no vidriado a lo mejor no se usó por un bailador, pero la pintura de blanco y negro junto con víboras pequeñas sobre una cara de color rosa son las características del Maringuilla, que es un hombre vestido de mujer que participa en las danzas de los Negritos. En algunas regiones no aparecen víboras en la máscara de la "Pequeña María" y este papel hasta puede ser interpretado por mujeres y niñas que no llevan máscaras.

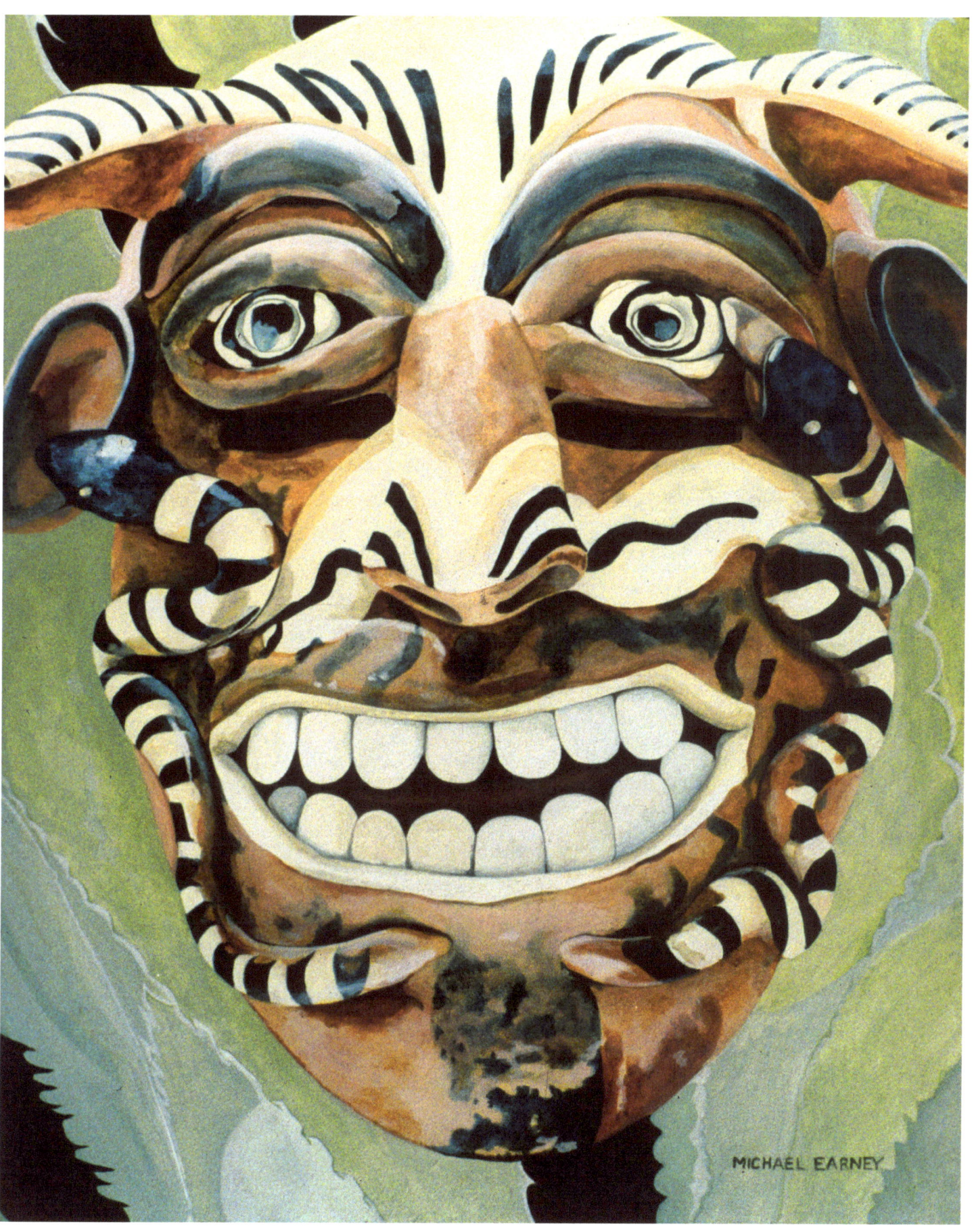

MICHAEL EARNEY

16. Tigre Fighter

2001 Acrylic on board (48" x 28")

Each May, just as they have for eons, annual jaguar fights are held to bring much needed rain. Fighters beat each other with knotted ropes in heated battles. Blood is shed for the gods to ensure abundant crops, to petition for rain, or for protection from the destructive forces of nature. The jaguar represents fierce nature, and when tamed, becomes the symbol of fertility. In the background, a jaguar with a rope around its neck is part of a stucco frieze at the ruins of Tula, in the state of Hidalgo.

16. Tigre Luchador

2001 Acrilico en fibracel (122cm x 71cm)

Cada año en mayo, como ha pasado durante varias épocas, hay peleas de jaguares para traer a la lluvia que siempre falta. Los luchadores se golpean uno al otro con sogas que llevan nudos durante batallas furiosas. Se ofrece sangre a los dioses para asegurar cosechas abundantes, para pedir lluvia, o para la protección de las fuerzas destructivas de la naturaleza. El jaguar representa la violencia de la naturaleza y cuando está domado se convierte en un símbolo de la fertilidad. Un jaguar que lleva una soga alrededor de su cuello forma parte de un friso de estuco que se encuentra en las ruinas de Tula, en el estado de Hidalgo.

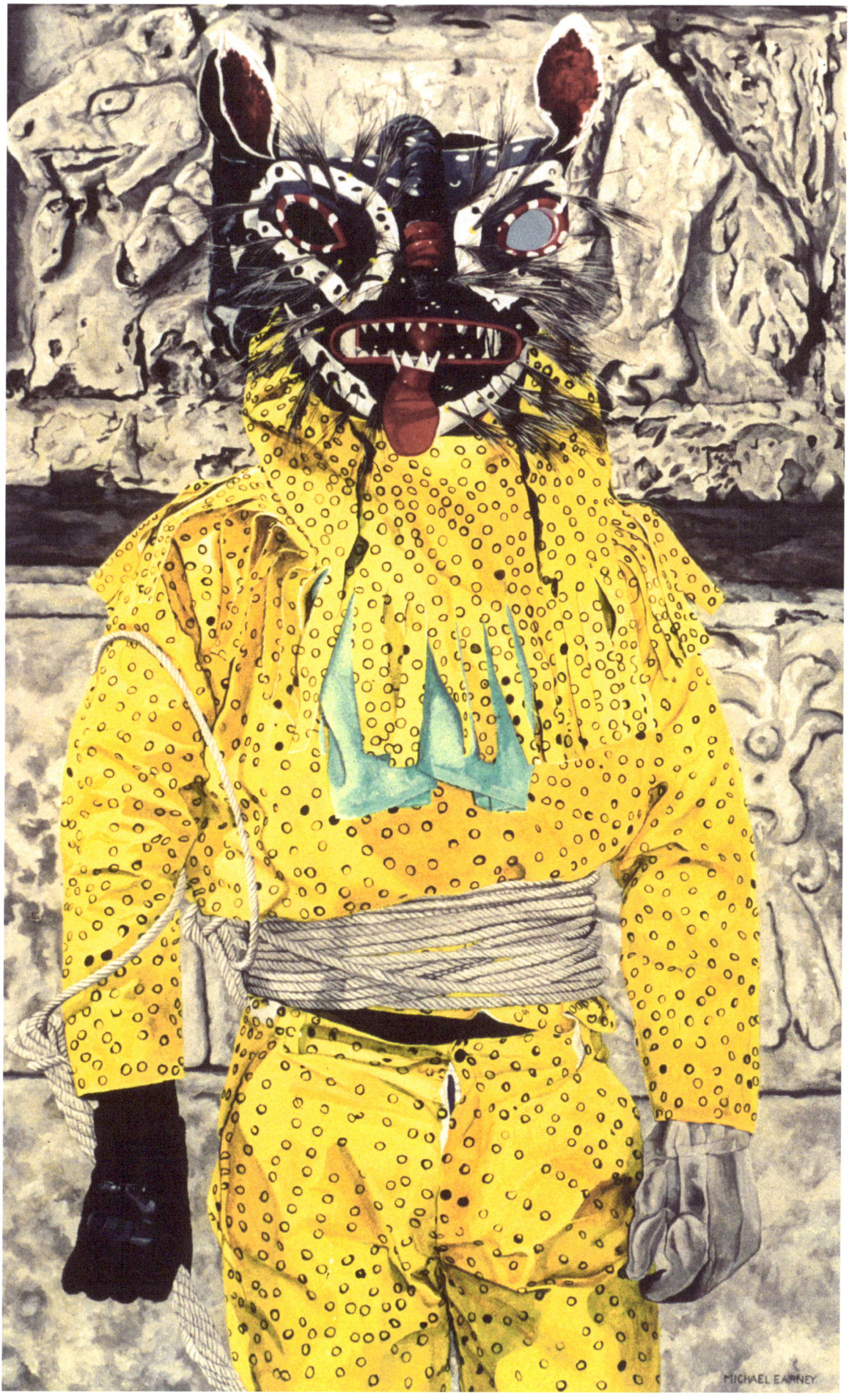

17. Kristin and Tlaloc

2001 Acrylic on board (48" x 36")

A mural at Teotihuacán, bordered by water plants, depicts a turquoise-masked Tlaloc, God of Rain, water pouring from his hands. This seemed like the appropriate background for this "Creature from the Black Lagoon" mask, bought on the street in Nuevo Progreso, Tamaulipas. Or perhaps instead, Kristin represents the young girls sacrificed each year to Chalchiuhtlicue, the Goddess of Water.

17. Kristin y Tlaloc

2001 Acrilico en fibracel (122cm x 91cm)

Un mural en Teotihuacán, rodeado de plantas acuáticas, que representa a Tlaloc, Dios de la Lluvia, con una máscara de turquesa, agua brotando de sus manos, pareció ser el fondo apropiado para esta máscara inspirada por "El Monstruo de la Laguna Negra", una película muy popular de Hollywood de los años 1950, que compré en la calle en Nuevo Progreso, Tamaulipas. O tal vez sea la joven muchacha sacrificada cada año a Chalchihuitlicue, la Diosa del Agua, la representada aqui.

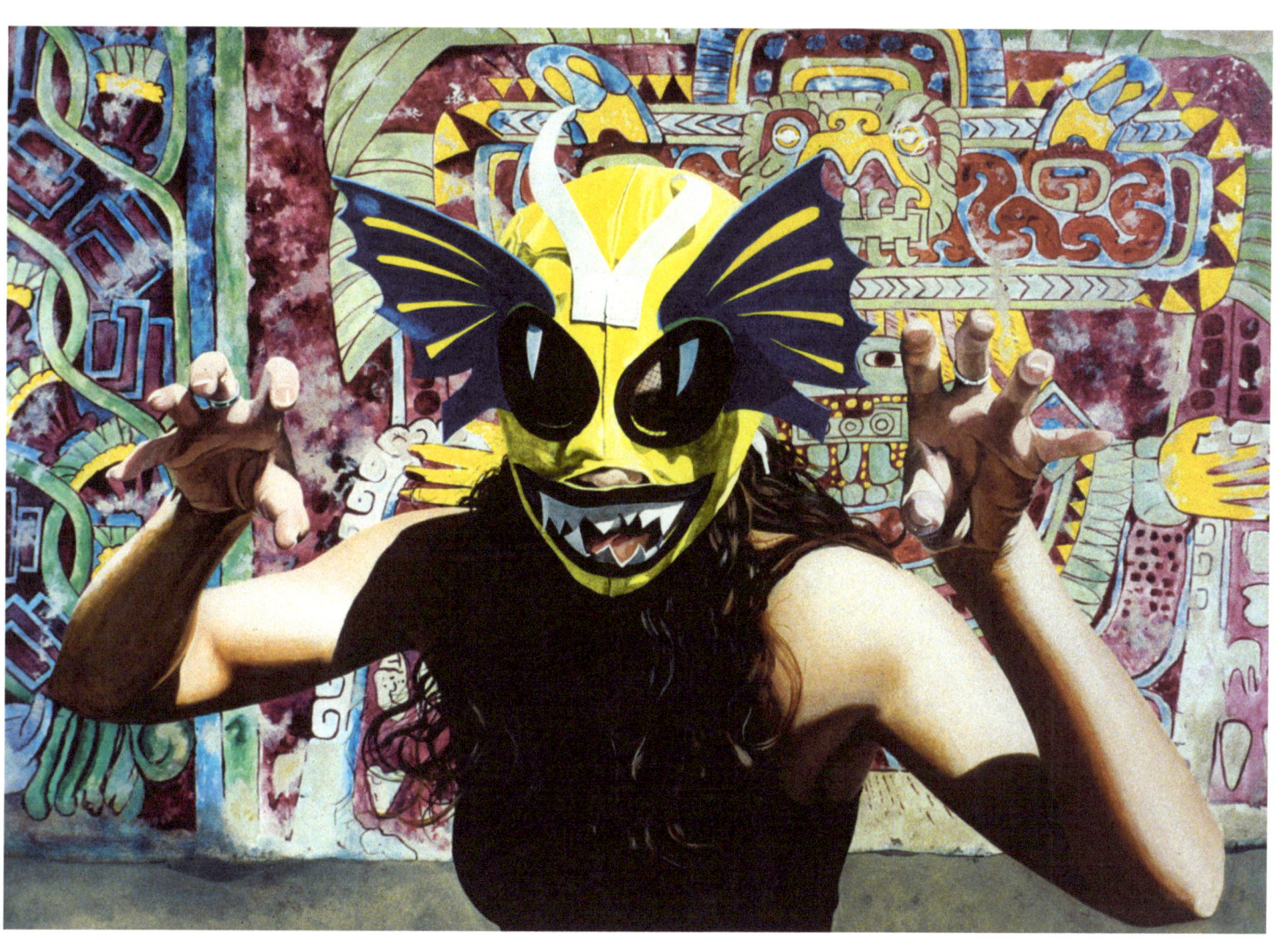

18. Negrito y Flor de Limon

2002 Acrylic on board (32" x 24")

The importation of African slaves by the Spanish would seem to be the source for the Dance of the Negritos, especially since it is most popular in the coastal states. However, these masks may have conveniently evolved from depictions of Pre-Columbian black gods reconfigured as a means to hide their true nature from the church fathers.

18. Negrito y Flor de Limón

2002 Acrilico en fibracel (81cm x 61cm)

La importación de esclavos africanos por los españoles parecería ser la raíz de la Danza de los Negritos dado que es la danza más popular en las zonas costeras. Sin embargo, estas máscaras quizás evolucionaron de representaciones de dioses negros precolombinos y fueron configurados para ocultar el verdadero significado de ellas.

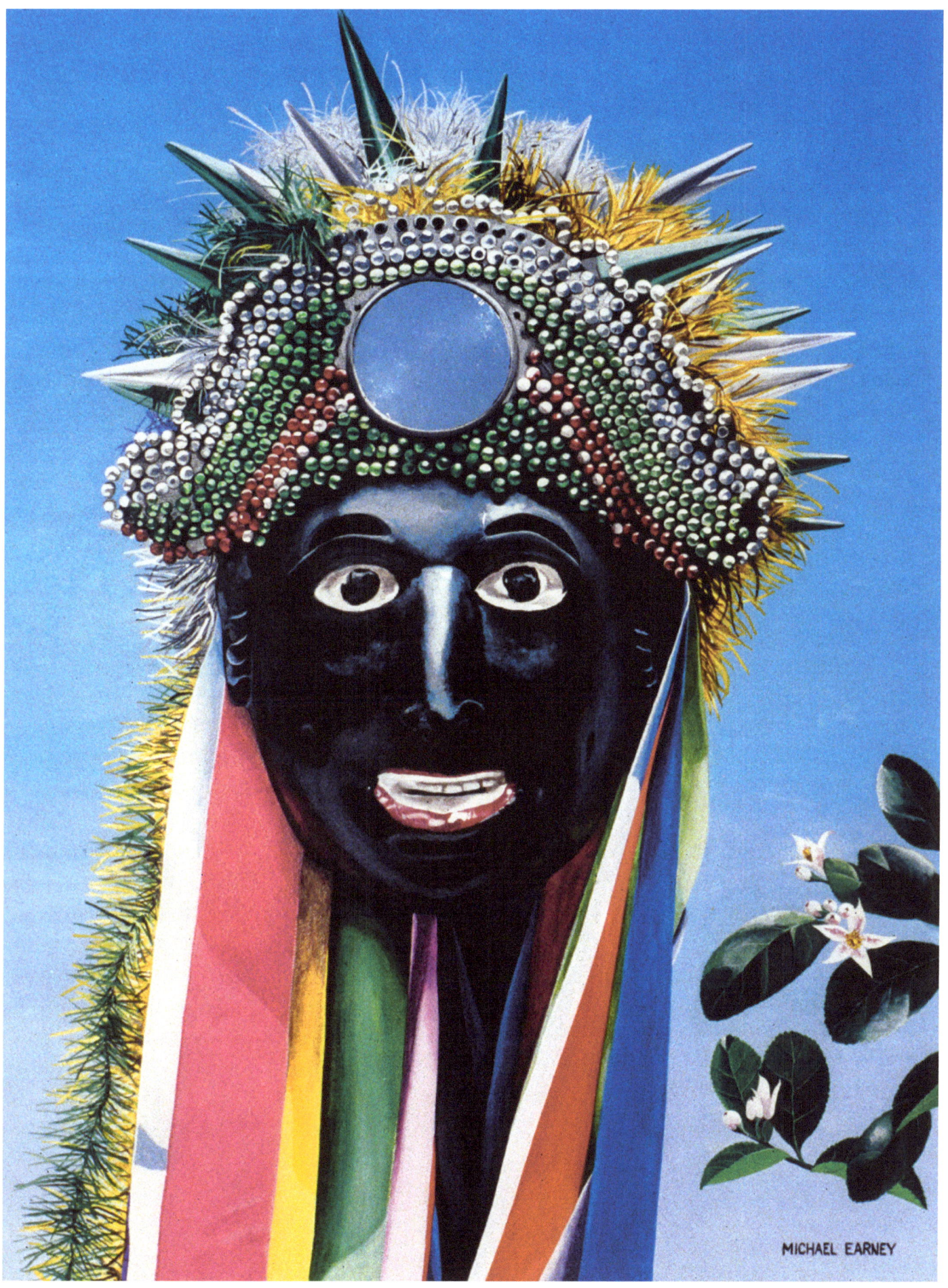

MICHAEL EARNEY

19. Tigres Antiguos

2002 Acrylic on board (32" x 24")

"O tigre, animal most noble and agile of ancient Mesoamerica, deified by Olmecs, Zapotecs, Teotihuacans, Toltecs and Aztecs since a thousand years before the birth of Christ, don't become frightened in your brave struggle, continue to die as you have died thousands of times in thousands of small town fiestas!" (Horcasitas 1971)

Background: Mural at Cacaxla, Tlaxcala. A jaguar skin draped rainmaker standing atop a jaguar serpent pours drops of water from a rainstick. Jaguar serpents live at the bottom of rivers and only Shamans can reach them. This mask of stiff rawhide protected the wearer during the annual rain-making festivals dedicated to Tlaloc, the Rain God.

19. Tigres Antiguos

2002 Acrilico en fibracel (81cm x 61cm)

"Oh, tigre, el mas noble y ágil animal de la antigua Mesoamérica, venerado por Olmecas, Zapotecas, Teotihuacanes, Toltecas y Aztecas mil años antes del nacimiento de Cristo, no te acobardes en tu estoica lucha, sigue muriendo como has muerto miles de veces en miles de pequeñas fiestas de los pueblos!" (Horcasitas 1971)

Fondo: Mural en Cacaxla, Tlaxcala. Un hacedor de lluvia vestido con pieles de jaguar parado sobre una serpiente-jaguar vierte gotas de agua de un palo de lluvia. Las serpientes- jaguar viven en el fondo de los ríos y solo los Chamanes pueden alcanzarlas. Esta máscara de cuero duro protegía al usuario durante los festivales anuales de hacer lluvia dedicados a Tlaloc, el Dios de la Lluvia.

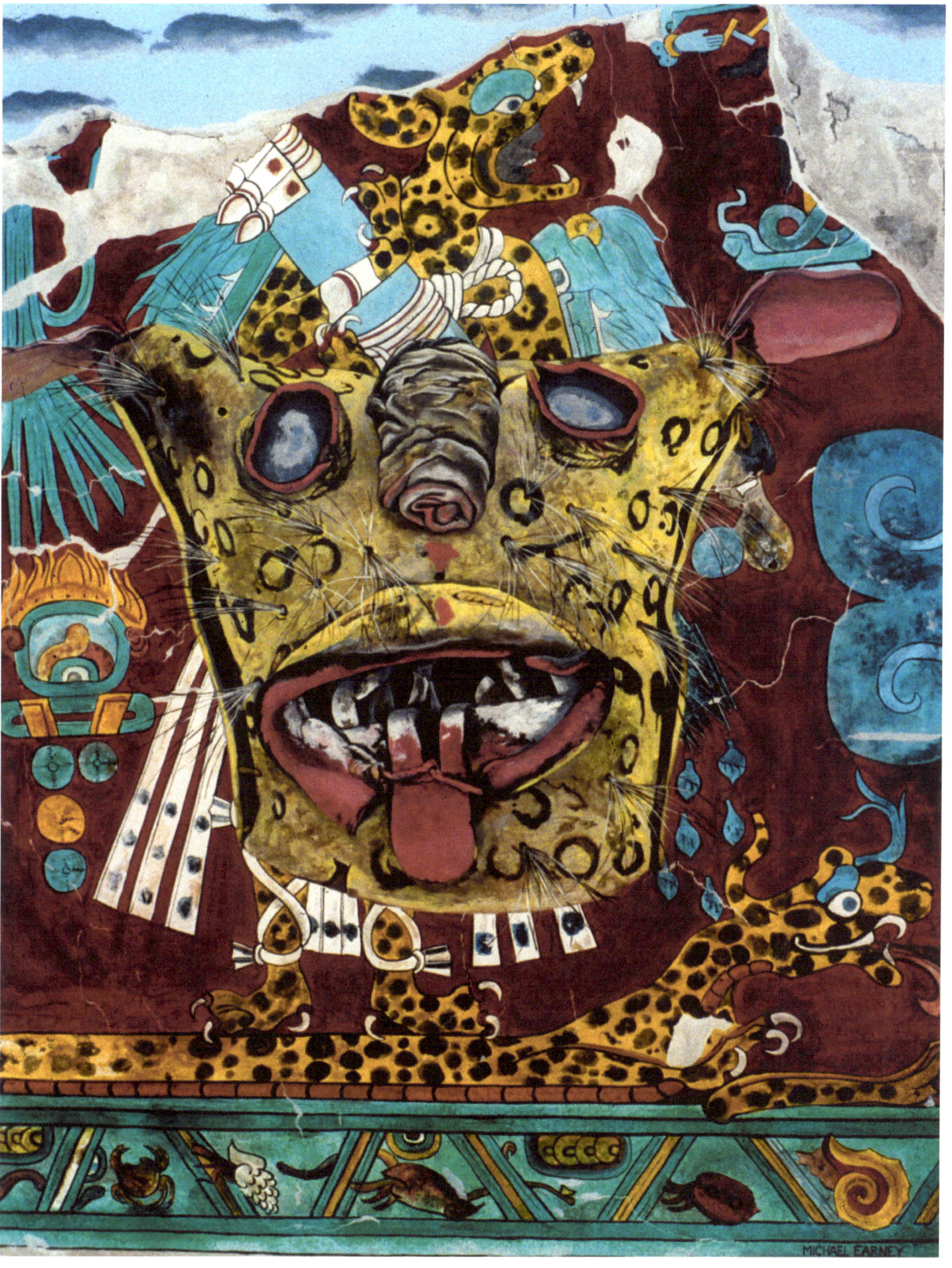

MICHAEL FARNEY

20. Tres Tejorones

2002 Acrylic on board (48" x 38")

The tiny Tejoron masks are intended to make those wearing them appear taller than they are. Male dancers, playing the part of females, once wore the traditional woman's huipil and wrap-around skirt. As fashions change so has the dancers' choice of costume. Although here played by men, women are increasingly filling the female roles, to the chagrin of the more traditionally-minded.

20. Tres Tejorones

2002 Acrilico en fibracel (122cm x 97cm)

Las pequeñísimas máscaras de Tejorones tienen el propósito de hacer que quien las lleva puestas se ve más alto. En el pasado, los bailadores varones hacían el papel de mujeres y se ponían un huipil y una falda tradicional. Con el cambio de la moda, también ha cambiado el disfraz que usan los bailadores. Cada vez son más las mujeres que juegan el papel que antes jugaban los hombres, algo que no le gusta a la gente conservadora.

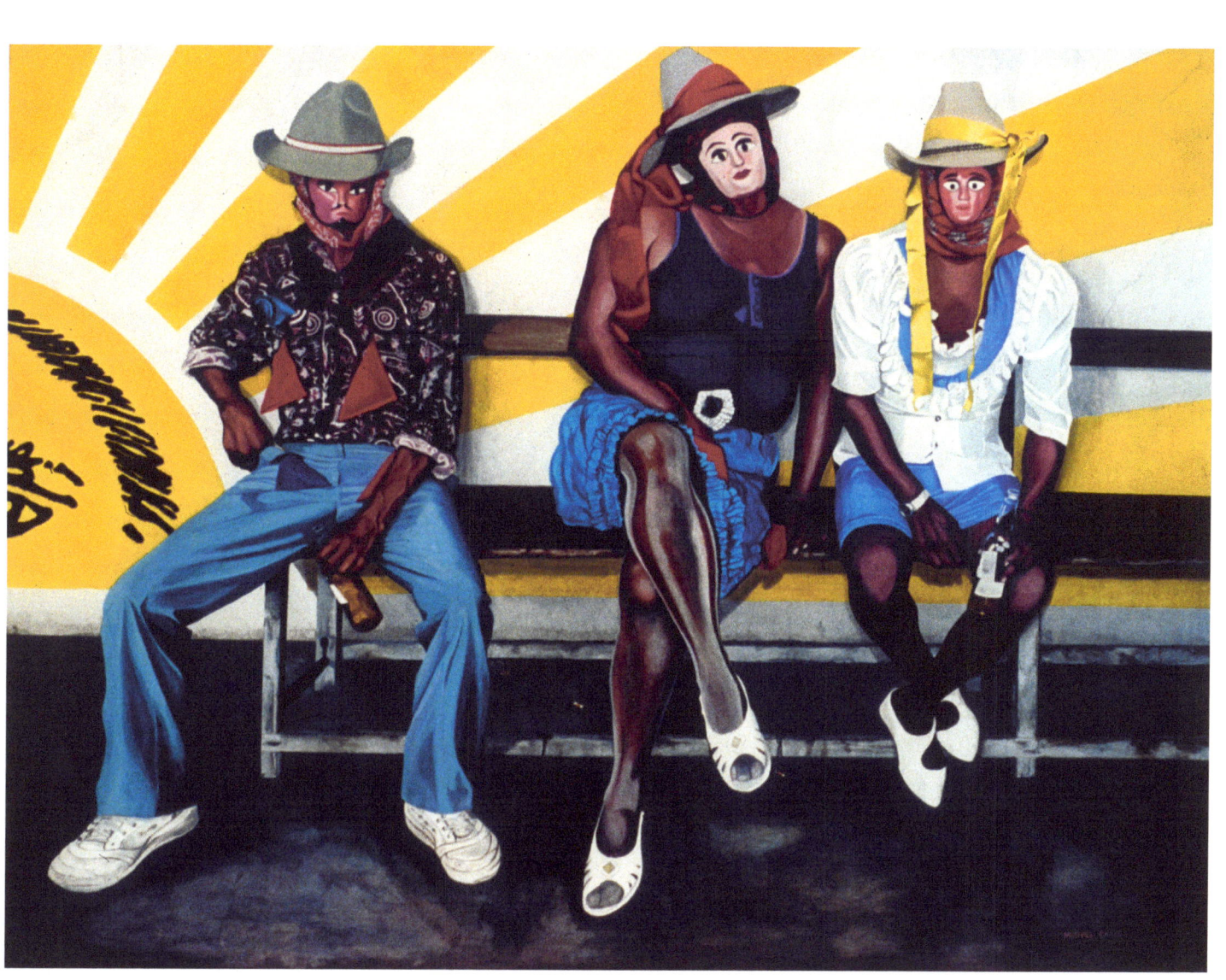

21. Nariz de Plata

2002. Acrylic on board (32" X 24")

Protruding, exaggerated tongues can represent wisdom, power, defiance or evil. In some Tigre dances, after the jaguar has been hunted and killed, the performer switches to a tigre mask with a protruding tongue which, in this instance, indicates death.

In the background, on recycled vellum, the old ink showing through, we see a warrior clad in a jaguar skin. In the resource scarce days after the conquest, this material was provided to natives by Spaniards wishing to preserve some knowledge of the past.

21. Nariz de Plata

2002 Acrilico en fibracel (81cm x 61cm)

Las lenguas prominentes y exageradas suelen representar sabiduría, poder, reto o maldad. En algunas danzas del Tigre, después de que el tigre es cazado y muerto, el ejecutante se cambia a una mascara de tigre con una lengua protuberante que en este caso significa muerte.

En el fondo, sobre pergamino reciclado, vislumbrándose la antigua tinta, vemos un guerrero vestido con piel de jaguar. En los primeros días después de la conquista, los españoles suministraban este material a los nativos tratando de preservar algún conocimiento del pasado.

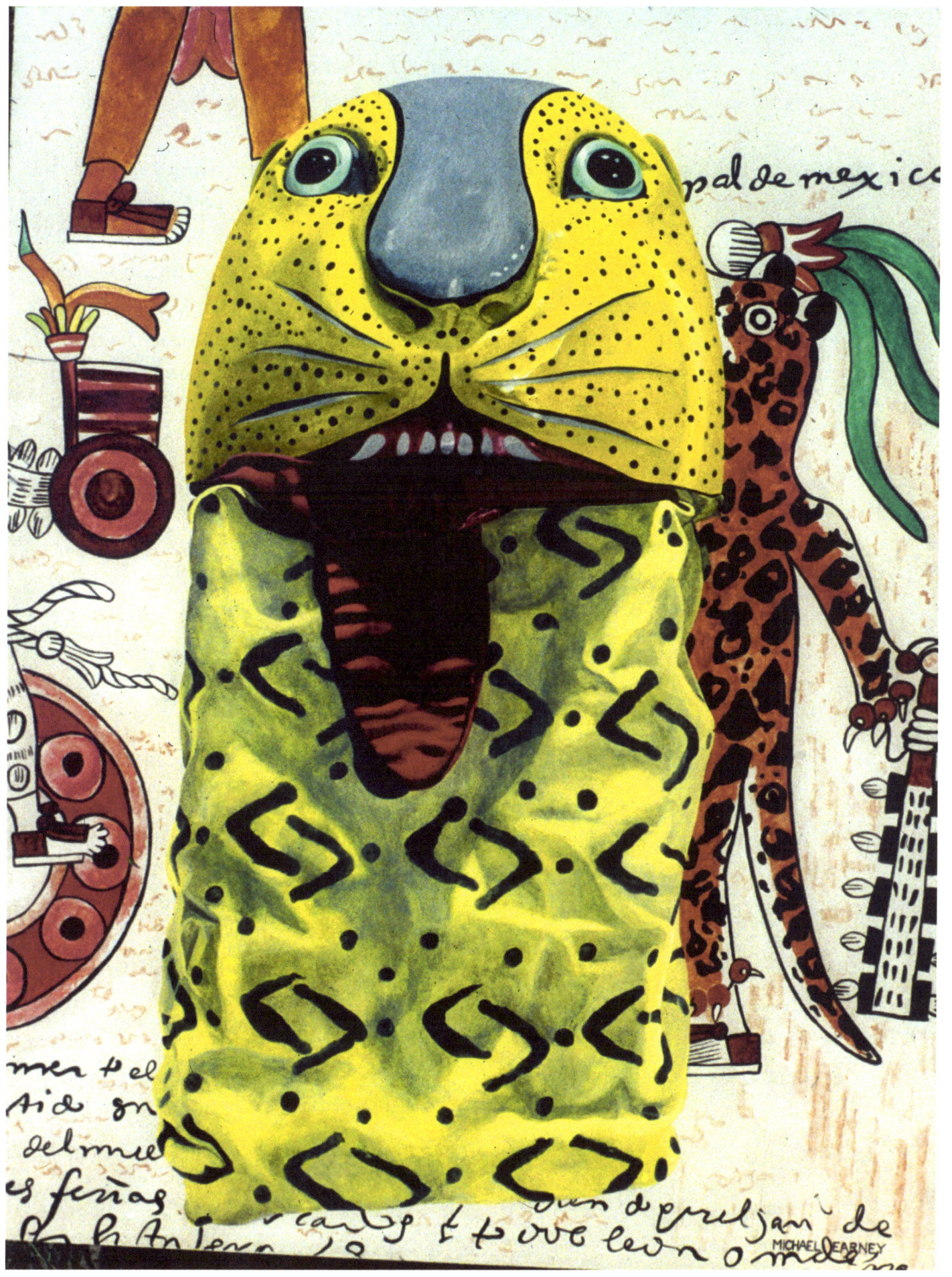

22. El Moro

2002 Acrylic on board (32" X 24")

The manner in which one religion supplants another in the wake of a conquest is neatly displayed in the juxtaposition of church and temple ruins at Mitla, Oaxaca. The Dance of the Moros y Cristianos, celebrating the victory of Christian Spanish over their Moslem rulers, served as an object lesson for the natives of the New World. White, blue-eyed Christians trump dark-skinned Pagans. Ironically, the Indians got to play both victor and vanquished when the play was brought over to Mexico.

22. El Moro

2002 Acrilico en fibracel (81cm x 61cm)

La manera en que una religión suplanta a otra después de una conquista se muestra claramente en la yuxtaposición de las ruinas de una iglesia y un templo en Mitla, Oaxaca. El Baile de los Moros y los Cristianos celebra la victoria que lograron los cristianos españoles sobre los moros que los gobernaban y servía como una lección ejemplar para los indígenas del Nuevo Mundo. Los cristianos blancos con ojos azules triunfan sobre los paganos de piel oscura. Irónicamente, los indígenas hacían el papel tanto del ganador como del perdedor.

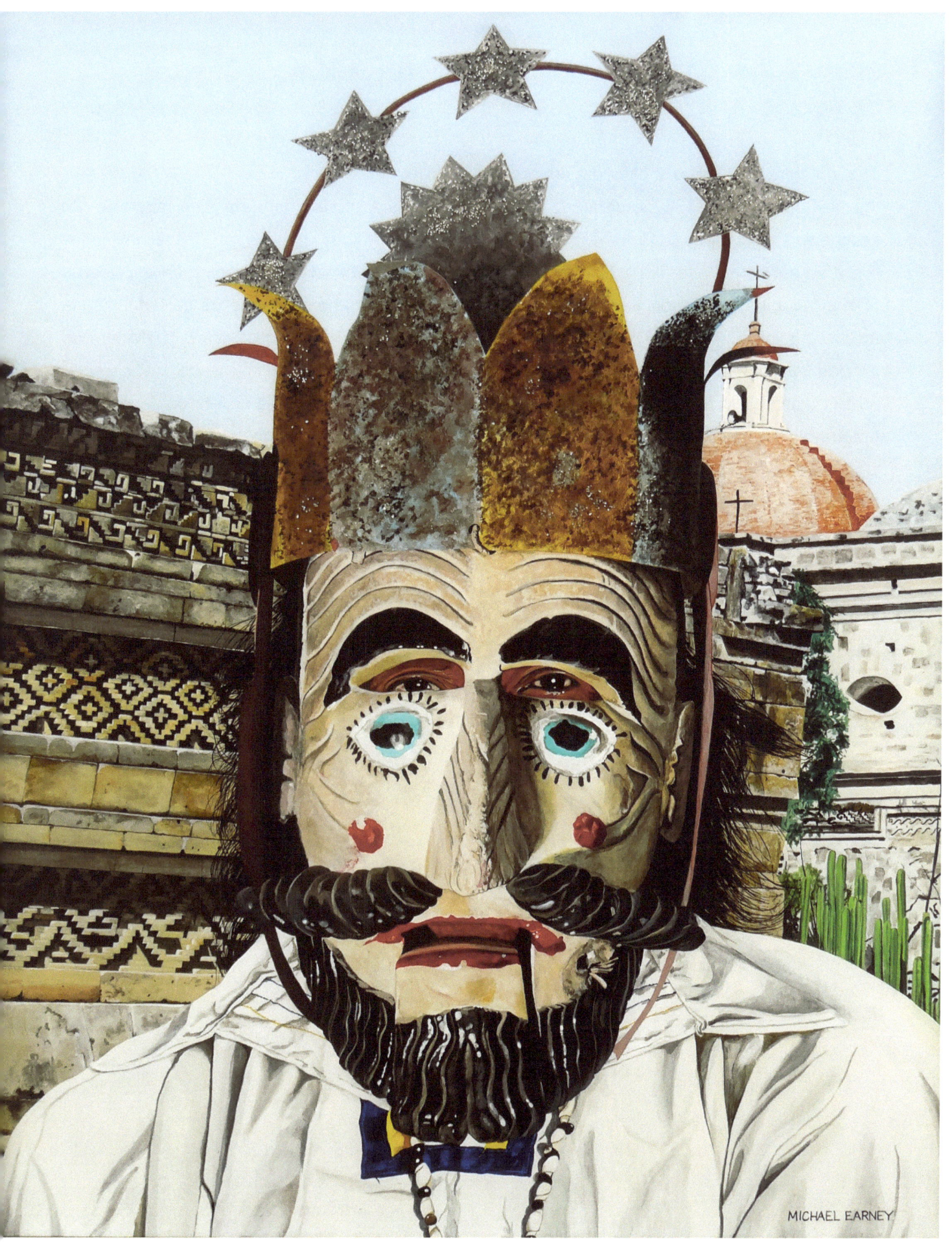

MICHAEL EARNEY

23. Conquest

2003 Acrylic on board (58" X 48")

The painters of Mexico's calendar art from the 1930's to the 1960's created heroic fictions worthy of Cecil B. DeMille, portraying a mythic past that never was. This is by one of my favorites, Jesus de la Helguera. For me, combining Sr. Helguera's painting entitled "Grandeza Azteca" with a Santiago mask represents the end of the Azteca empire, overcome by the Spanish Conquistador. This is an example of the Santiago mask used in Moros y Cristianos, Santiago dances and their variants. "Santiago!" (Saint James) was adopted as the battle cry of the Spanish after that saint's appearance during a crucial clash with the Moors enabled a Spanish victory. Subsequently, the much-travelled saint is said to have assisted in the conquest of the New World.

23. Conquista

2003 Acrilico en fibracel (147cm x 122cm)

Los pintores del arte que apareció en calendarios mexicanos desde los años 1930 hasta los años 1960 crearon ficciones heroicas (dignas de formar parte de una película de Cecil B. DeMille) que representaban un pasado mítico que jamás existió. Ésta pintura de Jesús de la Helguera es una de mis favoritas. Para mí, la combinación de la pintura del Sr. Helguera (titulada Grandeza Azteca) con una máscara de Santiago representa el fin del imperio azteca, que fue vencido por los conquistadores españoles. Éste es un ejemplo de la misma máscara que se ve en moros y cristianos y en las variantes de este baile. "¡Santiago!" se volvió el grito de guerra para los españoles durante las guerras con los moros después de haber visto una aparición del santo durante una batalla crucial que ganaron. Posteriormente se decía que el santo les ayudaba con la conquista del Nuevo Mundo.

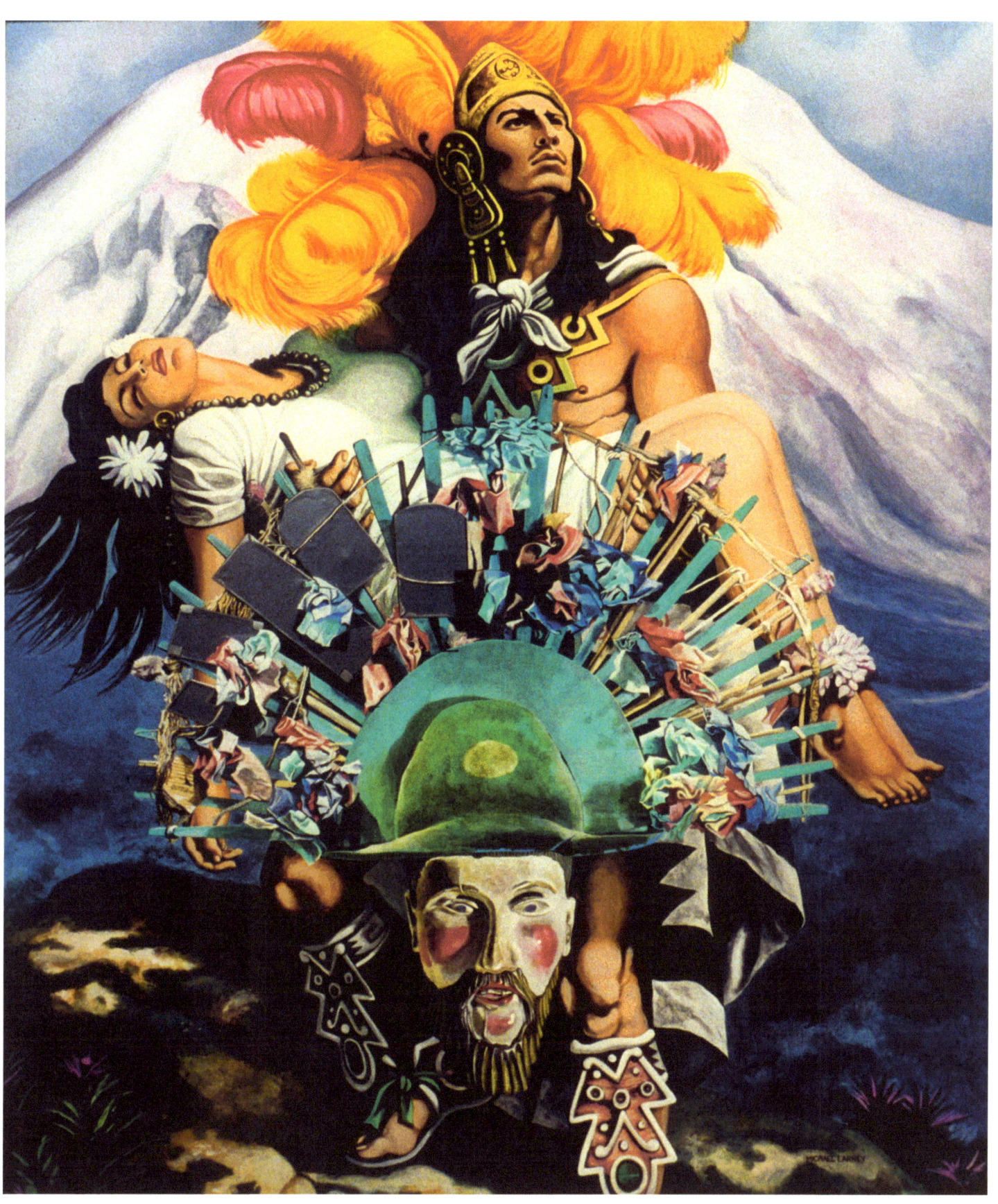

24. La Rana (The Frog)

2003 Acrylic on board (48" X 40")

Frogs and toads were associated with rain. During
certain Aztec rain-petitioning rites, young boys were tied to each corner of the altar, from where they were required to croak like frogs throughout the ceremony, and at the end of which, they were often drowned. Nothing was or is more important to agrarian populations than the rains that will ensure good crops. A good downpour seems imminent!

24. La Rana

2003 Acrilico en fibracel (120cm x 100cm)

Las ranas y los sapos se asociaban con la lluvia. Durante ciertas ceremonias de los aztecas para hacer que lloviera, se ataba a un niño joven a cada esquina de un altar. Desde allí, el niño tenía que croar como una rana durante toda la ceremonia y al terminar ésta, el niño normalmente era ahogado. No hay nada que fuera, o que ahora sea, tan importante para las comunidades agrarias como que la lluvia traiga buenas cosechas. No había ningún esfuerzo que fuese demasiado extremo como para ganar la benevolencia de las fuerzas de la naturaleza. ¡Parece que está por llegar un aguacero!

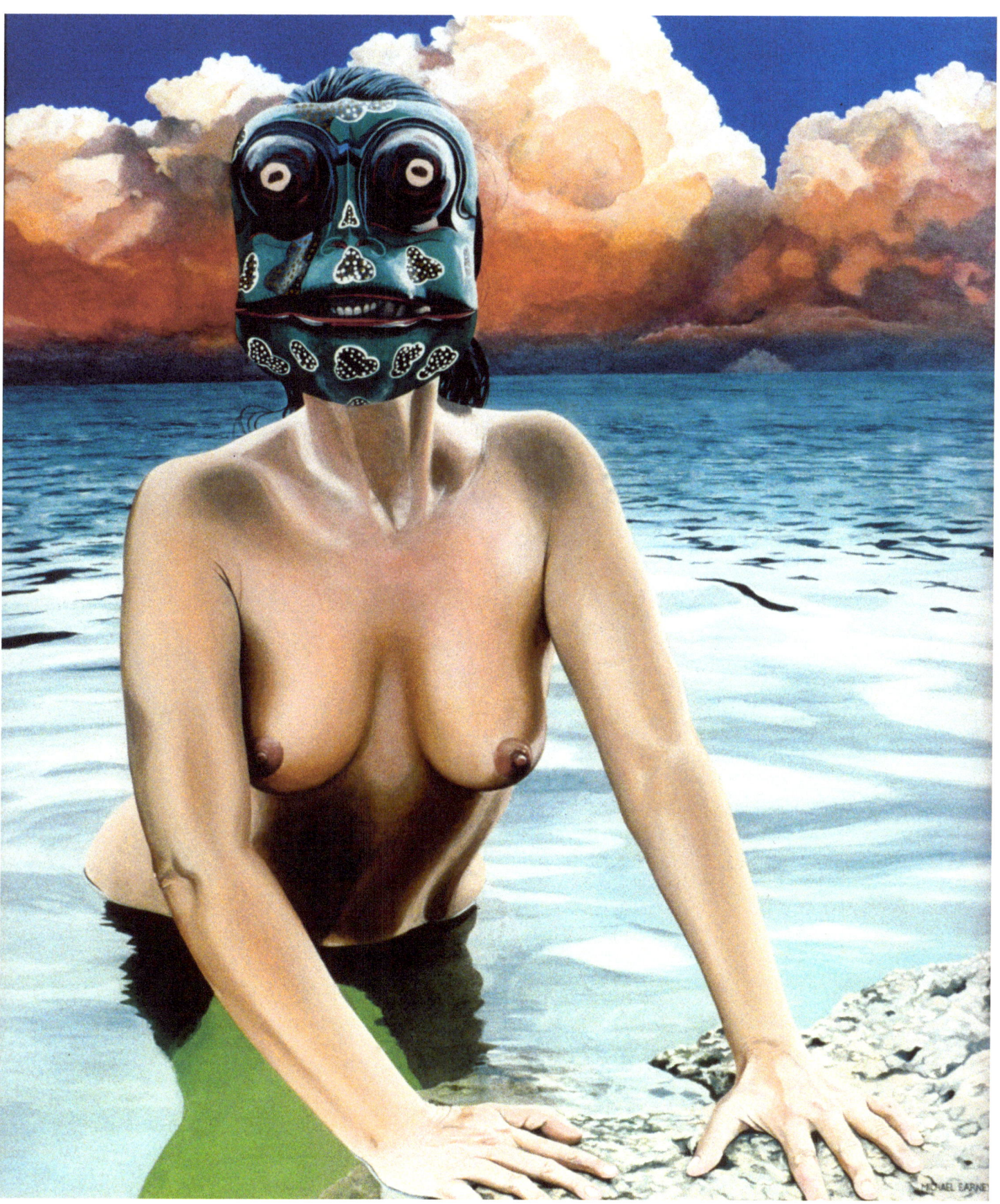

25. Had Folk Air

2003 Acrylic on board (48" X 27")

For those who do not recognize the wearer of this mask, the title of this painting is an anagram of her name. "Had Folk Air" is particularly appropriate considering that she was at the forefront of artists and intellectuals of her time embracing Mexican native arts and crafts. She invariably wore traditional tribal dress with native crafted jewelry. Another clue - the background is from one of her paintings. I chose this mask for her because of the fine little moustache.

25. Tenía Aire Folklórico

2003 Acrilico en fibracel (122cm x 69cm)

Para aquellos que no reconocen la persona que lleva puesto esta máscara ya lo adivinarán, al saber que el titulo de esta pintura es un anagrama de su nombre. "Had Folk Air" (en español, "Tenía Aire folklórico") es muy apropiado, dado que ella se encontraba en la vanguardia de los artistas e intelectuales que durante su época adoptaron la artesanía de los indígenas mexicanos. Siempre usaba ropa tradicional de diferentes tribus y joyería hecha por los indígenas. Otra pista: el fondo de esta pintura es igual al que se ve en una de las pinturas de ella.

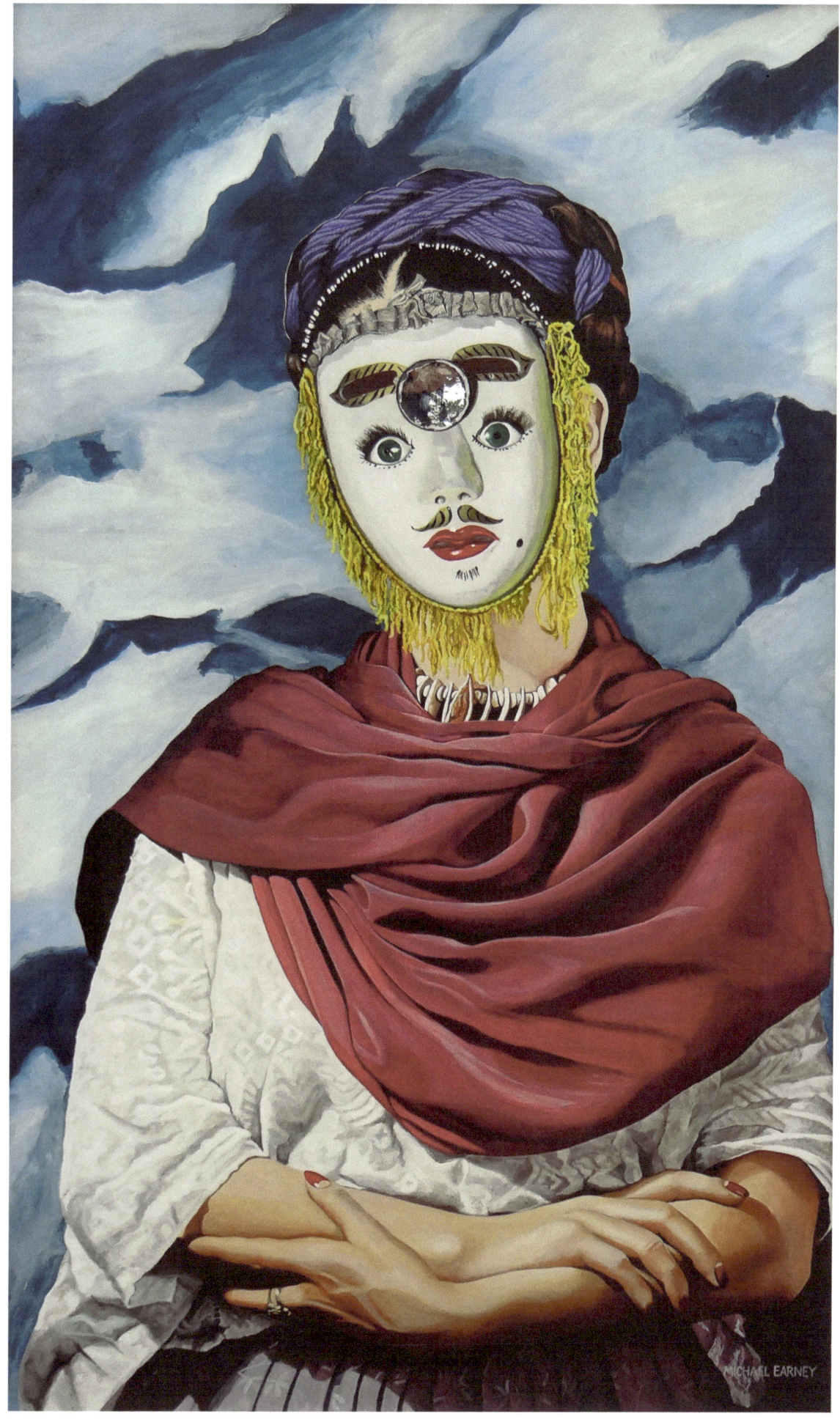

26. Una Posada, Una Calavera

2003 Acrylic on board (28" x 48")

The ubiquitous graphic art of Jose Guadalupe Posada (1851-1913) continued the age-old native tradition of taking a lighthearted approach to the terrors of death. Laughter, to keep up one's spirit in the face of our greatest fear, has provided Man the means to confront the ultimate darkness. This mask continues the tradition.

26. Una Posada, Una Calavera

2003 Acrilico en fibracel (71cm x 122cm)

El arte gráfico de José Guadalupe Posada (1851- 1913), que se ve por todos lados, continua la tradición ya establecida de burlarse de los terrores de la muerte. La risa nos ayuda a mantenernos felices cuando nos encontramos frente a nuestro miedo mayor y le ha dado al ser humano una manera de enfrentarse con la oscuridad final. Esta máscara continúa la tradición.

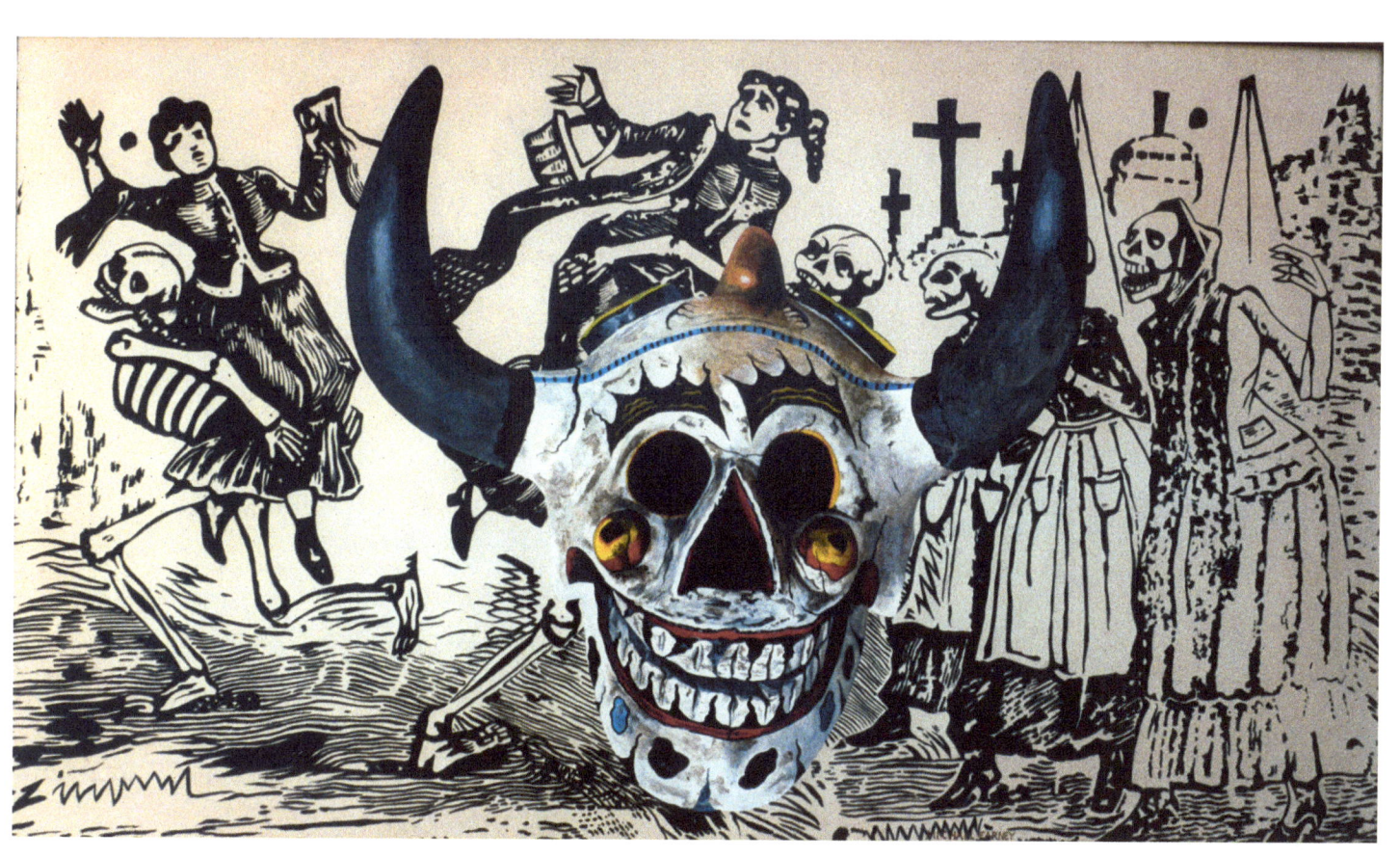

27. The Plumed Serpent

2004 Acrylic on canvas (72" x 60")

This large mask, called Giganton, was worn on the back of the dancer. Quetzalcoatl to the Aztec, Kukulcan to the Maya, the plumed serpent was a symbol of the vision serpent, the instrument by which the king communicated with the ancestors. Quetzalcoatl was also the planet Venus. Moctezuma should have known that the exiled Quetzalcoatl would return from the east as the morning star, not as Hernán Cortés.

The rattlesnake is the likely source of the plumed serpent cult. It has been asserted that the Mayan nobility altered the heads of their children, in a very painful procedure, so that their heads resembled that of the rattlesnake. The carved serpent upon which the Aztec couple are standing, from a painting by Jesus de la Helgera, and the feather mask in front bear little resemblance to the ancient Mexican depictions of the plumed serpent, but the connections are clear.

27. La Serpiente Emplumada

2004 Acrilico en tela (183cm x 152cm)

Llamada Giganton, esta gran máscara es usada sobre la espalda del bailarín. Quetzalcoatl, para los Aztecas, Kukulcan para los Mayas, la serpiente emplumada era un símbolo de la serpiente de la visión, el instrumento a través del cual el rey se comunicaba con sus ancestros. Quetzalcoatl también era el planeta Venus. Moctezuma debió saber que el exiliado Quetzalcoatl retornaría del oriente como la estrella de la mañana, no como Hernán Cortés.

La serpiente cascabel es muy probablemente el origen del culto de la serpiente emplumada. Se asegura que los nobles Mayas alteraban las cabezas de sus hijos, con un procedimiento muy doloroso, para que las cabezas se pareciesen a las de la serpiente cascabel. Aunque la serpiente tallada sobre la cual está parada la pareja Azteca (de una pintura de Jesús de la Helgera), y la máscara de plumas al frente, tienen poco parecido con la antigua descripción Mexicana de la serpiente emplumada, es clara la relación.

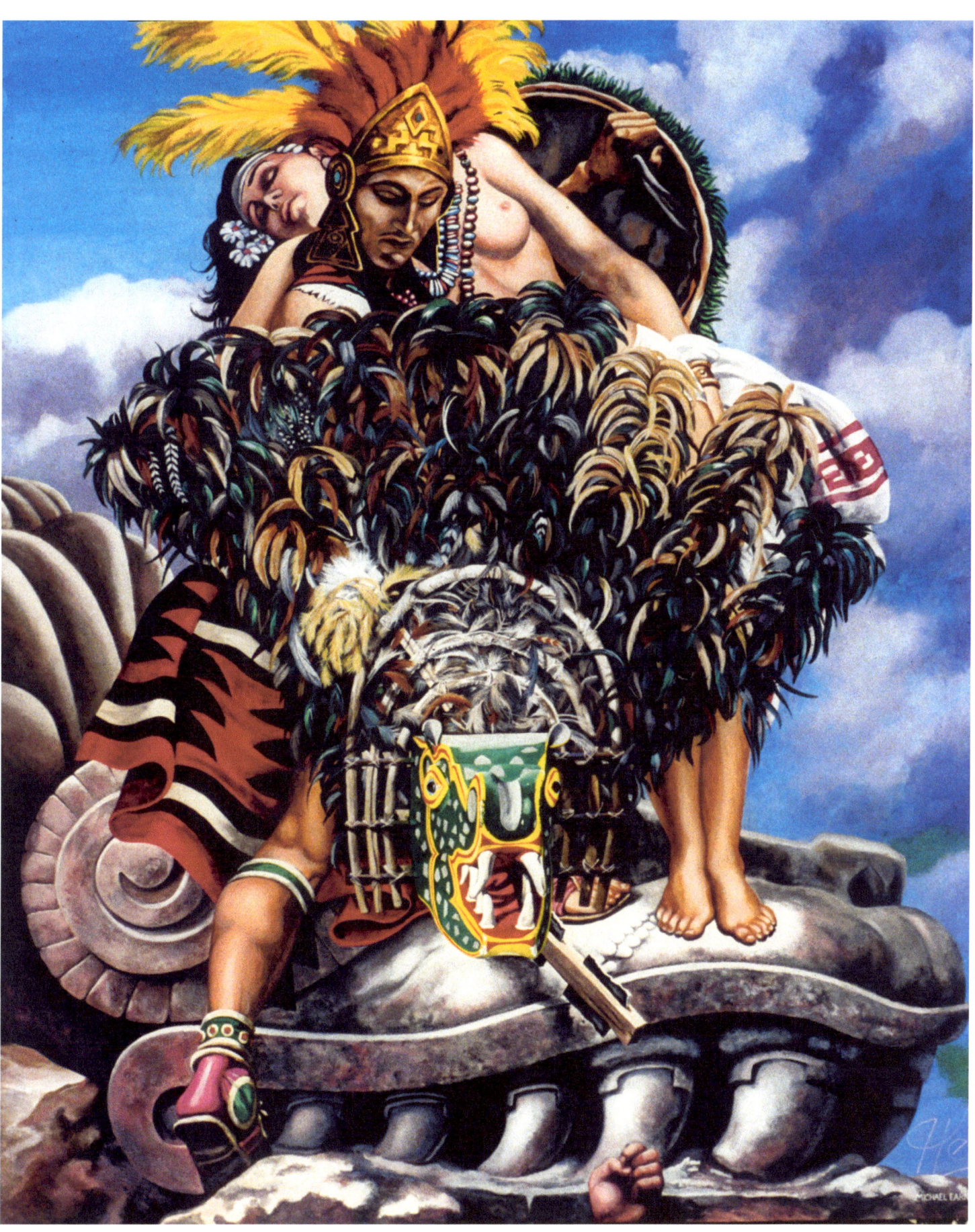

28. Pura Latina

2004 Acrylic on canvas (30" x 30")

Carnival masks such as this represent city people. A white skin indicated that a person did not labor in the fields. The sun was assiduously avoided by anyone wishing to appear refined. The whiter a young lady's skin, the more beautiful she was considered to be. Pura Latina is an expression of pride in accepting one's heritage, of combating the Caucasian values and norms imposed on subject races.

The two milagros reproduced here record the dangers encountered by illegal aliens seeking work in the USA, as when crossing the Rio Grande into Texas and again when returning home with cash in their pockets.

28. Pura Latina

2004 Acrilico en tela (76cm x 76cm)

Máscaras de carnaval como ésta, representan a la gente de clase alta que vive en la ciudad. La piel blanca es una señal de que la persona no trabajaba en los campos. Todos los que querían parecer más refinados, evitaban el sol a toda costa. Entre más blanca la piel de una mujer joven, más bella se le consideraba. "Pura latina" es una expresión que se usa para mostrar el orgullo que uno se siente por su patrimonio y para combatir los valores y normas del hombre blanco que se han impuesto sobre las razas subyugadas.

Los dos milagros que se ven aquí muestran los peligros que enfrentan los trabajadores indocumentados que buscan trabajo en Estados Unidos, primero cuando cruzan el Río Bravo para llegar a Texas, y luego de regreso con dinero en los bolsillos.

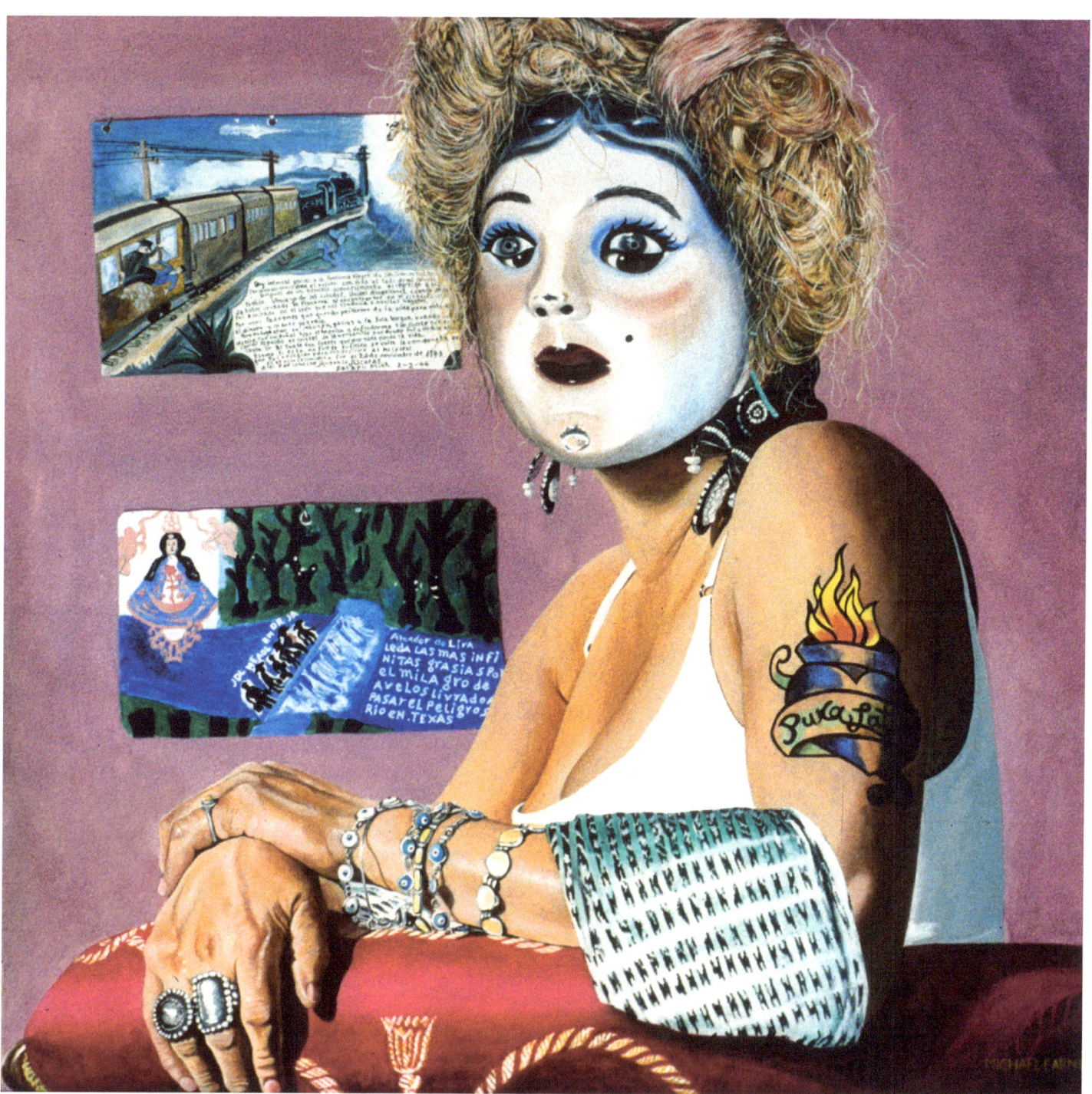

29. Plate XV
2004 Acrylic on canvas (40" x 30")

This mask is from the collection of the Rafael Coronel Mask Museum in Zacatecas, Zac. combined with a portion of plate XV, (La casa de las Monjas) from "Views of Ancient Monuments in Central America, Chiapas and Yucatan" by Frederick Catherwood.

John Stephens, Frederick Catherwood and Samuel Cabot went to Uxmal in 1841. It was Stephens' and Catherwood's second trip there. Stephens and Cabot came down with malaria almost immediately and were carried off to recover, leaving Catherwood alone at the ruins for six weeks during which time he completed more than fifty drawings.

In the past the long nosed god portrayed on the temple façade has been identified as Chac the Rain God. Snakes are also associated with rain. A good combination of images, I thought. However, in 1987, David Stuart determined that this image identifies the building as a "mountain" as well as a sacred place, essentially, a substitute for real hills and mountains, which are the homes of the Ancestor Gods.

Snakes can also represent the sky in classic Maya iconography. All of which illustrates the pitfalls of trying to draw parallels between ancient and modern uses of motifs in art.

29. Lámina XV
2004 Acrilico en tela (102cm x 76cm)

Esta máscara pertenece a la colección del Museo de Máscaras Rafael Coronel en Zacatecas, Zac. combinada con una porción de lámina XV, (La casa de las Monjas) de "Views of Ancient Monuments in Central America, Chiapas and Yucatan" ("Vistas de antiguos monumentos en América Central, Chiapas y Yucatan" por Frederick Catherwood). John Stephens, Frederick Catherwood y Samuel Cabot fueron a Uxmal en 1841; era el segundo viaje de Stephens y Catherwood allá. Stephens y Cabot contrajeron malaria casi inmediatamente y se les trasladó para su recuperación, dejando a Catherwood solo en las ruinas durante seis semanas en cuyo tiempo él realizó más de cincuenta dibujos.

En el pasado el dios de nariz larga que aparece en la fachada del templo se creía representaba al dios de la lluvia Chac. El dios de la lluvia Chac y serpientes son asociados con la lluvia, y yo por lo tanto pensé, que sobreponiendo esta máscara con prominentes serpientes se lograba una buena combinación de imágenes. Sin embargo, en 1987, David Stuart determinó que esta imagen en realidad identifica al edificio como una "montaña" así como un lugar sagrado, en esencia, un sustituto para una verdadera colina o montaña. Pero, como las nubes, lluvia, truenos y relámpagos se forman en las cimas de las montañas, ¿en que otra parte moraría el dios de la lluvia?

Las serpientes también pueden representar al cielo en la iconografía Maya clásica. Todo lo cual ilustra las dificultades encontradas al tratar de lograr demasiados paralelos entre los usos antiguos y modernos de motivos en el arte.

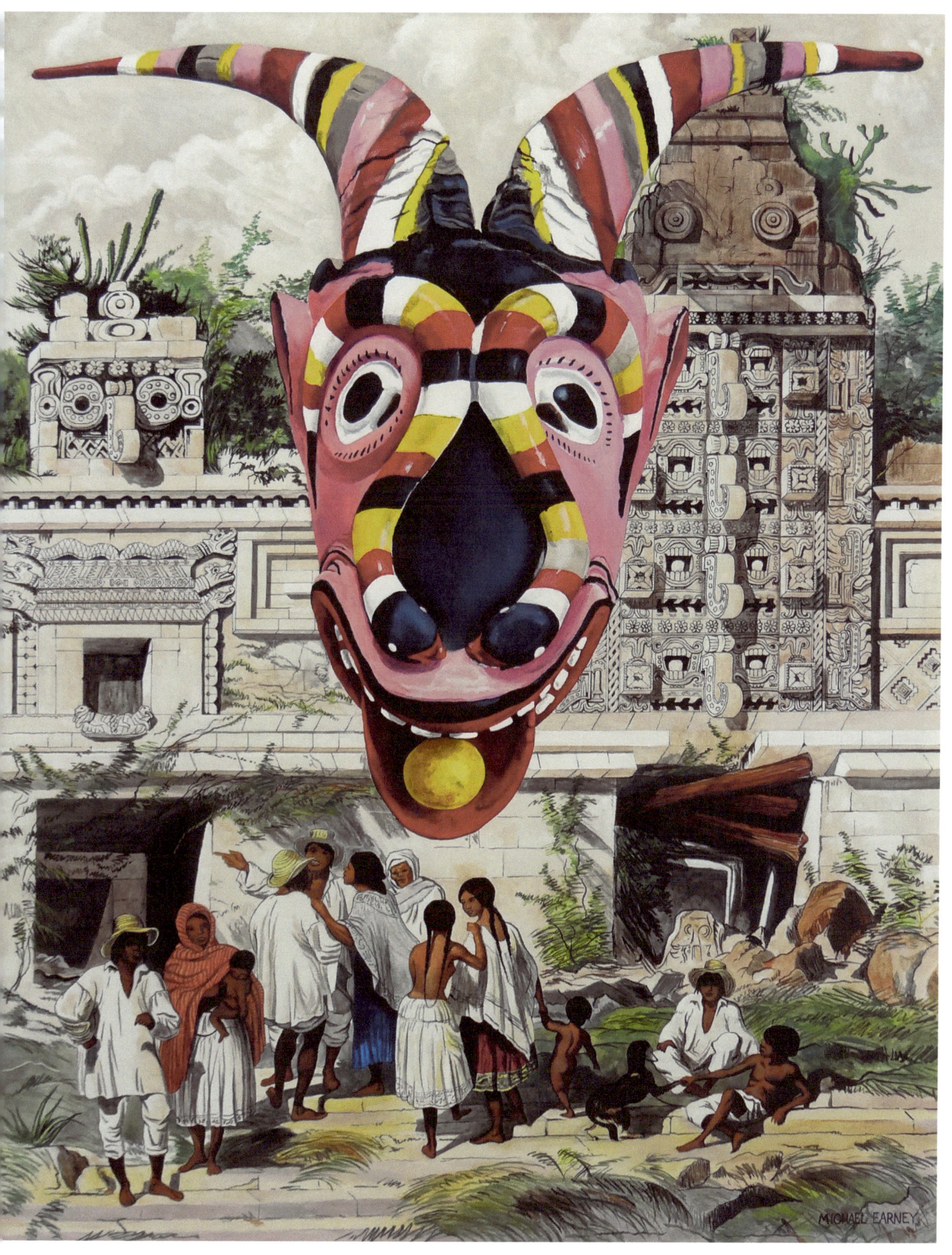

MICHAEL EARNEY

30. Costumes and Customs

2004 Acrylic on canvas (36" X 24")

In the years following the Conquest, some Catholic priests realized that their efforts of conversion were destroying much of the native people's history, lore and traditions. These priests provided converts with the means to document Aztec culture before it disappeared altogether.

The page from the Codex Mendosa, showing items of tribute made to the ruler of Tenochtitlan, has costumes used in pre-Columbian times. The Muerte in the foreground, participating in the festival of the Holy Cross, in Cerro Azul, Acatlan, Guerrero, is from a photograph by George O. Jackson Jr. Combined, they indicate that a continuity of sorts has survived the the centuries.

30. Disfraces/Costumbres

2004 Acrílico en tela (91cm X 61cm)

En los años después de la Conquista, unos pocos sacerdotes Católicos, dándose cuenta de que sus esfuerzos de conversión estaban destruyendo demasiado de la historia, saber popular y tradiciones del pueblo nativo, les suministraron a sus convertidos medios para documentar la cultura Azteca antes de que desapareciera del todo.

Los trajes mostrados en esta página del Código Mendoza, uno de los documentos producidos por convertidos, que se dice muestra elementos de tributo dados al Emperador de Tenochtitlan, sugiere que una continuidad de las clases ha sobrevivido a los siglos si son vistos con esta Muerte, de una fotografía por George O. Jackson Jr., participando en el festival de la Santa Cruz en Cerro Azul, Acatlan, Guerrero.

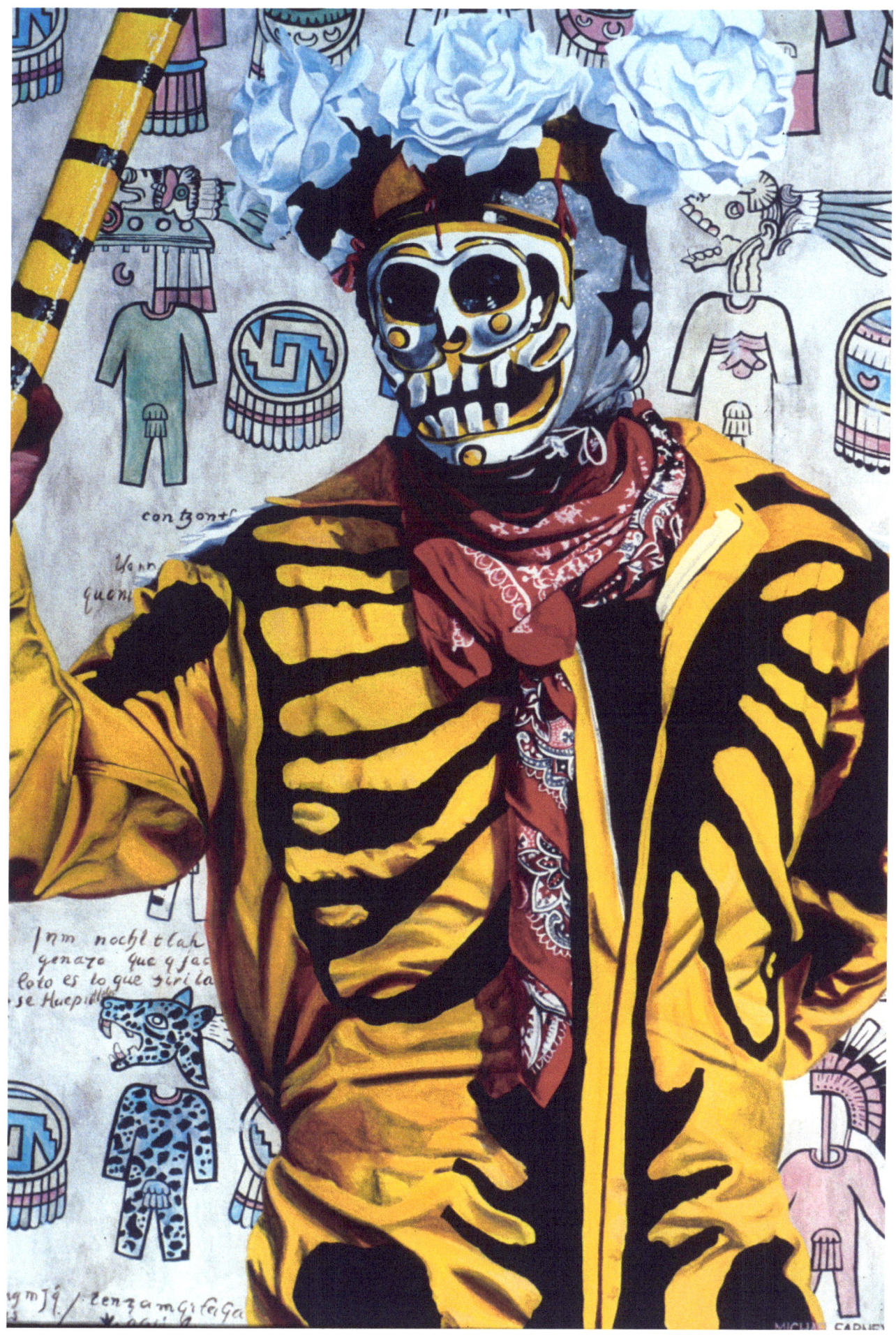

31. Devil
2004 Acrylic on canvas (40" x 40")

On September 16th, Mexico's Independence Day, a contest, known as the "Mojinanga de los Diablos", takes place in the town of Teloloapan, Guerrero. This mask, recognizable as the work of Fidel De la Fuente, would have been worn by one of the young men vying to be chosen as the best devil.

Behind the mask is the image of the Goddess Coyolxauhqui carved into a massive circular stone that was dug up in Mexico City in 1978. It remained at the foot of what had been her brother Huitzilopoztli's great temple, which was destroyed by Hernan Cortés.

In the eternal struggle between light and dark, the Aztec god Huitzilopoztli represented the Sun, Coyolxauhqui was the moon. Atop this temple the hearts of countless victims were offered to the Sun, their bodies then tumbled down the steps to land upon Coyolxauhqui, herself having been killed and dismembered by her brother. She represented the dark of the underworld. Each sacrifice graphically demonstrated the dualistic, cyclical nature of the cosmos.

31. Diablo
2004 Acrílico en tela (100cm X 100cm)

Los 16 de septiembre, Día de la Independencia de México, se celebra un concurso, conocido como la "Mojinanga de los Diablos", en la plaza del pueblo de Teloloapan, Guerrero. Esta máscara, reconocible como obra de Fidel De la Fuente, pudo haber sido usada por uno de los jóvenes compitiendo para ser elegido como el mejor diablo.

Tras esta máscara está la imagen de la Diosa Coyolxauhqui tallada en una piedra maciza circular que fue desenterrada en la Ciudad de México en 1978. Permaneció a los pies de lo que fuera el Templo Mayor de su hermano Huitzilopoztli, el cual fue destruido por Hernán Cortés. En la eterna lucha entre luz y oscuridad, el dios Azteca Huitzilopoztli representaba al Sol, Coyolxauhqui era la Luna. En la cima de este templo los incontables corazones de víctimas eran ofrecidos al Sol, sus cuerpos luego tirados por las escaleras para aterrizar sobre Coyolxauhqui, quien, según el mito, se hizo matar y desmembrar por su hermano. Ella representaba lo oscuro de inframundo. Cada sacrificio mostraba gráficamente la naturaleza dual, cíclica del cosmos.

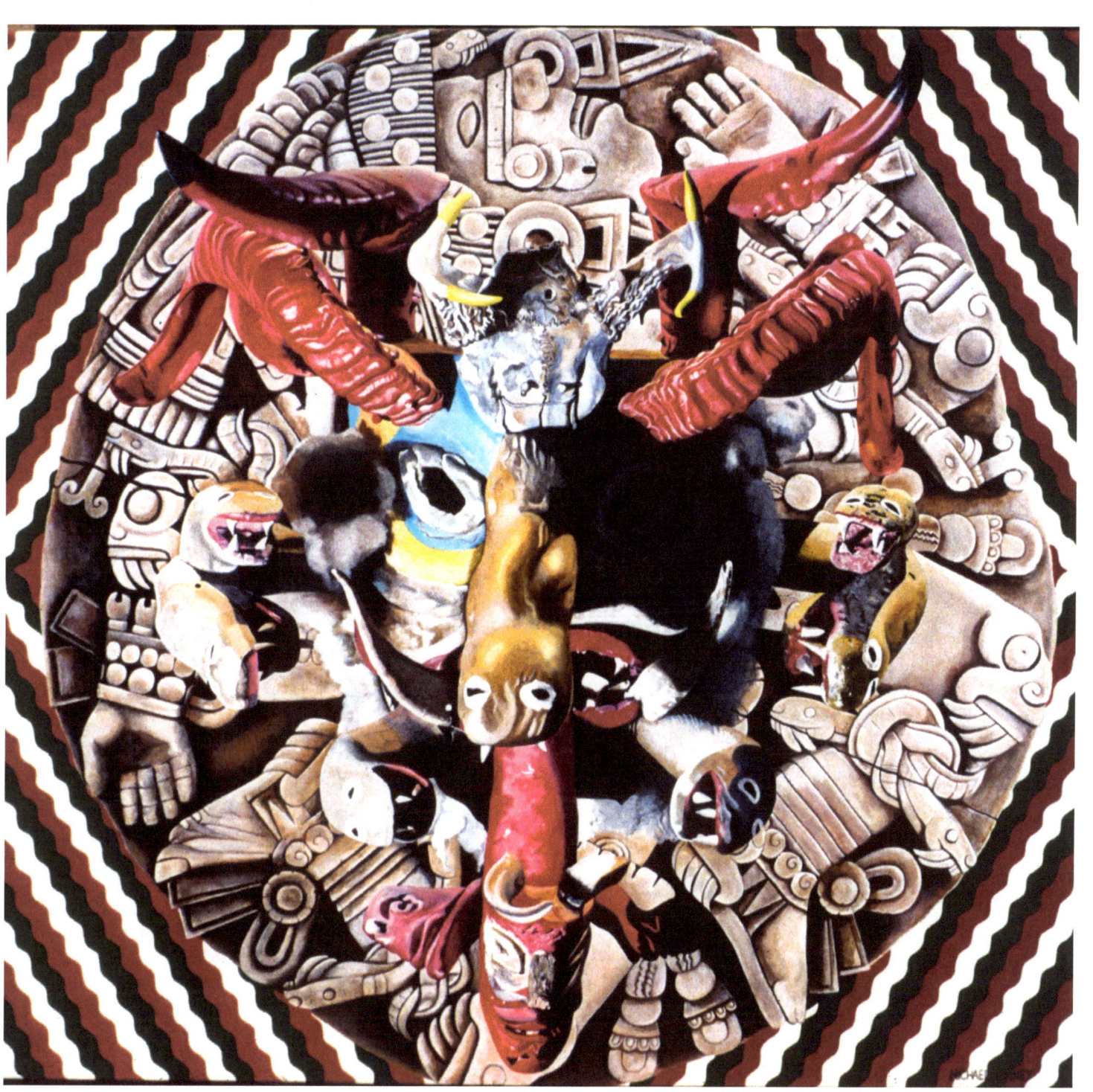

32. Slave
2004 Acrylic on canvas (40" x 30")

Portugal and Spain had been carrying on a thriving trade in black African slaves for most of the fifteenth century. Consequently, once discovered, the Americas became the newest and biggest market. Between 1492 and 1870 approximately eleven million slaves were transported to American ports by Portuguese, Spanish, French, English, Dutch and North Americans. (Many New England whalers were slavers on the side.) During Spanish rule, 250,000 slaves were imported to Mexico. After independence, Mexico received only 3,000 slaves, by which time there were nearly two million Mexican born children of African parents and those of part African descent in Mexico. In 1824 Mexico prohibited the slave trade and in 1829 outlawed slavery altogether. This prohibition was partly responsible for the establishment of the Republic of Texas by those wishing to reinstate slavery.

Many of the first black slaves came directly from Spain. Having long been trusted members of many households, they were sent to oversee the holdings of their Spanish masters, holdings that the owners themselves may have never seen. In fact there were more blacks than whites in Mexico in the beginning. For many indigenous people the blacks *were* the Spanish, the authorities, the overlords. Highly respected, blacks were readily equated with the pre-conquest rulers, the lords and nobles who had painted themselves black to honor their black gods and with the valiant warriors who blackened themselves before going into battle. "Blackmen" therefore, already had a place of honor in native dances. With the new religion a place was made for Jesus, the Virgin Mary and the Black African. In the painting rusted shackles from a sunken 17th-century slave ship rest atop a map of the period.

32. Esclavo
2004 Acrílica en tela (100cm x 75cm)

Portugal y España mantenían un próspero comercio de negros esclavos africanos durante la mayor parte del siglo quince, por tanto, una vez descubiertas, las Américas se convirtieron en el mayor y mas nuevo mercado. Entre 1492 y 1870 aproximadamente once millones de esclavos negros fueron transportados a puertos Americanos por Portugueses, Españoles, Franceses, Ingleses, Holandeses y Norteamericanos (muchos balleneros de New England –Nueva Inglaterra hacían también las veces como negreros), Durante el dominio español, 250,000 esclavos fueron importados a México. Después de la Independencia, México solo recibió 3,000, y para ese tiempo ya había dos millones de Africanos, niños nacidos en México de padres Africanos y aquellos en México descendientes en parte Africana. En 1824 México prohibió la trata de esclavos y en 1829 proscribió la esclavitud totalmente. Esta prohibición es en parte responsable de la fundación de la República de Texas por aquellos que querían restablecer la esclavitud.

Muchos de los esclavos negros procedieron directamente de España. Habiendo sido confiados sirvientes en muchos hogares, eran enviados a supervisar las tenencias de sus amos españoles, tenencias que sus propietarios tal vez nunca habían visto. En un comienzo habían más negros que blancos en México. Para muchos nativos, los negros eran los españoles, las autoridades, los jefes supremos. Siendo muy respetados, a los negros fácilmente se les igualaba con los gobernantes antes de la conquista, los señores y nobles quienes se habían pintado de negro para honrar a sus dioses negros y con los valientes guerreros quienes se ennegrecían antes de ir a la batalla, los "Blackmen"- Hombres Negros- por lo tanto, ya tenían un sitio de honor en las danzas nativas. En la nueva religión se les hizo un sitio a Jesús, La Virgen María y los Negros Africanos. En el cuadro oxidados grilletes de un barco negrero hundido en el siglo 17 reposan sobre un mapa de la época.

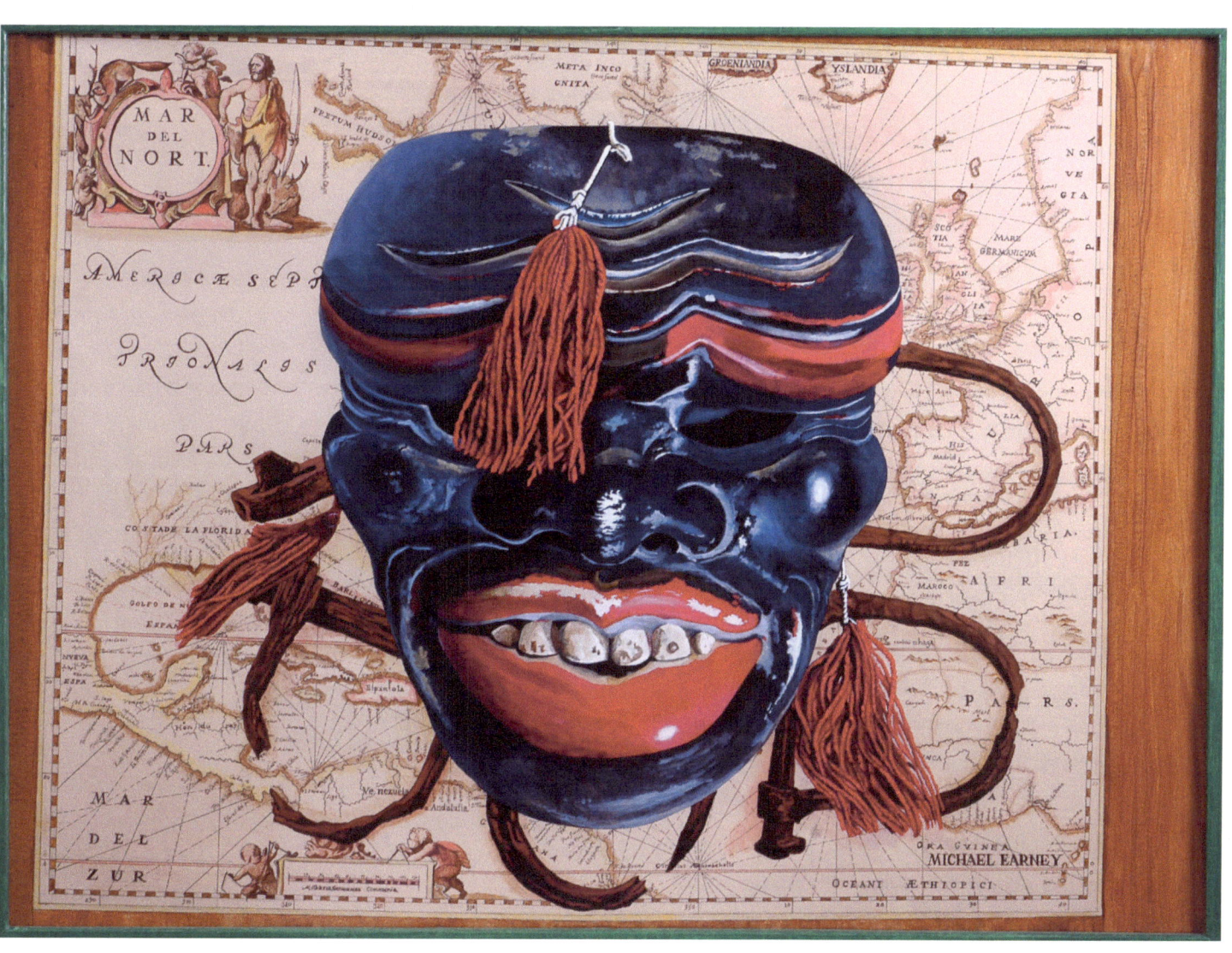

33. La Viejita

2005 Acrylic on canvas (40" x 30")

Combining a Viejito mask with the Chavez Marion, (another fine calendar artist), Pin-up appealed to me as a way to exemplify the core theme of this ancient dance. In the Dance of the Viejitos youngsters masked as old ones mimic the movements and mannerisms of old age before breaking into energetic dance steps, to the amusement of the audience. The dance is one of the best known in Mexico. It is primarily performed by the Tarascan Indians of Michoacan during Christmas and New Years', thus betraying its Pre-Columbian origins. The shortest day of the year in December once filled people with dread. Elaborate ceremonies were carried out in order to halt the sun's southerly progress and restore its waning power. The Dance of the Viejitos is all that remains of this concern. The dancers demonstrate that new life and energy can spring from the old and recognize the inevitability of life's cycle from birth to death and renewal. They are evidently successful, for the days begin to lengthen and new growth emerges from the earth again. The dance was dedicated to Huehueteotl, the God of Fire and the personification of life after death, who was portrayed as a bent, smiling old man.

33. La Viejita

2005 Acrilico en tela (100cm x 75cm)

Combinar una máscara de Viejito con este retrato de una modelo de Chavez Marion, (otro buen artista de calendarios), me pareció una manera de mostrar el tema central de esta antigua danza. En la danza de los Viejitos, jóvenes con máscaras de viejos hacen mímica de los movimientos y amaneramientos de los viejos antes de cambiar a pasos de baile enérgicos, para entretenimiento de la audiencia. Esta danza es una de las más conocidas en México. Primordialmente es ejecutada por los Indios Tarascan de Michoacan durante las Navidades y el Año Nuevo, así pues traicionando sus orígenes pre-Colombinos. El día más corto en Diciembre en una época llenaba a la gente con temor. Se realizaban elaborados esfuerzos para detener el progreso del Sol hacia el sur y devolverle su menguante poder. La danza de los Negritos es todo lo que queda de esta preocupación. Los bailarines demuestran que nueva vida y energía pueden surgir de lo viejo y reconocen la inevitabilidad del ciclo de la vida desde el nacimiento hasta la muerte y la renovación. Evidentemente tienen éxito, porque los días empiezan a alargarse y nuevos brotes surgen otra vez de la tierra. El baile estaba dedicado a Huehueteotl, el dios del fuego y la personificación de la vida después de la muerte, el cual era representado como un viejito encorvado y sonriente.

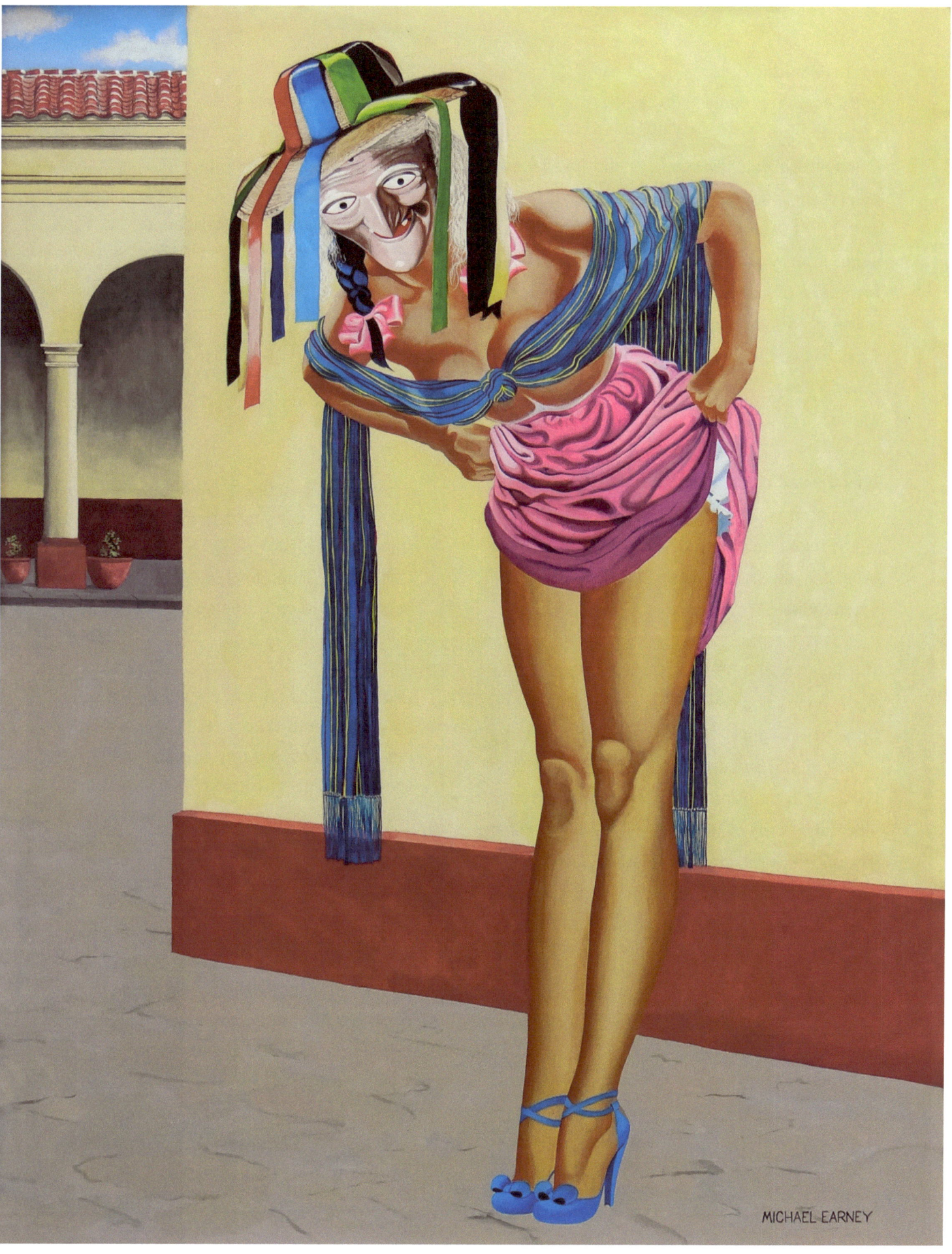

MICHAEL EARNEY

34. La Vanidad
2005 Acrylic on canvas (30" x 24")

Manuela Ballester was one of the few female artists who painted Mexican calendar art. She and her husband, the artist Joseph Renau, were from Valencia, Spain. They had been members of the vibrant art scene there and militant antifascists. When Generalisimo Franco overthrew the government and took power, they, like so many others, fled to Mexico.

This untitled piece, dating from 1940, appealed to me as a basis for the Nahua whistling mask, which might be giving a "wolf" whistle or simply reflecting the fact that in time the beauty of youth fades.

Whistling was once considered a power for both good and evil, a practice not to be undertaken lightly. Spirits were summoned by whistling. It may be that this mask was used to "whistle up the wind", to bring clouds and rain. Ehecatl, Lord of the Winds, was depicted wearing a wind mask painted red with black stripes by the eyes and blue areas on the forehead, colors derived from the Mexican whistling toad.

34. La Vanidad
2005 Acrílico en tela (75cm x 61cm)

Manuela Ballester fue una de las pocas artistas femeninas que pintaron calendarios artísticos Mexicanos. Ella y su esposo, el artista Joseph Renau, eran de Valencia, España y miembros de la vibrante escena artística y militantes antifascistas. Cuando el Generalísimo Franco derrotó el gobierno y tomó el poder, ellos, como muchos otros, huyeron hacia México.

Esta pieza sin título, fechada en 1940, me atrajo, como base para la máscara silbante Nahua, la cual podría estar dando un aullido de lobo o simplemente reflejando el hecho de que con el tiempo la belleza de la juventud se desvanece.

Silbar era considerado en una época como un poder tanto para el bien como para el mal, una práctica a no ser emprendida a la ligera. Se convocaban los espíritus silbando. Puede que esta máscara fuera usada para "silbar al viento", para llamar nubes y lluvia. Ehecatl, Señor de los Vientos, era representado usando una máscara pintada de rojo con rayas negras cerca de los ojos y áreas azules en la frente, un poco de los cual se puede ver en esta máscara, los colores son los mismos del sapo silbador de México.

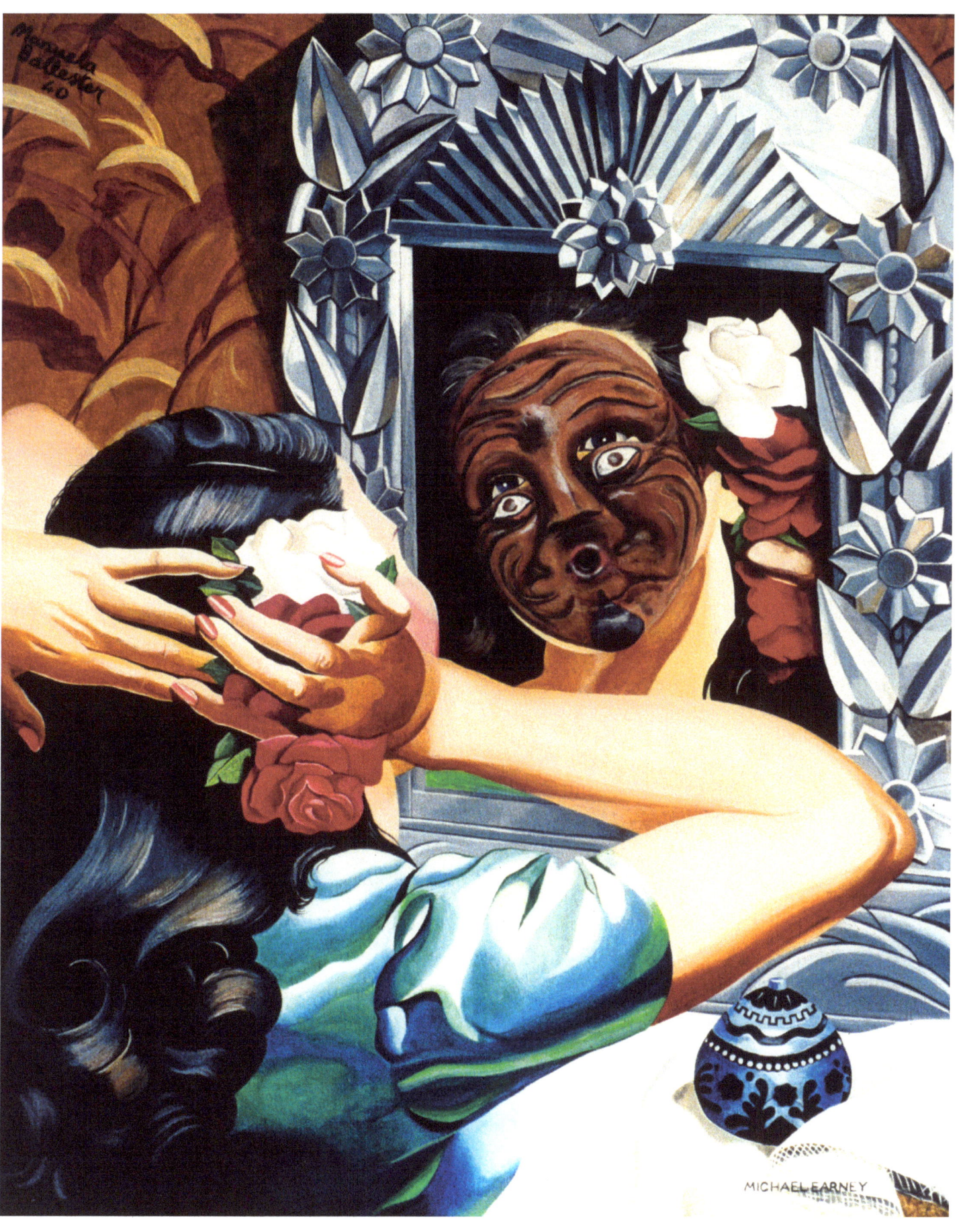

MICHAEL EARNEY

35. La Tigresa del Valle

2008 Acrylic on canvas (54"x 48")

Some years back I went with a friend to the Lagunilla market in Mexico City where she had previously bought masks from Indians who came down from the mountains to sell their wares. Unfortunately, heavy rains had caused mudslides, making it impossible for them to leave their village, a common occurrence where logging and agriculture on steep slopes destabilize the land*.

Lagunilla market covers several blocks, offering virtually anything anyone could want or need. Eventually we found masks, one of which is the tigre in this painting. The mask is carved from a solid block of wood. The wearer would normally see through the mouth but it was not clear to me exactly how it would be worn during an event. Disregarding the need for authenticity, I photographed "La Senorita del Valle" wearing it as shown. Of the processed roll of film only three exposures came out. While convinced that I had insufficient reference to work with, I nevertheless continued to search for the particular Diego Rivera calla lily painting I wanted for my background. My desultory search ended when I found that friends in San Marcos, Texas had a large print of it on their wall. At the time of painting this work I was unaware of Rivera's nude with calla lilies using Frida Kahlo as his model. Once I had stretched the canvas, with all the components on hand, the painting came together just as I had envisioned it so many years before.

* This is not the place to discuss the social conditions of Mexico that lead to such utilization of marginal lands.

35. La Tigresa del Valle

2008 Acrilico en tela (135cm x120cm)

Hace unos años fui con una amiga al Mercado de Lagunilla en la Ciudad de México donde ella anteriormente había comprado máscaras a Indios que bajaban de las montañas para venderlas. Lamentablemente, fuertes lluvias habían causado avalanchas de lodo imposibilitándolos de bajar de sus pueblos (algo que ocurre frecuentemente donde la tala y agricultura en empinadas laderas desestabilizan la tierra*

El mercado de Lagunilla cubre varias cuadras, ofreciendo virtualmente cualquier cosa que quieras o puedas necesitar. Por lo tanto eventualmente encontramos máscaras, una de las cuales es el tigre en esta pintura. La máscara está tallada en un bloque macizo de madera. El usuario normalmente veía a través de la boca pero yo no comprendí claramente como sería usada durante un evento. Descartando la necesidad de autenticidad, yo fotografié a "La Señorita del Valle" usándola como aquí se muestra. Del rollo de película procesado solo se obtuvieron tres exposiciones, porque el obturador de la cámara estaba fallando. Aunque estaba convencido de que no tenia suficiente referencias con que trabajar, seguí buscando la específica pintura lirio cala de Diego Rivera que quería para mi fondo. Mi poca metódica búsqueda terminó cuando descubrí que amigos en San Marcos, Texas tenía una gran reproducción de la misma en su pared. Al momento de pintar esta obra yo desconocía el desnudo de Rivera con lirios calas con Frida Kahlo como modelo. Habiendo clavado la lona sobre el bastidor, con todos los componentes a mano, la pintura salió tal y como la había vislumbrado muchos años antes.

* Este no es el lugar para discutir las condiciones sociales de México que conllevan a tal uso de las tierras marginadas

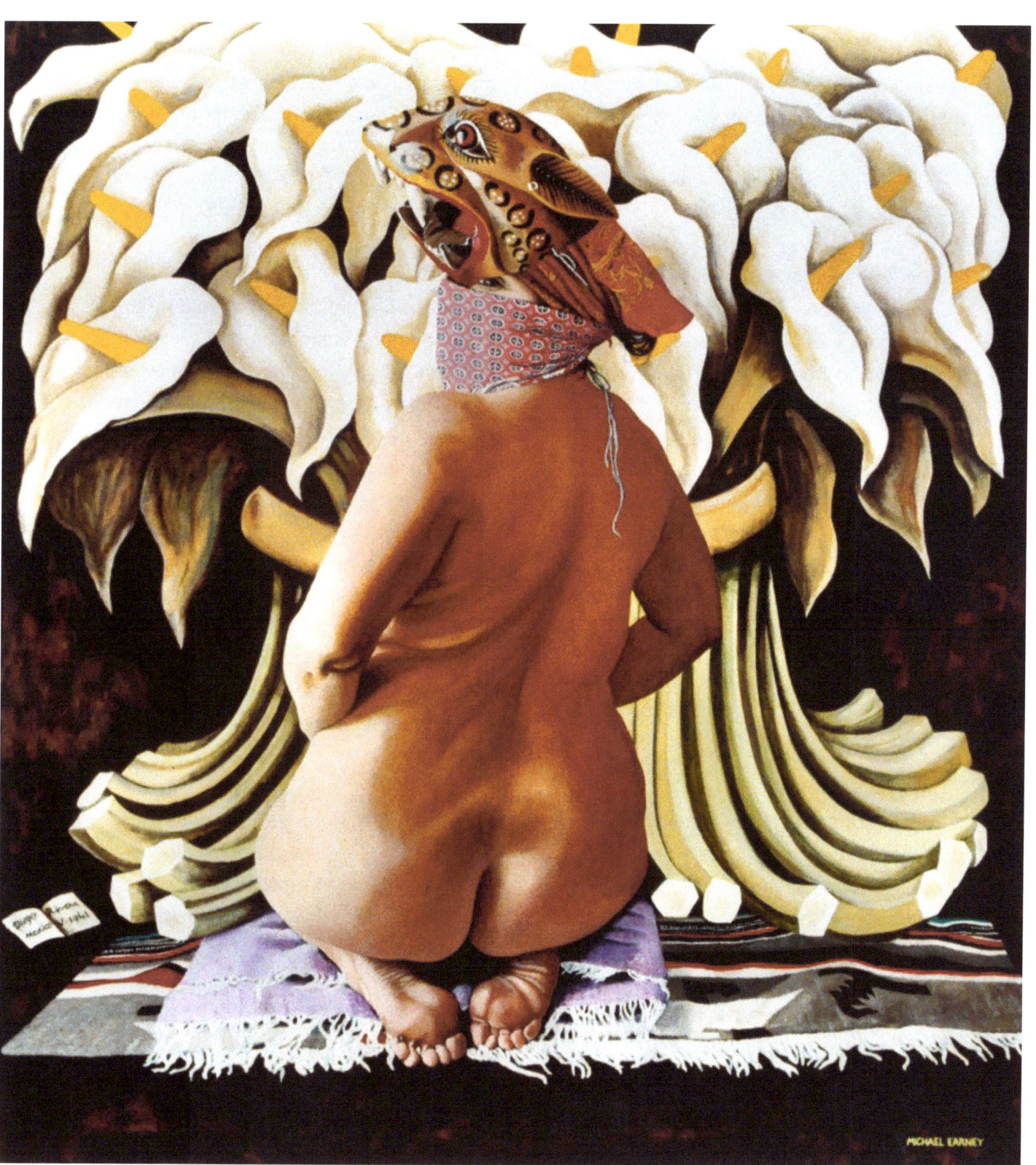

Drawings

Donald Cordry's, "*Mexican Masks*" was the first source for my mask paintings. These drawings are all based on photographs of masks from that book.

1. Bat Mask (*6.5"x 6") Pastel*

Cordry had several bat masks but I never saw another in any of the many collections I viewed. This was surprising given that the bat plays such a large role in Pre-Columbian mythology. It is primarily associated with death because it generally inhabits caves, considered to be entrances to the underworld, and because it comes out at night, the time when ghosts and spirits are abroad. The Maya, living today in Zincantan, "Place of the Bat", in the mountains of Chiapas, call themselves "Bat People".

2. Tigre (*10" x 10") Ink and pastel*

The photograph of a tigre mask in Cordry's book that served as the source of this drawing was taken at an angle. I altered it to full-face while drawing. It became the basis for the first painting in the series.

Dibujos

Las "*Mascaras Mexicanas*" de Donald Cordry fue mi primera fuente para mis pinturas de máscaras. Estos dibujos están todos basados en fotografías de máscaras de ese libro.

1. Máscara de Murciélago (*16.2cm x 15cm) Pastel*

Cordry tuvo muchas máscaras de murciélagos pero yo nunca vi ninguna otra en sus múltiples colecciones, como esta; la cual me sorprendió que el murciélago jugara un rol tan importante en la mitología pre-Colombina ; principalmente asociado con la Muerte, Debido a que generalmente habita en cuevas, consideradas como entradas al inframundo y a que usualmente sale por las noches a la hora que fantasmas y espíritus acostumbran vagar. Los Mayas que viven en la actualidad en las montañas de Chiapas específicamente en Zincantán llamada "Lugar del Murciélago" se autonombran Gente –Murciélago.

2. Tigre (*25cm x 25cm) Tinta y pastel*

La fotografía de la máscara del tigre en el libro de Cordry que sirvió como fuente para este dibujo fué tomada en ángulo. Yo la dibujé enderezandola en linea recta. Convirtiendose asi como base para la primer pintura de la serie.

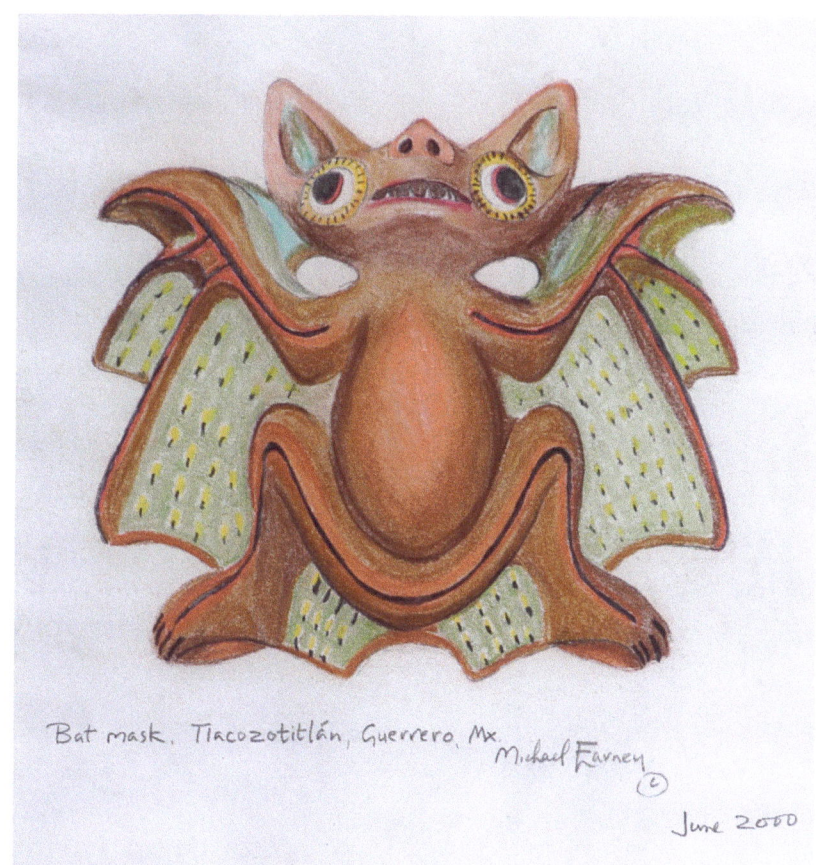

Bat mask. Tlacozotitlán, Guerrero, Mx.   Michael Farney
                                                    ©
                                          June 2000

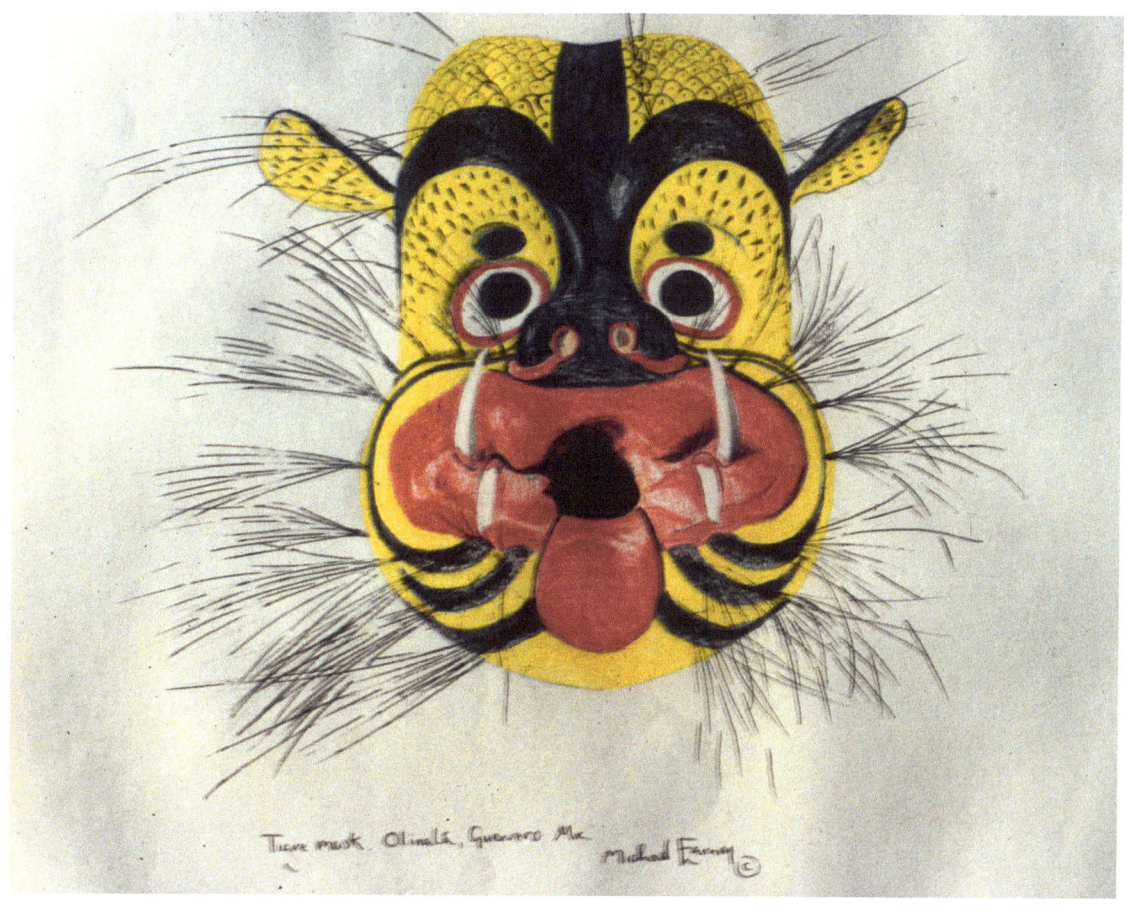

Tigre mask. Olinalá, Guerrero Mx   Michael Farney ©

3. Tres Potencias (20" x 18") Pastel

The Dance of the Tres Potencias (the Three Powers) is another of the morality plays imported by the Spanish for the edification of immigrants and natives alike. There is a written text with the good, (Jesus and Mary, etc.) battling the bad, (the Devil, Sin, and Death), for the souls of all mankind. This, presumably was after the Pope had decided that the natives, indeed, possessed souls. The horns mark this mask as one of the bad guys.

3. Tres Potencias (50cm x 45cm) Pastel

La danza de las Tres Potencias (los tres poderes) es otra de las obras morales importadas por los españoles para la edificación tanto de inmigrantes como de nativos. Existe un texto escrito, con el bien, p.ej. Jesús y María, etc. Luchando contra el mal, p.ej. el Diablo, Pecado y Muerte para las almas de toda la humanidad. Esto, probablemente fue después de que el Papa decidiera que los nativos, de hecho, tenían almas. Los cuernos señalan esta máscara como una de la gente mala.

4. Pastorela Dance (16" x 18") Pastel

The widely popular Pastorela Dance, like the Tres Potencias, (Three Powers), was a morality play, among many, introduced by the Spanish after the Conquest. The forces of good and evil battle each other in staged dramatizations. Devils, (this Pastorela Mask is clearly one of those, although it's Pre-Columbian features are just as obvious), fight with sword-wielding angels, presumably for the souls of their audience.

4. Danza de La Pastorela (40cm x 45cm) Pastel

Las muy populares danzas de la Pastorela y Las Tres Potencias son ambas representaciones de moralidad que entre muchas otras fueron introducidas por los españoles despues de la Conquista., La batalla entre las fuerzas del bien y del mal es escenificada dramaticamente en esta mascara de la pastorela, aunque su contenido Pre-Colombino es mas que obvio , el diablo pelea contra los angeles blandiendo su espada en favor de las almas de la audiencia.

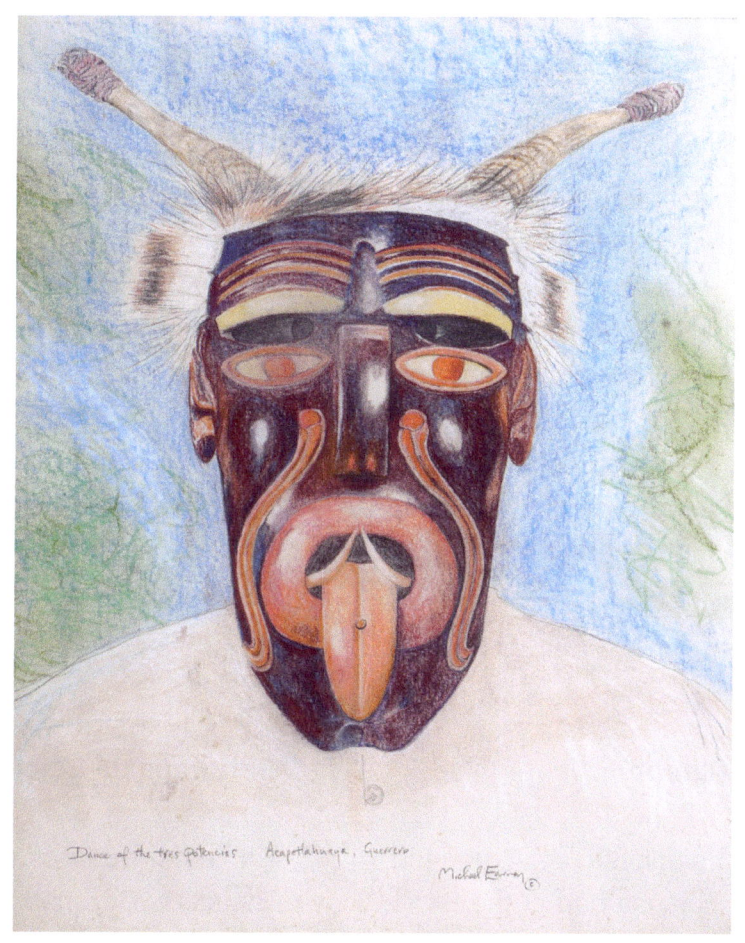

Dance of the tres potencias. Acapetlahuaya, Guerrero   Michael Ewing ©

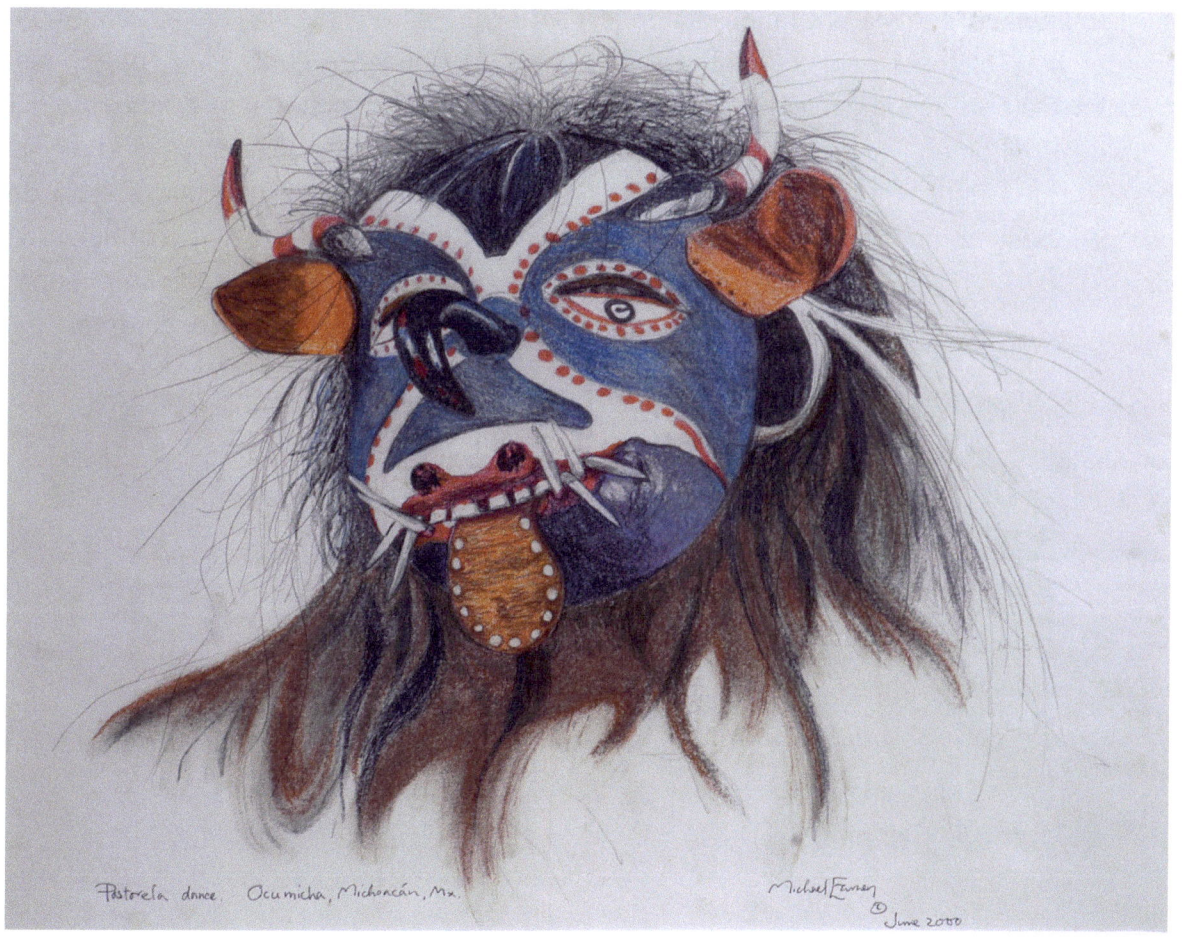

Pastorela dance. Ocumicha, Michoacán, Mx.   Michael Ewing ©
June 2000

5. Yacatecuhtli *(11" x 12") Pastel*

The Aztec god of merchants and travelers, Yacatecuhtli was one of the names under which Quetzalcoatl was worshiped. The name means Lord of the Vanguard or, One Who Goes Forth. Other names for the same personage were, Yacacoliuhqui and Yacapitzahuac, meaning, respectively, He With The Aquiline Nose, or, Pointed Nose. Ski Nose would be more appropriate for this mask.

Limited Edition Serigraph

In this serigraph, completed at Coronado Studios in Austin, Texas, as part of the Serie Print Project, I placed this funerary mask from Teotihuacán against a "papel picado", made for Day of the Dead celebrations. It shows La Catrina accompanied by an owl, the bird of ill-omen. I tried to give the impression of a dark and stormy night when all should best be at home behind closed doors.

5. Yacatecuhtli *(27.5cm x 30cm) Pastel*

Dios Azteca de mercaderes y viajeros, Yacatecuhtli era uno de los nombres bajo el cual Quetzalcoatl era venerado. El nombre significa, Señor de la Vanguardia o, Aquel que va al frente. Otros nombres para el mismo personaje eran Yacacoliuhqui y Yacapitzahuac, significando respectivamente, El de la naríz aguileña, o Nariz Puntiaguda. Nariz de Gancho sería más apropiado para esta máscara.

Serigrafía de Edición Limitada

En esta serigrafía, terminada en los Estudios Coronado de Austin, Texas, como parte de la Serie Proyecto Impreso, yo situé la máscara funeraria de Teotihuacán sobre un "papel picado", hecho para las celebraciones del Día de los Muertos. Muestra a La Catrina acompañada de un búho, pájaro de mal agüero. Traté de dar la impresión de una noche oscura y tormentosa cuando todo sería mejor en casa tras puertas cerradas.

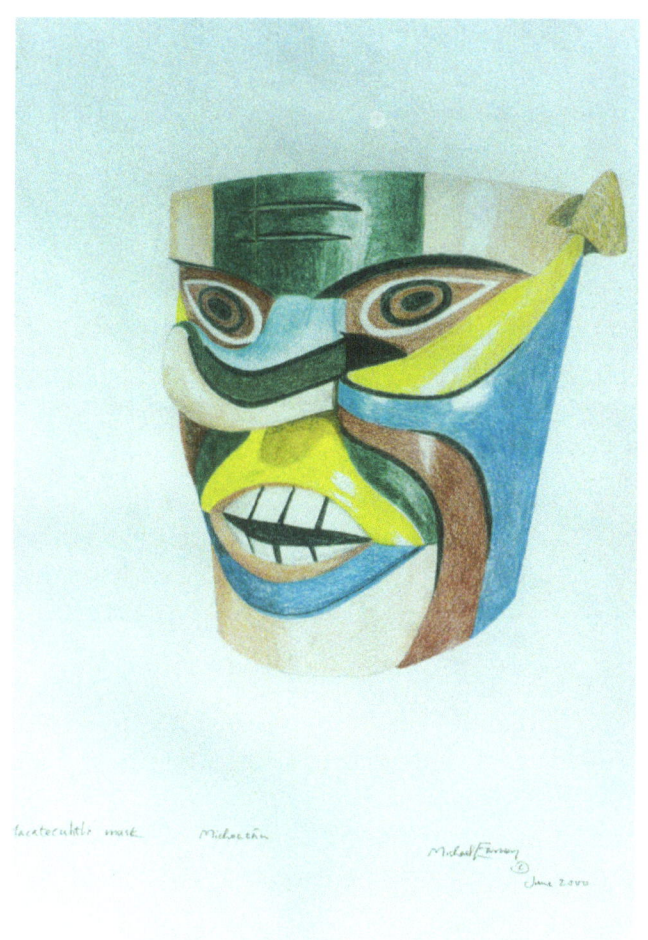

Iacateculali mask   Michoacán   Michael Ramsey ©
                                                        June 2000

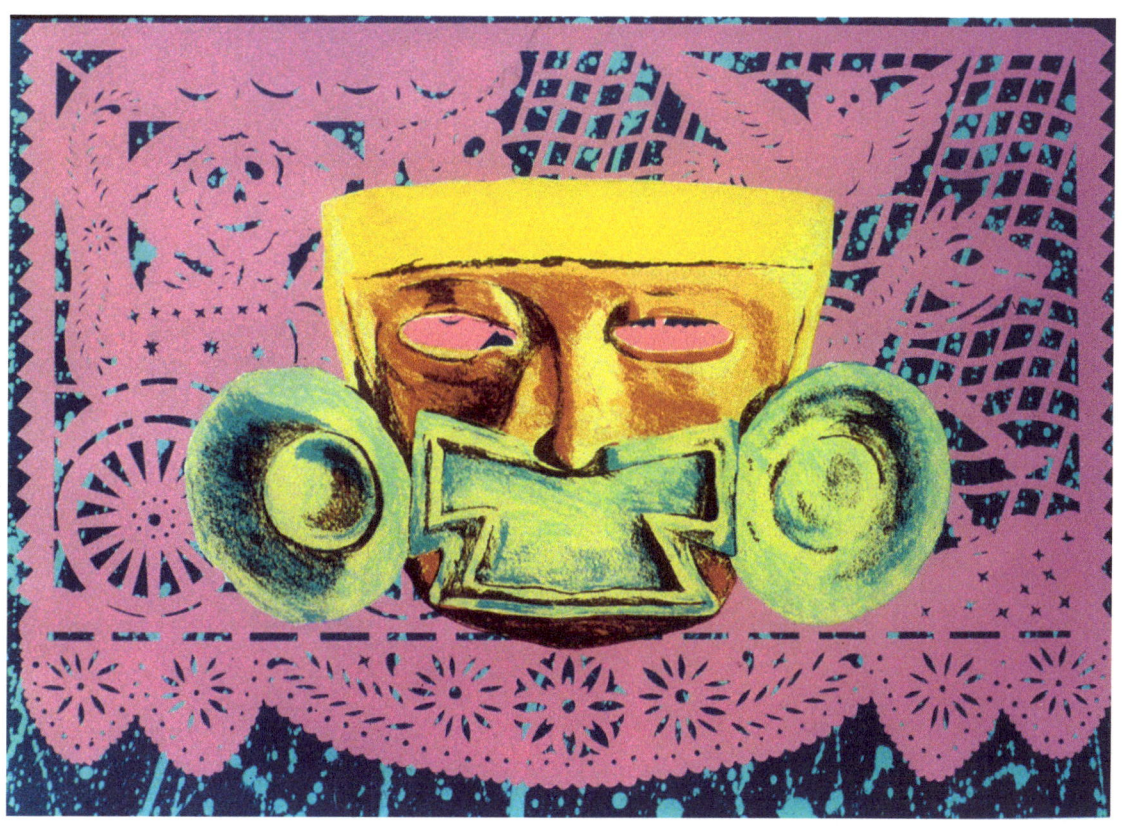

If you enjoyed this book, Michael P. Earney would be most appreciative if you would leave a review on Amazon, Goodreads, or any other Review site you like.

Also, don't forget to tell your friends! Word of mouth advertising is the most precious Thank You, a reader could give to an author.

Visit www.MichaelEarney.com to learn more about this author's books and various achievements.

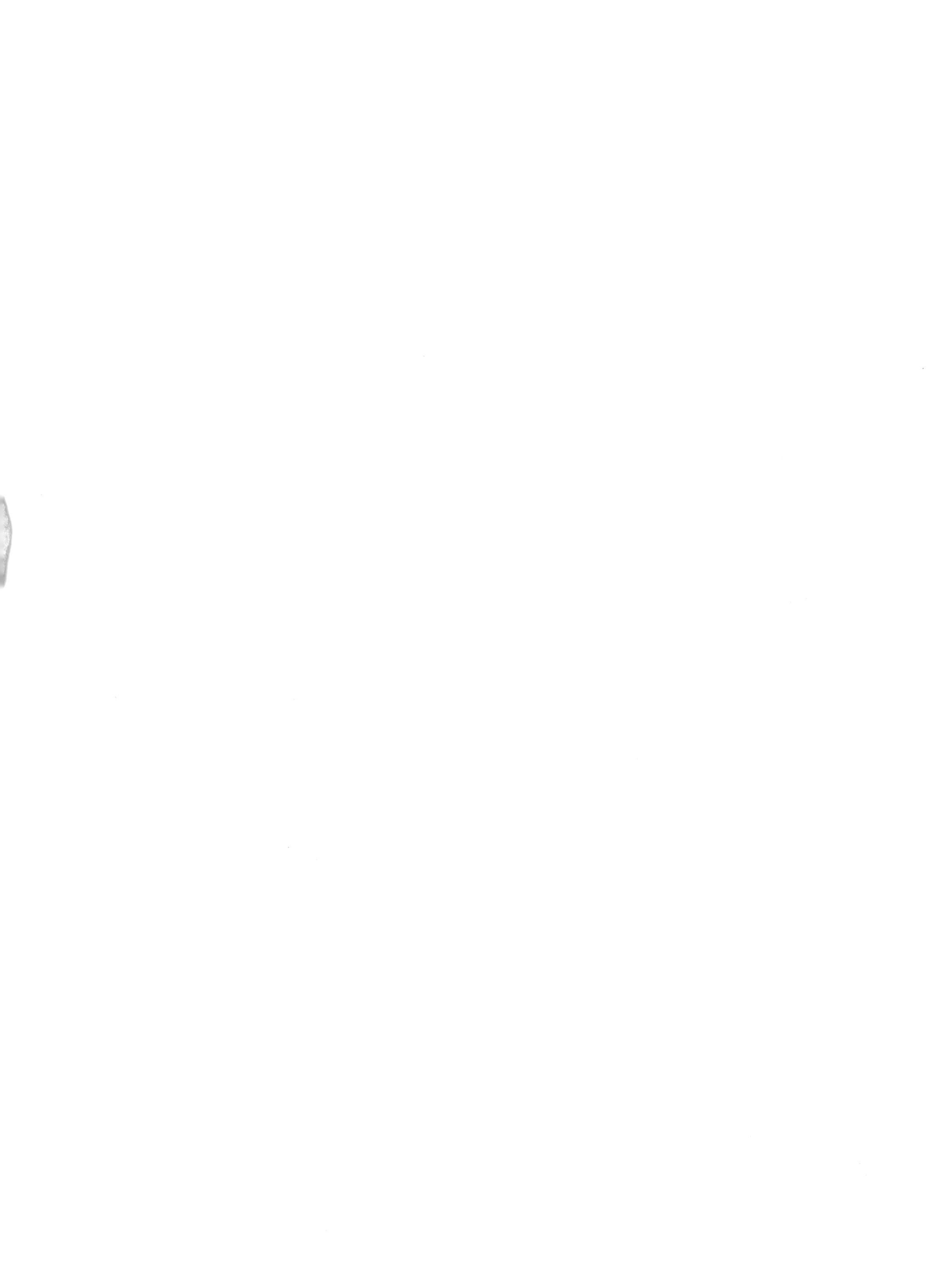